The Canadian Housewife

AN AFFECTIONATE HISTORY

❧

By Rosemary Neering

Edited by Elaine Jones
Copyedited by Ben D'Andrea
Proofread by Lesley Cameron
Designed by Diane Yee
Printed and bound in Canada by Friesens.

Library and Archives Canada Cataloguing in Publication
Neering, Rosemary, 1945–
      The Canadian housewife : an affectionate history / Rosemary Neering.
Includes index.
ISBN 1-55285-717-4
      1. Housewives—Canada—History.   2. Housekeeping—Canada—History.
I. Title.
HQ759.N44 2005   640'.971'09   C2005-903039-9

The publisher acknowledges the support of the Canada Council and the Cultural Services Branch of the Government of British Columbia in making this publication possible. We acknowledge the financial support of the Government of Canada through the Book Publishing Industry Development Program for our publishing activities.

Please note that the recipes in this book are unedited, from historical sources, and not tested or recommended. Some ingredients and methods may not be safe for modern use.

Front cover images from left to right, Glenbow Archives ND-3-5802, A.W. Barton, Ontario Archives, C 121-1-0-8-2, Andy Graetz, Weekend Magazine, Library and Archives Canada PA-115226.

Back cover image from City of Toronto Archives, John H. Boyd, Fonds 1266, 108431.

✥ Acknowledgements ✥

Thank you to all those who provided information, helped with translations, read chapters, and made suggestions. Among them: Selma Adams, Robert Bott, Peter Calamai, Paola Durando, Julie Gedeon, Katherine Gibson, Rosemary Holenchuk, Beth Hooson, Kevin Joynt, Kathe Lieber, Colette van Haaren, Tony Owen, Marial Shea, Madeleine Stulikova, Julie Watson, Wilma Wood; to publisher Robert McCullough, for his steadfast support; to AnnMarie MacKinnon for her patience; to Elaine Jones for her editing skills and perseverance; and to Diane Yee for her design skills.

A book like this could not exist without the efforts of researchers and writers who have gone before. I owe a debt of gratitude to those who edited diaries, unearthed tidbits of knowledge about the domestic sphere, and published analyses of the history of women in Canada. Some of their books can be found in the bibliography.

And thanks once more to Joe Thompson for all his support, including never needing me to be a housewife.

TABLE OF CONTENTS

❧ Introduction ❧

My mother was a housewife.

Born in England before World War I, she worked in an office between the wars. When she married my father early in World War II, she quit her job—as was the custom then—and settled down to being a wife and mother. Like so many others, my parents immigrated to Canada after the war, with their two very young daughters, looking for more opportunity than war-weary, class-conscious Britain could offer.

For the rest of her life, she cooked and sewed, cleaned house, and did laundry. She darned socks, canned peaches, and pickled cucumbers. With my father, she bought used furniture at auctions and sacks of potatoes and bushels of apples from the farmer. She kneaded bread, cooked roast chicken and two veg for Sunday dinner, and fancied up the leftovers for Monday. She baked apple pies and chocolate cakes.

She sewed our clothes and her own, often from remnants thriftily bought at the fabric store. She made handkerchiefs from old sheets, already turned sides to middle and worn through. She knitted sweaters and occasionally crocheted doilies. She washed the clothes in a fat, round washing machine and hung them to dry outdoors or in the basement next to the coal furnace. She swept and vacuumed and dusted. She put calamine lotion on our sunburns and insisted we take our cod liver oil. She made sure we did our homework and chastised us when we misbehaved. She had dinner on the table when my father came home from work. Two of her fingers turned white in cold weather, a legacy of the time they were dragged into the washing machine wringer.

For her time, she was not unusual: all the women in the neighbourhood were housewives, some better at the job than others.
She was one of that last generation of women for whom full-time
domestic work was the norm, full-time paid work outside the home
uncommon.

I took my mother for granted. All children do. "I'm not your
servant, you know!" she snapped at me once—or maybe more than
once—and I thought, though I had sense enough not to say out
loud, "You're not?!"

We all took housewives for granted; we always have. Yet colonies died without them and settlements foundered. From the
seventeenth-century New France housewives who staged illegal
protests in the streets because they didn't want their families to eat
horsemeat to the 1950s housewives who protested at the legislature for lower grocery prices, they have fought for the best for their
families. From the nineteenth-century backwoods housewife who
boiled pork fat and wood ash to make soap to the 1940s housewife
who saved metal and remade clothes to aid the war effort, they have
made sacrifices both for their families and for their country. From
the Acadian housewife who broke flax and carded wool to the 1950s
housewife who adored plastic and—or so the advertisements told
us—wore high heels to do her vacuuming, they have ensured that
the domestic sphere was well looked after. And from the Victorian
housewife who closed her eyes and thought of England to the 1930s
housewife who smiled and douched with disinfectant, they have
been at the centre of our lives.

Still, somehow, their unpaid labour has seemed to us much
less interesting than men's heroic explorations or titanic clashes in
politics or economics. By these traditional measures of worth, they
just didn't count. As more than one commentator has noted, if a
man marries his paid housekeeper and ceases to pay her wages, he
has reduced the gross national product.

This book looks back with affection at the time from the seventeenth century to 1960 when most women were full-time housewives—providing food, cleaning house, making clothes, doing
laundry, nursing the family, being mothers, being wives. It would
be impossible for one book to describe all the work of housewives
in all of those years. Instead, I focus on some significant times and

places in that span, following the history of the housewife from the days of spinning and soap-making to the days of multi-tasking sewing machines and multi-function washing machines.

By the time I came of age late in the 1960s, the era of the full-time housewife was coming to an end. Major feminist tomes such as *The Feminine Mystique*, the arrival of the birth control pill, increasing numbers of women going to university and seeking careers, full-time employment outside the home, prosperity, fast food, increasing automation, a reluctance to spend one's life focused mainly on the domestic sphere: all these meant major changes in the way that women spend their lives.

Few of us want to go back to wringing out laundry by hand, cooking over an open hearth, or fearing that our babies—or we, ourselves—will die in childbirth. Yet many of us feel a certain nostalgia for the skills that were once a woman's birthright. Young women are renewing the tradition of knitting, older women are quilting, and women young and old are experimenting with making jam and preserves. We're even hand-kneading and baking bread, that long-time staple.

The more we know about those skills and about how Canadian housewives coped with their many challenges through the centuries, the more we can look back with appreciation and affection at the grit, hard work, and love they invested in their homes.

She rose before daylight made crimson the east
For duties that never diminished
And never the sun when it sank in the west
Looked down upon work that was finished.
She cooked unending processions of meals,
Preserving and canning and baking.
She swept and she dusted
She washed and she scrubbed,
With never a rest for the taking.
A family of children she brought into the world
Raised them and trained them and taught them.
She made all the clothes and patched, mended and darned
Till miracles seemed to have wrought them.
She watched by the bedside of sickness and pain
Her hand cooled the raging of fever.
Carpentered, painted, upholstered and scraped
And worked just as hard as a beaver.
And yet as a lady-of-leisure, it seems,
The government looks on her station
For now, by the rules of the census report
It enters her—No Occupation.

— An unnamed writer looks askance at classifications in
the Canadian census; *Farmer's Advocate and Home Journal*,
June 10, 1910, as quoted in Beth Light and Joy Parr, eds.,
Canadian Women on the Move, 1867–1920, pp. 189–90.

• I •

SALT PORK AND HOMESPUN:

Housewives in Acadia and New France

It was the absence of wives and settled families that may well have been the greatest handicap agriculture faced. It was demonstrated that the desired immigrant plants and animals would thrive in the soil and climate, and the need for the products of husbandry was great and continuous. But of women of their own kind to cook and sew, harvest and hoe, and provide the solace and affection of home, there were none, and to their absence, as much as to any other problem or difficulty, the lack of success may be attributed.

—*Andrew Clark*, Acadia: The Geography of Nova Scotia to 1760

For geographer Andrew Clark, the equation was simple: no housewives, no successful colony. Many other factors worked against the success of the little settlement on the Bay of Fundy, established in 1603 as the first French colony in the New World. But the absence of women spelled doom to any farming community. "It has been abundantly demonstrated," he opined, "that an agricultural colony needs its own women."

A few chapters later, though, writing about the greater success of the second colony in Acadia, the thriving settlements on the marshlands along the bay, he thought that he had said quite enough on domestic subjects. "There is no need," he wrote, "to elaborate on the household carpentry, metalwork, spinning, weaving, tanning, cobbling, salting and smoking of food, nor the endless chores that were part of the way of life for men and women in a largely subsistent frontier economy."[1] He thus dismissed with an airy wave of his author's hand the importance to the economy of the domestic life of both men and women. Inside the home was outside his consideration.

And so it goes. Search for the role of the housewife in old Acadia and New France from the early 1600s to the end of French rule in 1763, and you'll have to dig deep. Again and again, visitors and commentators on the French colonial way of life mention food, clothing, and houses. But seldom do they mention the human hands that accomplished the domestic tasks. Food was cooked, clothing was sewn, children were raised—but by whom? Presumably by the women who were the keystones of domestic life.

France founded its first lasting settlements in North America early in the seventeenth century. In New France, habitant families

A View of the Bridge Built over the River Berlie, By Order of General Haldimand in 1781.

farmed long narrow stretches of land fronting on the rivers, while professionals, tradesmen, and colonial officers and their families lived in the towns. In Acadia, colonists dyked the salt marshes along the Bay of Fundy and established farms on the meadows thus created, while military men and their families, plus those who served or sold to them, lived at the fort of Louisbourg.

A few observers of the French colonial scene penned descriptions of the women of Acadia and New France. Pehr Kalm, a Swedish scientist sent to examine the North American way of life, had something to say about them:

> The women in general are handsome here; they are well bred and virtuous, with an innocent and becoming freedom ... In their domestic duties they greatly surpass the English women in the plantations, who indeed have taken the liberty of throwing all the burden of housekeeping upon their husbands, and sit in their chairs all day with

About four out of five residents of New France lived on farms; this one was near the town of Quebec. Bread ovens like the one at the right in this scene were heavily used by housewives in New France. They were essential for the production of the many heavy loaves of bread that were a staple in the habitants' diet. (Library and Archives Canada C-045559, Acc. No. 1970-188-2142 W.H. Coverdale Collection of Canadiana)

Generally considered to be the first French housewife in New France, Marie Rollet came to New France in 1617 with her husband, farmer and apothecary Louis Hébert, and their three children. When Hébert died, she remarried and remained in New France until her death in 1649. (C.W. Jefferys I-97)

C.W. JEFFERYS

◇◇◇◇◇◇◇◇◇◇◇◇◇◇◇◇◇◇◇◇◇◇◇◇◇◇◇◇◇◇◇◇◇

The habitations, built chiefly of wood, were extremely convenient, and furnished as neatly as a substantial farmer's house in Europe. The people bred a great deal of poultry of all kinds, which made a variety in their food, and which was, in general, wholesome and plentiful. Their common drink was beer and cider, to which they sometimes added rum.

Their usual clothing was, in general, the produce of their own flax and hemp, or the fleeces of their own sheep; with these they made common linens and coarse cloths … If any of them had any inclination for articles of greater luxury, they procured them from Annapolis or Louisbourg, and gave in exchange corn, cattle, or furs.

— Abbé Raynal, *A Philosophical and Political History of the Settlements and Trade of the Europeans in the East and West Indies*, 1783, as quoted in Dave McIntosh, *When the Work's All Done This Fall: Voices of Early Canada, the Settling of the Land*, p. 20.

folded arms. The women in Canada on the contrary do not spare themselves, especially among the common people, where they are always in the fields, meadows, stables etc. and do not dislike any work whatsoever.

He had a criticism or two, but was impressed overall: "upon the whole . . . they are not averse to the taking part in all the business of housekeeping, and I have with pleasure seen the daughters of the better sort of people and of the governor himself, not too finely dressed, going into kitchens and cellars to see that everything is done as it ought to be. And they also carry their sewing with them, even the governor's daughters."[2]

Throughout the French colonial era, more than three-quarters of the population was rural. A woman's work depended on her class. The habitante—wife of the peasant farmer—did all the household chores, with the help of her children, and assisted her husband and sons in the fields when needed. The merchant's wife who lived in town could afford the help of servants. And the wives of the upper class, whether on the rural seigneury or in the lavish houses of the town, usually supervised rather than performed household work—though, as Kalm notes, even upper-class women did intricate and ornamental sewing.

Most women who came to Acadia came with their husbands and sometimes their young families, and almost all took up lands to farm. But there was a definite dearth of women in the colony along the St. Lawrence, where soldiers, farmers, and artisans sought in vain for wives. Yet commentators repeatedly stress that habitants in the New World were better off than their counterparts in France. In New France and Acadia, though the seigneurial system imposed certain rents and duties on the habitants, they farmed larger plots of land than the French peasants, ate better, and enjoyed more freedom. In the seventeenth century, the leaders of the colony arranged for several hundred young women, most of them orphans or young widows who thought life in the new world must be better than that in the old, to be sent to New France.

The king provided a dowry for the *filles du roi*—daughters of the king—and promised a present for the household when they married. Almost every one of them did so. After their arrival in the 1660s, the population increased rapidly, and housewife lore and duties were passed down from mother to daughter. Those who married professional men or those in the upper echelons of the colony lived as befitted their positions, in Quebec or Montreal, in good houses, and instructing servants in the proper conduct of the household affairs. But the majority married soldiers or other ordinary men, often choosing those who had had the forethought to have already built a house.

Throughout the colonies, women looked after the kitchen garden, prepared and preserved food for the winter, cooked, cleaned, and did their jobs as wife and mother. In winter, they spun and wove, sewed and mended. They worked as partners with their husbands, often looking after financial affairs and always helping out in the fields.

They might have other tasks. Allies of the Algonquins, the French were opposed by the Iroquois, who led surprise attacks on the farmer in the field or the family in the home. Barbe Poisson, married at 15 and widowed at 18 by an Iroquois attack, remarried

Marie de l'Incarnation, an Ursuline nun who arrived in Quebec in 1639, wrote letters to her son, born before she joined the Ursulines:

The hundred girls that the King sent this year have just arrived and already almost all of them are married.... He is also sending men to supply the needs of the marriages.... A great many girls have come, and more are expected. The first woman to marry was the Moor, who wed a Frenchman.... When they have eaten the cask of flour and the bacon that the King is giving them, they will suffer very greatly until they have cleared the land. It is intended to ask henceforth for only village girls that are as fitted for work as men; experience shows that those not thus reared are not fitted for this country, since they are in a wretchedness from which they cannot raise themselves.

— *Word from New France: The Selected Letters of Marie de l'Incarnation*, 1665 and 1668, pp. 314, 345.

The New France housewife had to be prepared to make do:

Just recently when I was at Fort St. Jean, Madame la Croix had no oil with which to prepare the salad. She used bear oil therefore, and the salad tasted almost as good as with the usual cotton seed oil, though the flavour was a bit peculiar.

— Pehr Kalm, *Travels in North America*, p. 566.

Acadian housewives (and male settlers) made use of the wild produce of the country. Many of the first Frenchmen at Quebec died of scurvy in their first winter on the St. Lawrence before they learned from the native people how to make spruce beer, rich in Vitamin C:

But only Beer, made from the tips of Fir trees is brewed there; a strong decoction is put into a Cask with Yeast & Molasses, which is a kind of sugar syrup the colour of Raisine. All this ferments together for two or three days; when the fermentation is over the substance settles, & the light coloured Liquor, which is not unpleasant, is drunk. But the most common beverage is Water, & those who drink nothing else are always vigorous; & can stand hard work because they eat a great deal, & do not have constant employment.

— Sieur de Dièreville, *Relation of the Voyage to Port Royal in Acadia or New France*, p. 91.

at 19. She was living in the outpost of Montreal and was alone at home, the men working in the fields, when the Iroquois attacked once more. "She saw that our men were fleeing in any way they could, since they had no longer any means of defence," wrote priest and historian François Dollier de Casson. "Realising, too, that there was no man in her house to go to their aid, she herself took a load of muskets on her shoulders, and fearless of a swarm of Iroquois whom she saw rush from every direction towards her house, she ran to our Frenchmen...When she reached [one of the men] she handed over her arms to him, thereby marvellously strengthening all our Frenchmen, and holding back the enemy."[3] Another woman, set upon by three Iroquois, pretended to faint, then leapt up and chased off her attackers. When a French rescuer, happy to see her alive, embraced her, she slapped his face.

And then there was the final judgement of Pehr Kalm:

The women in the country were usually a little better dressed than our [Swedish] women. They always had night-gowns, and the girls curled and powdered their hair on Sundays.... Everywhere the girls were alert and quick in speech and their manner rather impulsive; but according to my judgment and as far as I could observe, they were not as lustful and wanton as foreigners generally claim the French to be.[4]

❧ THE COOK ❧

"A workman will eat two loaves [of bread] a week, each six or seven pounds in weight," wrote one observer of the New France scene.[5] "The colonist eats two pounds of bread a day and six ounces of bacon," wrote another.[6] Salt pork, smoked eel and fish, vegetables from the garden—though never, except in famine, potatoes, a food considered fit only for animals—and bread were the staples that the Canadian housewife served to her family in Acadia and New France.

Lacking the packaged yeast that bakers today take for granted, housewives raised their bread with homemade yeast made by fermenting hops or warm water, sugar, and flour. Though farmers often hand-ground their grain in the early days, as time went on,

17ᵀᴴ CENTURY KITCHEN FIREPLACE *showing Turnspit, Crane, Pot Hooks and Hangers. Fowls and Joints of Meat were roasted before the fire by putting them on the Spit, which was revolved by a small Dog in a cylindrical cage, connected with the Spit. Sometimes a Boy turned the Roast by a handle on the end of the Spit.*

Meat Fork

Bake Kettle

Broiler

Basting Pan

End of Spit with handle

Boil it or bake it, roast it or fry it—stews, sweets and every other dish save bread were cooked on the hearth using a multitude of fireplace tools and vessels. (C.W. Jefferys I-144)

they were more likely to take it to a mill located in the country-side or in a nearby town. The several kilos of bread each person ate weekly may not have looked as large as that weight in bread today: in the seventeenth and eighteenth centuries, heavy bread, made without a great deal of liquid, was considered better bread, and mixing and kneading the stiff dough took extra effort from the housewife.

One of the first things the habitant family built was an outdoor, wood-fired, clay bread oven—so useful that many were still in use in Quebec through the 1930s. The wife or husband built a fire in the oven and let it burn until the oven was thoroughly hot. They then pulled out the embers and quickly washed down the oven floor. The oven retained heat for as long as a day or two.

By the eighteenth century, bakers produced bread for town dwellers in Quebec, Montreal, and Louisbourg, but many a house-proud wife continued the rigorous work of bread-making.

Preserving the products of farm, forest, or river took much time: salting pork, preserving eggs, making butter, keeping meat in the cold cellar under the house or shed, making conserves from fruit, were all part of the housewife's repertoire of recipes and methods. It was a poor family indeed that did not salt down bar-rel after barrel of eels each fall for use through the winter and into the spring. The colonists caught a great variety of saltwater and freshwater fish; it, too, could be salted or, at least in New France

Marie de l'Incarnation writes to her son from Quebec in 1668:

They [squash] are prepared in div-ers manners—as a soup with milk, or fried. They are also cooked in the oven like apples or under the embers like pears, and it is true that, thus prepared, they have the taste of cooked rainette apples. Melons grow in Montreal that are as good as those of France....There is also a certain species that is called watermelon that is shaped like squash and eaten like a melon. Some salt them, others sugar them; they are considered excel-lent and are not noxious. The other potherbs and vegetables are as in France. We harvest them like wheat for use all winter and till the end of May, when the gardens are covered with snow....We do not cook the plums in the oven, for then only a pit covered with skin remains, but make marmalade out of them with sugar, which is excellent....We also make jam from gooseberries and from piminan [marsh cranberry] a wild fruit that sugar renders very pleasant.

— *Word from New France: the Selected Letters of Marie de l'Incarnation*, p. 346.

The aristocracy of New France dined rather better, and in finer surroundings, than the habitant did. The mistress of the house was assisted by her servants in preparing and serving banquets such as this one; her job was to act as a sparkling and witty hostess. (Library and Archives Canada C-013543)

The common people in Canada may be smelled when one passes them by on account of their frequent use of onions. Pumpkins also are abundant in the farmers' gardens. They prepare them in several ways, but the most common is to cut them through the middle, and place each half on the hearth, open side towards the fire, until it is roasted. The pulp is then cut out of the peel and eaten. Better class people put sugar on it.

— Pehr Kalm, *Travels in North America*, p. 510.

where winters were reliably cold, frozen in a cold cellar. The most important animal was the pig, eaten fresh, salted, and, in New France, frozen. Salt pork—*lard salé*—was a staple in both colonies.

In the kitchen garden beside the house, women grew the same wide variety of produce as in France of that era: salad greens, beans, onions, leeks, turnips, beets. Wheat, oats, barley, field peas, and cabbages were the standard crops, used for bread, pea soup, and a dozen other dishes. The garden also provided herbs, such as thyme, that took the place of expensive spices that had to be imported to the colonies by ship.

There was no need to plant vines for fruit. Women and children collected wild strawberries, blackberries, raspberries, plums, cherries, and other fruits from the nearby woods. The colonists planted apple trees and ate the apples fresh or dried.

Town housewives bought much of their produce at market. Habitant families brought goods by cart or by sleigh in winter, taking up spots according to the produce they sold. Often, wives and daughters tended the stalls while fathers and sons headed for the tavern. Town residents also bought meat from the butchers and fish from the fishmongers in the markets. Montreal housewives, for example, could buy wheat flour, corn, cabbages, melons, cucumbers, apples, fish, milk—frozen in winter—maple sugar, pork, mutton, and live sheep, turkeys, geese, and chickens.

Products that could not be grown or gathered must also be bought at market. Especially in Acadia, a three-cornered trade between North America, the French West Indies, and France brought brandy, wine, molasses, and other delicacies to the table and supplied the salt for preserving fish and meat.

Town or country, the colonial housewife did her cooking at a fireplace that also heated the house. Suspended over the hearth from a hook or pole was a device that allowed use of a cauldron, grill, or rotisserie. A three-legged bake kettle placed over the coals served for the cooking of a great many different foods.

The restricted space and cooking methods meant that one-dish meals were very popular. Tourtières—originally stews made from wild birds such as pigeons or partridges in a pan called a tourtière, and made in later days with game and farm meat and sealed with a pie crust—became the signature dish of many a New France household. A soup-that-never-ends was common, simmering in a cauldron hanging over the fire, eaten and replenished with water, vegetables, and meat.

Swedish visitor Pehr Kalm meticulously noted the meals he ate with upper-class settlers in Quebec. "They" who do the preparing are presumably the housewives, or their servants:

Finally the fruit and sweetmeats are served, which are of many different kinds, viz. walnuts from France or Canada, either ripe or pickled; almonds; raisins; hazel-nuts; several kinds of berries which are ripe in the summer season, such as currants red and black, and cranberries which are preserved in treacle; many preserves in sugar, as strawberries, raspberries, blackberries and mossberries. Cheese is likewise a part of the dessert and so is milk, which they drink last of all, with sugar. Friday and Saturday, the "lean" days, they eat no meat according to the Roman Catholic rites, but they well know how to guard against hunger. On those days they boil all sorts of vegetables like peas, beans and cabbage, and fruit, fish, eggs, and milk are prepared in various ways. They cut cucumbers in slices and eat them with cream, which is a very good dish. Sometimes they put whole cucumbers on the table and everybody that likes them takes one, peels and slices it, and dips the slices in salt, eating them like radishes. Melons abound here and are always eaten without sugar....There is always salt and pepper on the table....They never put any sugar into wine, or brandy....Immediately after dinner they drink coffee without cream. Supper is commonly at seven o'clock, or between seven and eight at night, and the dishes are the same as at dinner. Pudding is not seen here, and neither is punch.

— Pehr Kalm, *Travels in North America*, pp. 474–75.

The Sieur de Dièreville, who travelled in Acadia in 1699 and 1700, describes Acadian crops and gardens:

With the exception of Artichoke & Asparagus, they have an abundance of every kind of vegetable, & all are excellent. There are fields of white-headed Cabbage & Turnips, which are kept for the entire year. The Turnips are put in the cellars; they are tender & sweet, & much finer than in France; moreover they may be cooked in the ashes, like Chestnuts. The Cabbages are left in the field after they have been pulled up, the head down & the stalk in the air; in this way they are preserved by the snow which comes & covers them to a depth of five or six feet, & they are only taken out as they are needed; the settlers never fail to put some in the cellar as well. Neither of these vegetables goes into the Pot without the other, & nourishing soups are made of them, with a large slice of Pork. It is necessary, above all else, to have a great many Cabbages, because the people eat only the hearts, & the Pigs are given what is left; during the Winter it is their only food, & these gluttonous animals, of which there are a great number, are not satisfied with a small quantity.

— *Relation of the Voyage to Port Royal in Acadia or New France*, p. 108.

A soldier with American Benedict Arnold's ill-fated campaign against Quebec after the English takeover of the colony was billeted with an habitant family:

In the evening before bedtime, the females of the house prepare the dinner of the following day. It may be particularly described, as it was done in our view for a number of days together, and during the time was never varied. This was the manner: a piece of pork or beef, a portion of each kind, together with a sufficiency of cabbage, potatoes and turnips, seasoned with salt, and an adequate quantity of water, were put into a neat tin kettle with a lid. The kettle, thus replenished, was placed on the stove in the room where we all slept, and there it simmered till the time of rising, when it was taken to a small fire in the kitchen, where a stewing continued till near noon, when they dined. The contents were turned into a large basin. Each person had a plate; no knife was used, except one to cut the bread, but a five or six pronged fork answered the purposes of a spoon. The meat required no cutting, as it was reduced to a mucilage, or at least to shreds.

— John Joseph Henry, in Kenneth Roberts, *March to Quebec: Journals of the Members of Arnold's Expedition*, pp. 361–62.

RECIPES

La Cuisinière Bourgeoise was Canada's first cookbook, appearing in Quebec in 1825, a copy of a book published in France in the mid-eighteenth century. Initially intended more for middle- and upper-class housewives who supervised staff, rather than for habitantes, many of whom did not know how to read, it was a compendium of recipes and household hints. Among the recipes were those for a duck casserole and for a very French type of doughnut.

DUCK CASSEROLE

Singe, clean, and cut a duck in four. Blanch it for a quarter of an hour, then cook it in a small pot with turnips, a quarter cabbage, parsnips, carrots, onions, all cut up and stirred together, plus some good bouillon, a small piece of salt pork with the rind off and cut in slices, a bouquet garni, a little salt. When it is all cooked, arrange the duck in a terrine to serve it, putting all the vegetables around it. Degrease the bouillon in the small pan where you cooked the vegetables, and reduce it. Pour a little around the duck and serve the rest as a sauce for the vegetables and the duck, taking care to taste it first to make sure it is good.

BEIGNETS

Take six eggs, beat them with a few spoonfuls of sugar, cut up apples very fine, mix them all together with a half-setier [a quarter litre] of milk, a little flour, so that batter is like that for crepes; add a little salt, half a glass of brandy, a little cinnamon, about a marble-size bit of pearl ash [potassium carbonate, an early leavening agent made from wood ash]. Let the mixture rise an hour next to the fire; then drop it by spoonfuls in boiling fat.

To make excellent black pudding, cut up some onion, and parboil it in water, then skim it and add the blood, and some salt, pepper, cloves, and cinnamon mixed together, and some bread cut into little pieces. Stuff it all into a small intestine that has been well scraped. Take the grease off and boil it in a saucepan of water on the fire, pricking it first so it doesn't burst. If you want to put milk with the blood, it will be even better. Milk pudding is made with pieces of roasted chicken and milk instead of blood, adding in the onion, the salt and the spices; some people put in some chopped fennel and a few grains of musk and amber. To cook milk pudding, after it has been boiled like the blood pudding, instead of simply putting it on the grill, cook it in a roasting pan, or a silver bowl, putting it in the fire or over charcoal; and as it browns, drain the fat often....Mustard, either Dijon or common, is the proper sauce of all black puddings and sausages.

— Nicolas de Bonnefons, *Les Délices de la Campagne*, 1661, as quoted in Bernard Audet, *Se Nourrir au Quotidien en Nouvelle France*, p. 151, author's translation.

❧ THE HOUSEKEEPER ❧

Observers were of two minds about the housekeeping of the New France housewife. Some found the kitchens and other rooms to be remarkably clean. But traveller Pehr Kalm, visiting in 1749, turned up his nose at the housekeeping he observed:

> They seem rather remiss in regard to the cleaning of the utensils and apartments, for sometimes the floors, both in the town and in the country, are hardly cleaned once in six months, which is a disagreeable sight to one who comes from amongst the Dutch and the English, where the constant scouring and scrubbing of the floors is reckoned as important as the exercise of religion itself. To prevent the thick dust, which is thus left on the floor from being noxious to the health, the women wet it several times a day, which lays the dust. And they repeat this as often as the dust is dry and begins to rise again.[7]

The truth is probably that some housewives were more house-proud than others. Busy with spinning, weaving, cooking, gardening, sewing, nursing, washing clothes, caring for the children, dealing with the winter cold, and keeping her husband happy, however, the New France or Acadian housewife might be forgiven if she spent as little time as possible scrubbing and sweeping floors, cleaning pots and pans, and airing the bedding.

There was often not a great deal to clean. Especially in the early years, simple houses had just one room, which served as kitchen, living room, and bedroom. Centred on the huge fireplace and hearth, the room had at one end the canopied bed of husband and wife, with the children's beds close by. The room was furnished with half a dozen wooden chairs, a table, a spinning wheel, a weaving loom, a wardrobe, a storage chest or two, and something to carry in the water. In the early days of the colonies, many windows in farmers' houses were covered with oiled paper rather than with glass, so the housewife was spared the task of washing windows. Prosperous town dwellers and country land-owners occupied larger houses—but housewives there were likely to have servants and, perhaps, slaves.

Habitant housewives had to make their own cleaners and other substances. *La Nouvelle Cuisinière Canadienne*, published in the mid-19th century, listed a variety of recipes for household potions, handed down from generation to generation. Among them:

BOOT-BLACKING
Take a quarteron [about 125 grams] of noir d'Ivoire [a type of black colouring], three ounces of common sugar, a big spoonful of olive oil and a chopine [half a litre] of spruce beer— mix it all up without heating.

PAPER GLUE
With two big spoonfuls of flour, put as much crushed resin as will fit on the tip of a knife; mix this with beer and boil it for half an hour.

Instead of candles, they use lamps in country places, in which they burn the train-oil of porpoises, a common oil here. When they have none of it, they use the train-oil of seals.

—Pehr Kalm, *Travels in North America*, p. 486.

a Canadian Woman

a canadian man

The Canadians not only make their own cloaths, but

The climate of New France demanded warm clothing, spun, woven, and sewn by the housewife. A visitor in the early 19th century sketched this couple in winter. (Library and Archives Canada C-014835)

In the seventeenth century, especially in the country, floors were made of packed earth. By the mid-eighteenth century, floors were generally made of seasoned boards. The housewife threw fine sand—sand from Acadian beach dunes was ideal—on the floor, then scrubbed and swept the floor clean. In spring, the whole house got a good cleaning or airing: floors, furniture, household goods, mattresses, bedding, household linens, and rugs.

Winter posed its own problems. The housewife in the days before matches were invented had to make sure that the fire did not go out. It should be kept, it was said, at a temperature to keep the soup simmering nicely. Much of the time, light from the fireplace was all that was needed, but the housewife also looked after the candles and oil lamps. Making candles was a finicky chore that required dipping and redipping long oiled wicks into melted, filtered mutton or beef tallow, or pouring hot tallow into candle moulds. Poor habitants, who could not afford tallow and wicks, used simple oil lamps, with oil rendered from seals, porpoises, or whales.

Cold was the colonists' enemy. In later days, colonists heated their houses and cooked food on iron stoves:

Every crevice through which cold air could penetrate, was carefully pasted with strips of paper of every color. To permit the cold air to intrude is not the only evil which results; but the smallest interstice admits the air with an almost impalpable snow, which is very inconvenient, particularly at night, when the winds blow most sharply. A stove of iron stood a small space from the wall of the kitchen chimney, but in such a way that it might be encompassed by the family or the guests. This stove was kept continually hot, both by day and by night. Over the stove there is a rack so constructed as to serve for the drying of wet clothes, moccasins, etc, etc.

—John Joseph Henry, in Kenneth Roberts, *March to Quebec: Journals of the Members of Arnold's Expedition*, p. 361.

❧ THE SEAMSTRESS ❧

Off to New France sailed the *filles du roi*, to marry and help populate the St. Lawrence lands. They would need some material help: the king gave to each a dowry that included, as well as money and other goods, 100 sewing needles, a spool of white thread, a pair of scissors, and 1,000 pins.

All were articles much needed, for most of the housewives of New France and Acadia made their own clothes and those of their families, mended those clothes, sewed bedcovers and other household linens, and stuffed feathers from barnyard fowl into pillows and quilts. While the upper class could depend for the most part on clothing and fabric brought by the trade ships from France, even they would need to direct their servants in the making of clothes and coverings that suited the climate of the colony. Habitant families had few clothes; those of the upper class had many more.

Observers of the colonial scene frequently point out that the colonists did not eat lamb: sheep were raised mainly for their wool and ended up in the stew pot only when they were older. In the spring, the colonists sheared sheep and washed fleeces. Over the next months, the wives and daughters carded and combed the wool, spun it into yarn that they might dye or leave undyed, wove it into cloth, and made the cloth into clothes or coverings.

The colonists also grew flax and hemp, turned into cloth through a long and laborious process. Hemp or flax plants were pulled up in the early fall, roots and all, then laid in wet fields or a swampy area and turned from time to time, so that they would rot, and the fibres could be separated from the stalks—a process known as retting. The fibres were then broken, cleaned, combed, spun, and woven, with women, girls, and boys involved in various parts of the process.

Winter was the time for making and mending clothes. Old clothing served as patterns for new. When, after many remakings, an article of clothing could no longer be used, it was cut up for use in *catolognes*—bedcoverings woven from thin strips of cloth—or for rag rugs.

The Canadians not only make their own cloaths, but the stuff with which they are made up is manufactured by themselves (the women)—the colors are always blue or grey.

—Notes from the sketchbook of artist Sempronius Stretton.

As for the women, they are always busy, and most keep their husbands and children in serviceable linen materials and stockings which they make skilfully from the hemp they have grown and the wool produced by their sheep.

—Sieur de Villebon, *Memoir on the settlements and harbors from Minas at the head of the Bay of Fundy to Cape Breton*, 27 Oct. 1699, in John Clarence Webster, *Acadia at the End of the Seventeenth Century*, p. 132.

No factory-made clothing for the residents of New France. This illustration created in the 20th century shows habitant women carding (left), spinning (right), and weaving (background) wool. (Library and Archives Canada C-002481)

❧ THE LAUNDRESS ❧

There's a tale told that washerwomen were unwittingly responsible for the fall of French Quebec to the English. General Wolfe, encamped in 1759 with his men on the riverfront opposite the cliffs of Quebec, couldn't decide how to attack the strong French citadel. One day, several of his soldiers went for a walk along the shore. Across the way, women—servants or housewives—were washing their laundry on the riverbank. Later that day, the soldiers saw the laundry blowing in the breeze atop the cliffs. Ah-hah, they thought, so this is where the narrow path we seek snakes up the cliffs. The rest, as they say, is history.

True or not, the tale points up the difficulties of doing laundry in the days before running water. For housewives in early Canada, laundry was the toughest and dirtiest of a range of difficult tasks. In summer, it was frequently simpler to take the clothes to the water than to bring the water to the clothes, soaking, sudsing, and pounding them on the riverbank. If she laundered at home, the housewife must bring water to the fire, then heat it in tubs or cauldrons, introduce soap and clothes, agitate, rub on a scrub board, drain, wring, bring in more water for rinsing, heat it, rinse the

The Sieur de Dièreville waxes poetic in his description of the women of Acadia:

They make the things they lack;
     their wool
Is fashioned into Clothing, Caps
     and Socks.
They are no way distinguished by
     new styles,
And still wear hooded Capes;
     their Shoes
Of Elk and Seal skin are flat-soled
And made for comfort. From their flax
Linen is also woven, and thus by
Their industry, their nakedness is
     veiled.

— *Relation of the Voyage to Port Royal in Acadia or New France*, p. 96.

clothes, drain, and wring. The clothes were dried in the fresh air throughout the year, freeze-drying in the cold air of winter. Little wonder that the colonial housewife washed heavy woollen outer clothes perhaps once a year, indoor clothing several times a year, and only underclothing on a weekly or monthly basis—about as often as people washed themselves.

Though soap was commercially produced in France and, eventually, in New France, many housewives made their own soap. That required wood ashes, readily available from the fireplace, and animal fat, rendered down from the fall butchering of cows and sheep. The whitest possible ashes from the hottest fire were mixed with water—preferably soft water—and left to stand. The resulting lye water was then mixed with animal fat that had been melted, strained, hardened, and cleaned. That mixture was boiled, poured into moulds, left to harden, and dried and aired for about two weeks, to produce a variety of soaps, from coarse to fine. Each housewife had her own recipes, passed down in the family or taught to her by nuns or neighbours.

᪵ THE NURSE ᪵

Physicians diagnosed illness in Acadia and New France, while surgeons actually laid hands upon patients, cutting and sewing them back together. But their ability to care for and cure their patients was limited by contemporary medical wisdom. To treat illness, doctors got rid of bodily fluids, purging, bleeding, or administering enemas as the situation seemed to dictate. Regardless of the results they might obtain, few families could afford to summon doctors, and, in any case, there were few physicians or surgeons in the colony.

Inevitably, most of the family's health care fell to the housewife. She had many ailments to deal with. The link between cleanliness and health would be not be established for some years yet. Despite various attempts, including one in 1673 that made it obligatory for householders to have adequate latrines and privies, "to avert the infection and stench that such filth occasions when people are allowed to deposit it in the streets,"[8] servants still emptied chamber pots into the street as late as 1750. Colonists suffered from

"Il est assez gras pour faire du savon." "He's fat enough to make soap from." Old Acadian saying about a dog. If the dog dropped his head upon hearing the verdict, it was said that he understood the comment.

Merchandise in the dowry of a *fille du roi*: a small chest to hold the dowry; 1 bonnet; 1 taffeta handkerchief; 1 pair of shoe ribbons; 100 sewing needles; 1 comb; 1 spool of white thread; 1 pair of stockings; 1 pair of gloves; 1 pair of scissors; 2 knives; 1,000 pins; 4 lace braids; and 2 livres in silver money.

DRINK THIS FOR A COLD
Infuse a fistful of almonds for 12 hours in a pint of water, pour off the infusion and add a pint of water; reduce the whole to a chopine [half-litre].

— *La Nouvelle Cuisinière Canadienne.*

dysentery caused by poor sanitation and worms entered the system through contaminated food. More serious diseases, such as cholera, measles, scarlet fever, and smallpox swept through the colony from time to time, often spreading from sailors or passengers aboard visiting ships. Neither physicians nor housewives had much success in curing these diseases.

To treat the daily run of bruises, sprains, pains, poisonings, chilblains, and minor illness, the housewife used infusions from plants or folk remedies. Some of these remedies, handed down from mother to daughter or learned from the native people of the colony, seem strange and even laughable to modern eyes. Yet there was much wisdom in the use of plantain leaves to soothe stings of plants or insects, an infusion of yarrow leaves to reduce fever, or poultices of comfrey leaves to heal wounds. Comfrey, in particular, was widely used, as it had been from the days of ancient Rome, for dysentery, for coughs, even for knitting bones. If a child had worms, mother prescribed a good dose of garlic.

Not all remedies were equally useful. The museum of Maison Saint-Gabriel in Montreal notes that maple syrup, urine, and sheep excrement were used to cure coughing; lead grains to remove corns; crushed lice to treat jaundice; and oil from small dogs to treat rheumatism.[9] But if a folk remedy could not cure a major illness, then, in all likelihood, neither could any other remedy known in the colony. If all else failed, there was always prayer.

❧ THE MOTHER ❧

Cook, seamstress, nurse, housekeeper, wife: all these roles were necessary in Acadia and New France. But the most respected female role of all was that of mother. How else would a country be populated except through the fecundity of its women? When the French government sent *filles du roi* to Quebec in the 1660s, it was with the firm expectation that they would become wives and—more important—mothers, and in so doing, strengthen the colony.

Most of them did. Between 1663 and 1672, the population of New France more than doubled, from 3,200 to 6,700, with much of the increase resulting from births, not immigration. In Acadia, women had an average of four living children; in New France, they

Pehr Kalm describes the Acadian method for dealing with pain:

The fresh leaves [of northern white cedar] are pounded in a mortar and mixed with hog's grease or any other grease. This is boiled together until it becomes a salve, which is spread on linen and applied to the part where the pain is. The salve gives certain relief in a short time. Against violent pains which move up and down in the thighs and sometimes spread all over the body, they recommend the following remedy. Take of the leaves of a kind of polypoly [a type of fern] four-fifths, and of the cones of the Thuya one-fifth, both reduced to a coarse powder by themselves and mixed together afterwards. Then pour milkwarm water on it so as to make a poultice, spread it on linen, and wrap it around the body; but as the poultice burns like fire, they commonly lay a cloak between it and the body, otherwise it would burn and scorch the skin.

— *Travels in North America*, p. 469.

People in this country love their children madly, imitating in this sense the Savages, and this prevents them from disciplining them and forming their characters (honour).

— Administrator Jacques Raudot, 1706, as quoted on http://www. civilization.ca/vmnf/popul/habitant/ famil-e.htm, consulted 26/04/05.

A later artist recreates the visit of the Intendant Jean Talon to a habitant home, where several mothers look on with their children. (Library and Archives Canada C-011925, Acc. No. 1983-45-3)

Perhaps parents doted on their children because so many died young:

In Lord Giffard's house on April 30th, 1655, Toussaint Giroux and Marie Godard's son was delivered by Lord Giffard. On May 7th this son was baptized by Father Raganeau, a Jesuit. Godfather—Joseph Giffard; Godmother—Louise Giffard, Lord Charles de Lauson's wife. The name Charles was given to him. The child deceased and was buried the same day, May 7th, 1655.

— entry in a New France parish register, as quoted on http://www.lacefairy.com/Giroux/Toussaint2.html, consulted 27/04/2005.

averaged six or eight, and up to a dozen, though many died in infancy or early childhood. Women might well be pregnant about half the time between the average age of marriage—23—and menopause at around 50.

No habitant woman worth her salt—a phrase with real meaning then—took to her bed when pregnant. Women were most likely to get pregnant in spring, with spring and summer the seasons of hardest work for women and men alike. Women continued to work in the fields and in the house until close to their due date.

A midwife who lived in the area or neighbour women aided at the birth. These helpers swaddled the baby tightly; a few days later, it was taken to a priest for baptism. Soon after that, mother was back at work. She—or, if necessary, a wet nurse—breast-fed her child for about 14 months.

It was the mother's job to make sure her children were properly instructed in all matters religious. In the early days, when priests were only occasional visitors to each parish, mothers taught their children the rudiments of the Catholic faith. Family prayers were said morning and evening and rosaries counted. Both mother and father took very seriously their task of making sure their children followed the rules of the church.

If she knew these skills she would teach her children to read, write, and do simple arithmetic. She passed on to her daughters her household skills of sewing, weaving, cooking, and housekeeping. Children were expected to become part of the working household by the age of seven, helping in the kitchen garden, looking after some of the animals, tending the fire, and sweeping the floor. Yet, from all accounts, mothers were very indulgent with their children, and many an observer complained that the sons and daughters of the habitants did too little work and were too much protected.

⊱ The Wife ⊰

Pehr Kalm was dismayed when he observed that women in New France rarely washed their floors. We can speculate that he might have been less critical if the job of washing floors had fallen to him, but the age had its expectations, and Kalm was far from the only man who expected a clean house and an obedient woman. The married woman in New France and Acadia was legally under the sway of her husband.

In most cases, the marriage was harmonious, a partnership between husband and wife, where both worked hard to sustain farm or profession and family. Sometimes, neither husband nor wife could read or write; in others, only the woman knew how to do so. In those families, she did the household accounts and looked after any written contracts the family might have, such as one to build a house. If the man traded in furs and left his family while he travelled the back country, he might leave her with a power of attorney, so that she could look after family affairs.

But if the marriage was bad, the wife had little recourse. She might petition for the separation of their financial affairs if her husband were a drunk or a wastrel, but only rarely could she legally leave his bed and board. In such cases, a compelling argument had to do with her own worth: if she was considered a fine housewife and mother, her chances were better—though still not good. In seventeenth-century Louisburg, Jeanne Cromé petitioned the court that her husband drank, abused her physically and mentally, insulted her viciously in front of his drunken comrades, punched

The Sieur de Dièreville comments on children in Acadia:

In almost every family five or six Children are to be found, & often many more; the swarming of Brats is a sight to behold; although no Pilgrimages are made, here as elsewhere, in order to obtain them, they follow one another closely, & appear to be almost the same age. . . . But when they are fit to work, which is at an early age, Children are the wealth of the Country; they save their Fathers the day labour of a Man, amounting to twenty-five or thirty sols, an outlay they could not afford.

— *Voyage to Port Royal*, p. 93.

A woman had to be perceptive about prospective husbands. Marie de l'Incarnation writes about the choices made by the *filles du roi*:

Those better informed began to build a house a year before they were to marry, because those who had a house found a better match; it's the first thing the girls find out about, and it's wise of them to do so, because those who aren't at all established suffer a lot before they become comfortable.

— *Word from New France*, pp. 353–54.

Widows, orphans, and women without means came to New France to find husbands and have families. A 20th-century artist gives his impression of the arrival of the *filles du roi*, sponsored by the king. Unmarried men—most of the populace—flocked to the docks to see their prospective wives. (Library and Archives Canada C-020126, Acc. No. 1996-371-1)

∞∞∞∞∞∞∞∞∞∞∞∞∞∞∞∞∞∞∞∞∞∞

Upper-class women had their own tasks:

At the table, the eye of the mistress of the house must have the sharpness of the eagle and the softness of the dove....The great art of the house mistress consists of treating her guests in such a way that she makes the social inequality between them disappear....The spirit of the house mistress consists particularly in making others shine.

— *La Nouvelle Cuisinière Canadienne*, p. 6, author's translation.

her and kicked her thus causing a miscarriage, lifted her nightshirt and displayed her to his comrades, called her a whore, and continued to abuse her in front of the priest who was remonstrating with him. The court, always in favour of women obeying their men, must have refused her petition, since she had two more children with the husband.[10]

Disease, hard work, the Iroquois raids, and the fact that men were often considerably older than their wives meant that women had a fair chance of becoming widows. If their husbands died before the children were grown, the widows took on most of the tasks of their husbands—at least until they could find a new husband, not a particularly difficult task if they were still of child-bearing age. "Although the country is most healthy for both sexes," noted Dollier de Casson, "it is incomparably more so for the women, who are almost immortal here.... [I note] the ease with which members of the same sex may find husbands here. This ... may be admirably illustrated by quite an unusual example ... of a woman who, after losing her first husband this year, had banns proclaimed once, was [excused from] two other callings, and had her second marriage arranged and carried out before her first husband was buried."[11] If older, they were to be cared for, by written contract, by one or more of their children.

In times of famine or of war, women were not to be trifled with. In December of 1757, for example, a shortage of beef in Montreal promoted the governor to substitute horsemeat for half the beef ration allowed to families. Women marched in the street to protest: "They had an aversion to horse flesh; . . . he was the friend of man; . . . religion forbade the killing of horses."[12] Though the governor threatened them with hanging for their illegal protest, in the end they were allowed to go free.

In the country it is usual that when the husband receives a visit from persons of rank and dines with them, his wife stands behind and serves him, but in the town the ladies are more distinguished, and would willingly assume an equal if not superior position to their husbands.

— Pehr Kalm, *Travels in North America*, p. 417.

· 2 ·

CANDLES, COMPLAINTS, AND A STIFF UPPER LIP:

Housewives in the Backwoods

A settler's wife should be active, industrious, ingenious, cheerful, not above putting her hand to whatever is necessary to be done in her household, nor too proud to profit by the advice and experience of older portions of the community, from whom she may learn many excellent lessons of practical wisdom. . . . She must become skilled in the arts of sugar-boiling, candle and soap-making, the making and baking of huge loaves, cooked in the bake-kettle, unless she be the fortunate mistress of a stone or clay oven. She must know how to manufacture hop-rising or salt-rising for leavening her bread; salting meat and fish, knitting stockings and mittens and comforters, spinning yarn in the big wheel . . . and dyeing the yarn when spun to have manufactured into cloth and coloured flannels, to clothe her husband and children, making clothes for herself, her husband and children. . . . The management of poultry and the dairy must not be omitted. . . .

—Catherine Parr Traill, The Backwoods of Canada

꒰Ꙩ꒱

Perhaps the best-known housewife in Canadian history, Catherine Parr Traill was one of many women who settled in infant towns and backwoods in the late eighteenth and early nineteenth centuries, making a new life in the British colonies. She was not a typical housewife. She found time to complain about the servant problem and freely acknowledged that she was at least upper-middle class. But she left us a chronicle of everyday household life written with detail not seen before in this country.

Parr Traill came to what is now Canada at a time of great change. Between 1713 and 1763, Acadia and New France were turned over to the British and the Acadians were expelled from their paradise (though many returned after 1763). In the late eighteenth century, the American Revolutionary War sent United Empire Loyalists fleeing across the border, some 30,000 to the Maritimes, about 2,000 to Quebec, and some 7,500 to the almost untouched territories north of the Great Lakes that would soon be dubbed Upper Canada.

Some Loyalists were white, some were black, some were native. Some were true-blue English; some were Pennsylvania Dutch, of German origin and Amish or Mennonite background. Some were able to cling to their worldly goods and arrive in Nova Scotia, if not rich, then at least well-off. Others escaped with nothing more than the clothing they wore and a barrowful of belongings. What they had in common was their determination to make a new life under the British Crown. Each family received a grant of land and enough food to see them through the year.

They were followed over the next 50 years by a deluge of immigrants from Europe. Between 1806 and 1844, the population of

Encampment of the Loyalists at Johnstown, a New Settlement, on the Banks of the River S.ʳ Laurence in Canada, taken June 6.ʳ 74.
taken from ... marked in the Plan

Upper and Lower Canada (Ontario and Quebec) almost quadrupled, from just over 300,000 to almost 1,200,000. From a relatively static, unilingual, Catholic, seigneurial society centred along the St. Lawrence and the Bay of Fundy, the collection of colonies that would become Canada became a quickly changing region where the population spoke English, French, and other languages, followed different religions, owned their own land, and sprawled across the wilds from the Atlantic to Lake Huron.

Like Parr Traill and her husband, many nineteenth-century immigrants were driven to Canada by hard times in Europe, where an economic collapse saw families both wealthy and poor pushed to the brink. Some families went to the Maritimes, some to Quebec. In both places they found settled communities and established towns, but life could be difficult if they lacked pioneer skills, money, or possessions.

Most of the great numbers who pushed on to the bush-covered lands west of Quebec became farmers. By 1851, fewer than 15 per cent of the close to a million people in Upper Canada lived in towns. The backwoods farmers cleared the forest, built houses, established new routines, and revived or learned the skills that they needed. With transport almost non-existent, and few goods available even in the towns, they had to rely mostly on their own efforts.

The women who came were a diverse lot with varying traditions, which they adapted—or not—to the circumstances of their new

Fleeing overland in the America Revolution, families brought little to the backwoods of Canada. In this depiction of a camp and new settlement on the St. Lawrence River, housewives are at work washing clothes and tending cooking fires. (Library and Archives Canada C-002001 Acc. No. 1989-218-1)

The log cabin, the wash tub, the rough road to the home-stead—in the year or two after they arrived, housewives in Upper Canada lived a basic pioneer life. (Library and Archives Canada C-040048, Acc. No. 1970-188-333, W.H. Coverdale Collection of Canadiana)

Jan 25, 1839: I caught myself wishing an old long-forgotten wish that I had been born of the rougher sex. Women are very dependent here, and give a great deal of trouble; we feel our weakness here more than anywhere else.

June 10, 1840: The various methods of making bread, cheese, candles, etc., [and butter] were also commented upon, so you see what ladies talk about here. These useful topics are, however, not unmingled with a little general gossip.

— Anne Langton, *A Gentlewoman in Upper Canada*, pp. 73, 152.

homes. Some were desperately unhappy, unable to cope with separation from family and friends, afraid of the wilderness, disgusted by the change from their well-ordered lives in Britain or the United States. But most made do, following Parr Traill's instructions about working hard and adjusting to the country.

One custom quickly adopted was the work bee. Isolated for much of the year in their own homes, backwoods women treasured any chance to get together for quilting, sewing trousseaus, and apple paring and drying. They also cooked the huge amounts of food necessary for land-clearing and building bees.

Housewives of a certain class—even those with little money—complained frequently in their writings that servants were scarcely to be had. If they were hired, they left soon or worked poorly. And with good reason: many a couple that would have been poor and landless in Europe were able to purchase land of their own, and a woman could set up housekeeping in her own small cabin or shanty instead of hiring out to work in someone else's house.

Even those who could afford to hire a servant or get products from the faraway store were subject to the shortages that plagued the backwoods settler. When goods were available, they had to travel over execrable roads to reach the distant homesteads, and they might, or might not, arrive in decent condition—or at all.

Parr Traill was far from the only woman to chronicle her efforts. Among the Loyalists and later settlers were well-educated women who naturally turned to writing letters, diaries, and books about their lives as bush housewives. Their stories of cooking, cleaning, candle-making, and other activities, their accounts of childbirth, mothering, and wifely duties and worries, and their descriptions of chopping down trees, helping to build houses, looking after livestock, and fishing and hunting give us a picture of the backwoods housewife's life between 1790 and 1850.

Elsewhere in Canada, housewives continued their work:

The females of Labrador…engage in the hard and laborious toils of fishing with as much zeal and activity as the males. When the salmon and trout fishing commences, the women and children employ themselves assiduously in the sport, and are often out night and day while the season of the fishery lasts. At the fish stands, while the cod fishery is in the full tide of operation, the women are seen among the most constant and dextrous in dressing the fish, thrown up by the fisherman. Some of these females will dress two or three thousand fish in a single day.

— Ephraim W. Tucker, *Five Months in Labrador and Newfoundland During the Summer of 1838*, as quoted in Beth Light and Alison Prentice, *Pioneer and Gentlewomen of British North-America*, 1713–1867, pp. 119–20.

There are no manufactures carried on in the Colony [Prince Edward Island], except domestic ones for the use of the farmer's family. The settlers generally make of their wool a very useful cloth, called homespun, which serves the men for jackets and trowsers, whilst a finer sort serves the females with gowns for winter use; they also manufacture blankets, stockings or socks, and mittins. The wool is simply died with indigo. Some families make the greater part of their table, bed, and personal linen from flax, often using with it cotton warp of American manufacture…. The Colonists make a great part of the soap and candles they use, but the greater number burn fish oil for light.

— J.L. Lewellin, *Emigration: Prince Edward Island: A Brief but Faithful Account of this Fine Colony*, as quoted in Dave McIntosh, *When the Work's All Done This Fall*, p. 44.

I have not often in my life met with contented and cheerful-minded women, but I never met with so many repining and discontented women as in Canada. I never met with one woman recently settled here, who considered herself happy in her new home and country; I heard of one, and doubtless there are others, but they are exceptions to the general rule…. Women of the better class…seem to me to be perishing of ennui…for being in general unfitted for out-door occupations, unable to comprehend or enter into the interests around them, and all their earliest prejudices and ideas of the fitness of things continually outraged in a manner exceedingly unpleasant, they may be said to live in a perpetual state of inward passive discord and fretful endurance.

— Anna Jameson, *Winter Studies and Summer Rambles in Canada*, Vol. 2, pp. 133, 147–48.

"Do-it-yourself" was a necessity, not a choice, for the backwoods housewife. This 20th-century depiction of pioneer life shows her at work pouring cream into a butter churn; though the houses suggest a later community, the methods are still those of the earliest pioneers. (Russell Taber, courtesy of the International Nickel Company)

ᚷ The Cook ᚷ

Handwritten family cookbooks passed from generation to generation; recipes from France, England, Scotland, Ireland, and Germany; ingredients native to North America and some that came from far away; scarcity and abundance: the kitchen world of the backwoods housewife was a mixture of traditional and new.

Perhaps most important were the housewife's ingenious ways of improvising. English immigrant Mary O'Brien described a day of cooking in her journal for November 6, 1830:

> My little quarter of pork was dangling before the fire at the end of a skein of worsted, for having a loaf to bake I was unable to bake it as usual in the all-accomplishing bake kettle. I cast my eyes on the said bake kettle and, behold, its lid was raised upwards of an inch by the exuberant fermentation of the loaf within, which was threatening to run down its side into the ashes. Hastily I then was obliged to resume my labours and, seizing a knife, I cut from the top of the loaf the exceeding portion and placed it, much to my satisfaction, before the fire on a plate. There I hoped it would soon be converted into capital rusks. Of course the frying pan would have been the natural receptacle but that was engaged in enacting dripping pan for the pork. Oh,

KNICKERBOCKER PICKLES
Take six gallons of water 10 lbs of Salt 3 lbs of coarse brown sugar, 1 quart of Molasses 3 oz salt petre 1 oz Pear[l] ash. Boil and skim. When quite cold pour over pork or beef previously placed in a barrel. 16th January made this pickle but only put 6 pounds of rock salt, & used Sallerata instead of pearl Ash.

— Sarah Welsh Hill Diary, in Kathryn Carter, ed., *The Small Details of Life, Twenty Diaries by Women in Canada, 1830–1996*, p. 93, note 31.

who can number up the uses and perfections of a Canadian bake kettle and frying pan?

I had just turned from the complacent contemplation of my arrangements when a treacherous stick, on which was resting at once for support and heat a saucepan containing a stew of cabbage and an old cock, gave way and my stew was emptied on my rusks. The rusks were spoiled, that much could not be helped, but the lucky plate saved my old cock from being buried in the ashes and enabled me to restore my stew. Just then my guests arrived.[1]

Such ingenuity was often called for in the getting and cooking of provisions. You could grow it, you could buy it—or you could shoot it or fish for it. Some bought fish and game from the native people who lived in the region, while others went into the forests and streams themselves, bringing back deer and fish for their wives to cook. In those pioneer days, salmon still spawned in the creeks near Lake Ontario, and pike, whitefish, and herring swam in lake and river waters. Women could buy maskinonge, pickerel, white-fish, herring, bass, and a dozen other varieties of freshwater fish. And some women did the fishing themselves, then sold their fish for a little extra household cash. Even such a personality as the governor's wife thought ice fishing a fine occupation: Elizabeth Simcoe fished for trout from her carriole through the ice of rivers near York (soon to become Toronto). Housewives even seined for salmon with their flannel petticoats at the mouth of one salmon stream.[2] Hunters brought in venison, to be eaten fresh or dried.

Each housewife had her kitchen garden, where she grew vegetables, small fruits, and, if she was of a mind to, flowers. Wheat from the fields went to the mill for grinding into flour, paid for by a portion of the flour. Farmers butchered for beef, pork, and poultry. Most housewives kept their own small flock of chickens, ducks, and geese—though disaster could strike at any time. "Besides a fine brood of fowls," wrote Catherine Parr Traill, "... I have some ducks and am to have turkeys and geese this summer. I lost several of my best fowls, not by the hawk, but a horrid beast of the same nature as our polecat, called here a scunck... [who] comes like a thief in the night and invades the perch, leaving headless mementos of his barbarity and blood-thirsty propensities."[3]

RECIPE FOR HOP-RISING

Take two double handfuls of hops, boil in a gallon of soft water, if you can get it, till the hops sink to the bottom of the vessel; make ready a batter formed by stirring a dessert-plateful of flour and cold water until smooth and pretty thick together; strain the hop-liquor while scalding hot into the vessel where your batter is ready mixed; let one person pour the hop-liquor while the other keeps stirring the batter. When cooled down to a gentle warmth, so that you can bear the finger well in it, add a cup or basinful of the former barm, or a bit of leaven, to set it to work; let the barm stand till it has worked well, then bottle and cork it. Set it by in a cellar or cool place in summer, and in winter it is also the best place to keep it from freezing. Some persons add two or three mealy potatoes boiled and finely bruised, and it is a great improvement during the cool months of the year.

— Catherine Parr Trail, *The Backwoods of Canada*, p. 319.

Feb. 1, 1839: I am going to exercise my skill in shaping ham tonight. That I consider my special province. My mother shines in rolled pig's head, and Aunt Alice in pork pies.

July 2, 1839: I grumbled a little at the necessity of storing all your summer provisions in the winter, and at the annoyance of unpacking and repacking barrels of pork, boiling brine, etc., etc. Our caterer I find, instead of a box of candles, has brought us a cask of tallow, much to our disappointment, having already clear abundance of work on hand. I have sometimes thought, and I may as well say it, now that it is grumbling day—woman is a bit of a slave in this country.

May 10, 1841: We had the first nice spring rain to-day, which makes us look forward to a better supply of milk and butter.

May 29: Today I intend taking all the hams and the bacon down and inspecting their condition. This is an operation that must be very frequently performed. There is a little beetle in this country that I had rather get rid of than even mosquitoes or black flies. It infests all our provisions. We intend putting up a smoke house soon, which is the best way of keeping hung meat.

— Anne Langton, *A Gentlewoman in Upper Canada* pp. 101–102; 115; 182; 186.

Scorned by the French in Canada as food scarcely fit for pigs, potatoes were a staple for the Loyalists who came from the United States and for immigrants from the British Isles. Every backwoods farm and garden contained hills of the starchy tuber, and settlers strove to find new varieties that would mature earlier or keep longer. The housewife relied on potatoes to improve the yeast starter she used to make bread; for soup, potato cakes, and dumplings; for that most standard of meals, salt pork and potatoes; and even for laundry starch. By early in the nineteenth century, even Acadian and Quebec housewives had been won over by this useful food.

Not all innovations were equally welcome. Newfangled baking soda—bicarbonate of soda, a relative of pearl ash—could be used in baking, but it was unreliable and produced uneven results. For most housewives, a flat and heavy cake, leavened with eggs or even fresh snow, was the standard, while they continued to rely on salt-rising or hop-rising for their bread.

Many middle-class housewives kept a family cookbook, with recipes carefully written in and passed down from mother to daughter or garnered from the neighbours. Family treasures that served instead of the few published cookbooks, they specified ingredients available from field, garden, market, and store. A disappointed housewife wrote in her own comments on the various recipes: "Bad!"—or simply crossed out recipes that didn't work.

By about 1830, cast-iron stoves for heating and cooking were making their appearance in both town and country. Though the stoves provided convenience, with ovens, broilers, bake pans, and a flat surface for saucepans or heating irons, many housewives scorned them initially for cooking. There was nothing, they said, like the flavour developed on the hearth or above the fire.

When men gathered to work together on building or harvesting, women provided acres of food and oceans of drink. English immigrant Susanna Moodie—who frowned on the work bee as an occasion where more drinking than working took place, and suggested that, for the money expended, the Moodies could have hired several men to log their lands—described her preparations for one bee:

People in the woods have a craze for giving and going to bees, and run to them with as much eagerness as a peasant runs to a racecourse or a fair; plenty of strong drink and

A later artist saw pioneer life through somewhat rose-coloured glasses, but his thoughts on the housewife's work were accurate: though canning jars like those shown weren't on the scene until late in the 19th century, she did have to preserve fruits and vegetables by canning, drying, and pickling. (Russell Taber, courtesy of the International Nickel Company)

excitement being the chief attraction of the bee. . . . the maid and I were engaged for two days preceding the important one, in baking and cooking for the entertainment of our guests. When I looked at the quantity of food we had prepared I thought it could never be eaten, even by thirty-two men. . . . they all sat down to the table which I had prepared for them, loaded with the best fare which could be procured in the bush. Pea-soup, legs of pork, venison, eel, and raspberry pies, garnished with plenty of potatoes, and whiskey to wash them down, besides a large iron kettle of tea. . . . Someone was funning Old Wittals for having eaten seven large cabbages at Mr. T----'s bee, a few days previous, and his son, Sol, thought himself, as in duty, bound to take up the cudgel for his father. "Now, I guess that's a lie, anyhow. Father was sick that day, and I tell you he only ate five."[4]

As in Acadia and New France, food preservation was an important task. The housewife salted fish and laid them down in barrels, pickled vegetables, bottled fruit, dried apples, made jam, cured hams, and salted pork. Eggs and milk were available only when hens laid and cows freshened, usually from spring to late fall, so she must preserve eggs and produce cheese and butter. She kept meat through the summer by putting it in the ice house, a small cellar lined with timber and covered with earth and sod, filled in winter with ice from the lakes or rivers. Her husband sometimes took the products she made—butter, cheese, wool, and flax—to town where he traded them for such things as salt and tea.

In times of famine, such as those that struck Upper Canada in the 1790s and the 1820s, she improvised as best she could. One beef bone could be boiled repeatedly with a little bran, and the housewife soon learned which wild roots and leaves could be eaten. Yet in better times, dinner could be a complicated affair in upper- and middle-class households, set out in a pattern on the dining table. Anne Langton describes a company dinner, and various other aspects of cooking and preparation: "The dinner prepared was soup at the top, removed by a boiled fillet of veal, pork at bottom; corners, spring chickens, ham and veal steaks, and macaroni. Second course, pudding, tart, trifle, and cheese cakes."[5]

RECIPES

The Cook Not Mad, or Rational Cookery is considered the first cookbook published in English Canada. A copy of an American book, it circulated widely in Upper Canada. Among its suggestions:

NO. 104: NICE COOKIES THAT WILL KEEP GOOD THREE MONTHS

Nine cups flour, three and a half of butter, five of sugar, large coffee cup of water, with a heaping teaspoonful of pearlash dissolved, in it; rub your butter and sugar into the flour, great spoonful of caraway.

NO. 196: A NEW METHOD OF KEEPING APPLES FRESH AND GOOD, THROUGH THE WINTER AND INTO SUMMER

Take a quantity of pippins or other good winter apples; take them from the trees carefully when ripe, and before frost, make a hole through each one with a goose quill from stem to eye, fill this with sugar, lay in this position two weeks, till they are a little wilted, then put them in a tight cask and keep them from freezing.

NO. 263: TO PRESERVE EGGS

Rub the outside of the shell as soon as gathered from the nest, with a little butter, or any other grease that is not fetid. By filling up the pores of the shell, the evaporation of the liquid part of the egg is prevented; and either by that means, or by excluding the external air, the milkiness which most people are fond of in new-laid eggs, will be preserved for months, as perfect as when the egg was taken from the nest.

NO. 274: AN EXCELLENT KETCHUP WHICH WILL KEEP GOOD MORE THAN TWENTY YEARS

Take two gallons of stale strong beer, or ale, the stronger and staler the better; one pound of anchovies, cleansed from the intestines and washed, half an ounce each of cloves and mace, one quarter oz. of pepper, six large roots of ginger, one pound of eschalots, and two quarts or more of flap mushrooms, well rubbed and picked. Boil these ingredients over a slow fire for one hour; then strain the liquor through a flannel bag, and let it stand until quite cold, when it must be bottled and stopped very close with cork and bladder, or leather. One spoonful of this ketchup to a pint of melted butter, gives an admirable taste and colour, as a fish sauce, and is by many preferred to the best Indian soy.

❧ The Housekeeper ❧

Though the adage that "cleanliness is next to godliness" comes from eighteenth-century England, there is almost nothing about cleaning the house in all of Catherine Parr Traill's multitudinous instructions to women who settled in Canada. A fanatical devotion to a clean house was a trait of the city and the Victorian era. Faced with the eternal mud of the backwoods, her men tracking in dirt every day from their work in the fields, and the chores that awaited her each day, the backwoods housewife was not compelled to keep her house spotlessly clean. The small houses of early settlement meant that a minimal sweeping took little time. Outdoor toilets

RECIPES

The Jopling family cookbook, page after page of handwritten treasures that date from as early as 1796, was passed to daughters Sarah, Charlotte, and Alice Jopling from their mother. Each of the women added recipes and thoughts through the years.

FROM MOTHER, CA. 1796:

TONGUES

If it be a dried tongue, steep it all night in water, but if a pickled one only wash it well from the brine. Let it boil moderately three hours. If it is to be eat hot, stick with cloves, rub it over with the yolk of an egg, strew crumbled bread over it & when done, baste it with butter & set it before the fire until it becomes of a light brown. Dish.

SPRING BROTH

Take a crust of bread, about a quarter of a pound of fresh butter: put them into a soup pot or a stew pan with a good quantity of herbs as beet; sorril; chervil; lettuce, leeks & purslain, all washed clean and coarsely chopped, put to them a quart of water & let them stew until it is reduced to one half, then it will be fit for use: This is an excellent purifier of the blood.

FROM THE DAUGHTERS, CA. 1808–1840:

A GOOSE PIE

Take a goose and a fowl, bone them & season them well, put forcemeat into the fowl and then put the fowl into the goose. Place these into a raised crust & fill the corners with a little forcemeat. Put half a pound of butter cut into pieces on the top, cover it, send it to the oven.

PLUM WHISKEY

Pour a gallon of whiskey into a two-gallon jar with two pounds of loaf sugar when well dissolved fill the jar with butter plums.

Nov. 28, 1842: The putting in of double windows, and stuffing with cotton wool, has been a good part of my occupation today.

— Anne Langton, *A Gentlewoman in Upper Canada*, p. 212.

POT-POURRI

Gather your roses when perfectly dry pull them from the stalks leaving out the decayed leaves. Intermix them with a small quantity of lavender and orange flowers, put a thick layer of roses immediately fresh from the stalk into the jar glazed inside and having a glazed cover that fits close. Strew them over with common salt, pressing them down close with the hands and so proceed until the jar is filled. Put on the cover and let it remain undisturbed for 5 weeks. Then pour off the liquor from it and with the hands break into pieces. Prepare the following compounds: 1 oz nutmeg, 1 oz cloves, 1 oz mace, 1 oz cinnamon, 1 oz gum, 1 oz oris root cut in slices, shavings of calamus coronaticus, do [ditto] of Sandalwood, a small quantity of each with a few grains of musk. Mix it all well together with the rose leaves and put the whole into a porcelain jar observing frequently to stir it.

— Martha Field cookbook, Upper Canada, 1842–1858.

and no piped water caused their own problems, but at least there were no modern bathrooms to clean.

Which is not to say houses were not cleaned. Housewives could choose from a wide variety of brooms, home-made, store-bought, or acquired from a peddler who made the rounds of the backwoods once or twice a year—brooms for sweeping the floor, for the stairs, for corners, for carpets. Some backwoods brooms were made of evergreen branches, tied to a handle and trimmed, or a branch of a wood such as hickory, beach or birch, one end split into fine shreds, the other used as a handle. Some women swore by cedar boughs tied together for a hearth brush, because they gave forth such a pleasant scent when used. Housewives used coarse clean sand and hot water to scrub wooden floors, applying the sand once a week with a heavy broom and the water-the hotter the better-with a mop. Long-handled dusters were in vogue for those housewives who had possessions and knick-knacks worth dusting. Once or twice a year, the housewife undertook a thorough spring cleaning, hanging the bedclothes out in the wind (but keeping any feather comforters in the shade), sweeping and cleaning in every corner. This was the time to turn mattresses that were made of evergreen boughs, corn husks, straw, or feathers.

As in New France and Acadia, one of the housewife's chores was to keep the fire burning. Lighting a fire required striking a flint with a steel to produce sparks, or sending a child to a distant neighbour to bring back glowing coals. Hot coals were covered with ashes to keep them alive when they were not needed.

Every chronicler of backwoods life mentions the making of candles, still the light source preferred over oil lamps: "I have been engaged this afternoon making up my remaining supply of tallow into four dozen portly-looking dips, eight to the pound," wrote Anne Langton on April 13, 1839. "My last making was twelve dozen, and I think the larger number is very much as quickly accomplished as the smaller one, for they gather more tallow when thoroughly cooled, so that with many I need not go through them as often as with few."[6]

Year-round, the housewife had to battle two demons: damp and bedbugs. The authors of *The Cook Not Mad* recommended a yearly application of four egg whites and 10 cents' worth of quicksilver (mercury, commonly used in household preparations),

C.W. JEFFERYS

Not a witch's cauldron but a soap kettle— the artist shows the making of potash in a giant cauldron buttressed by stones and heated on an outdoor fire. Together with animal fat, potash—made from fireplace ashes—was a necessary component of the soap made by backwoods housewives. (Jefferys II-222)

Anne Langton cleans her brother's house:

I came back with a strengthened conviction of the importance of woman, and congratulating myself, that though I might be an old maid I never could be an old bachelor.

— *A Gentlewoman in Upper Canada*, January 25, 1839, p. 99.

No. 281 Ready mode of mending cracks in Stoves, Pipes, and Iron Ovens.

When a crack is discovered in a stove, through which the fire or smoke penetrates, the aperture may be completely closed in a moment with composition consisting of wood ashes and common salt, made up into a paste with a little water, and plastered over the crack. The good effect is usually certain, whether the stove, etc. be cold or hot.

— *The Cook Not Mad.*

beaten together to a froth, to every part of the bedstead where bugs might appear.[7]

Bedbugs weren't the only insects to threaten the home. The same book instructs the careful housekeeper in preventing moths: beat fur garments in April with a small cane or stick, wrap them gently in linen, putting small lumps of camphor between the folds, then place them into a well-closed box. Take them out when they are needed, beat them again, and hang them for a day to let the camphor smell dissipate. "If the fur has long hair," added the author, "as bear or fox, add to the camphor an equal quantity of black pepper in powder."[8] Alternatively, the housewife might sprinkle Scotch snuff—a fine, dry powdery snuff—into her furs.

The housewife, suggested the book, could make paste by stirring rye or wheat flour into cold water until it was the thickness of cream, then heating and stirring it. If she wanted only a little for some "trifling purpose," she should mix a small amount in a spoon and heat it over a lamp or candle.[9] A reader might also learn from this book how to clean woodwork by using that most handy of substances, pearl ash; how to make whitewash from that most handy of vegetables, potatoes; how to remove a glass stopper stuck in the mouth of a bottle; how to clean brass; how to air feather beds; how to make a cheap blue paint for ceilings (from blue vitriol and best whiting); and a whole variety of other useful hints.

But few needed a book to tell them how to keep house. Most did as their mothers had done, sweeping, dusting, washing, shining, as part of their weekly routine, and washing dishes, keeping the fire, and bringing in water every day.

‌ THE SEAMSTRESS ‌

Red flannel she could buy from the distant store, and bright gingham too, but the backwoods housewife was still much in the business of spinning and sewing, dyeing and darning. If rain fell out of doors, it was a fair bet that she was busy with her needle indoors, mending or remaking clothes, knitting, or converting worn-out outfits into rag rugs.

The new settler brought her own and her family's clothing with her, and could buy cloth from a store or an itinerant peddler. Such cloth was not cheap, however, and the thrifty housewife could save money by spinning and dyeing her own yarn, to be sent to the weavers or used for knitting. Less likely to have flax or hemp than the long-established farmer in Acadia or New France, she used the wool from sheep—provided those animals survived wolves and cold winters.

Once the sheep were sheared, women might gather at a picking bee, where they sorted out the coarse or matted wool that could be used to spin rough yarn. Then they worked grease evenly into the

Nov. 9/42: Today I have been stitching very diligently at a gingham gown of my mother's that I am altering for myself; and when I have done it I must attack a silk one, which I consider a very important affair, for a better gown here lasts for years.... There are certainly some advantages to living in the backwoods.

— Anne Langton, *A Gentlewoman in Upper Canada*, p. 206.

August 10, 1841: Venetian blind-making, sail-making, and stay-making have been my occupations this wet day, and my mother has been shoe-making, or rather covering a favourite pair of shoes the second time.

— Anne Langton, *A Gentlewoman in Upper Canada*, p. 188.

C W JEFFERYS

Far distant from stores—and lacking money to purchase—a backwoods housewife learned how to spin wool from sheep or fibres from flax. (Jefferys II-230)

<<<<<<<<<<<<<<<<<<<<<<<<<<<<<<<<<<<<<<<<<<<<<<<<

TO MAKE A RAG CARPET

1. Take a piece of old cloth and cut or tear it into a strip about six millimetres wide, cutting to the end of the cloth, but not all the way through, leaving enough to hold the piece together.

2. Turn at the end of each strip and cut from the other end, so that you produce one long piece of cloth.

3. If you want a carpet with no turned up pieces, cut the strips through and join them together; this is more work, but produces a finer carpet.

3. Wind each long strip into a ball, sewing the strip together if it tears. You can wind colours separately, or wind them into one large ball. Separate balls produce stripes in the final carpet; colours wound together less predictable patterns.

4. Send the balls to the weavers—or weave them yourself on cotton warp.

— adapted from Catherine Parr Traill, *The Canadian Settlers' Guide*, pp. 181–82.

wool so it could be more easily combed or carded. They might card the wool themselves, with teethed carding boards, or, once a region was more developed, send it to a carding mill so they could spin it into yarn and dye it.

"I often noticed, as we passed by the cottage farms," wrote Parr Traill, "hanks of yarn of different colours hanging on the garden or orchard fence to dry; there were all manner of colours, green, blue, purple, brown red, and white. A civil landlady, at whose tavern we stopped to change horses, told me these hanks of yarn were first spun and then dyed by the good wives, before being sent to the loom. She showed me some of this home-spun cloth, which really looked very well."[10]

Before they were dyed, the yarns had to be thoroughly washed to remove the grease that, only a few weeks earlier, the housewife had been at pains to put in. Maple bark for brownish grey; sumac bark for slate grey; purslane weed, logwood, and indigo plants, grown for just this purpose, for blue; madder for red; goldenrod flowers and onion skins for yellow and pale brown; the lye from wood ashes—that all-purpose substance—and copperas, a metallic sulphate that varied according to the metal used, for orange. A dyer needed to be both botanist and chemist.

Parr Traill advised of knitting, "If you do not understand this useful art, I strongly advise you to turn your attention to it as soon as possible. . . . Your boys and husband will need plenty of woollen socks and mitts in Canada. There is no country where there is so much knitting work done as in Canada." Socks and mittens, cradle covers and curtains: these and any number of other wearables and usables were products of the knitter's skill. If the housewife and her daughters knitted more socks than her menfolk could use, the extras could be sold at the general store. "Children and women will earn many a dollar if they are industrious, in the evening, between twilight and candle-light."[11]

Some women, proud possessors of a loom and the skill to go with it, wove cloth, but more sent their yarn to a weaving mill, which took half the wool in return for weaving it all. Women then made the cloth into trousers, shirts, and dresses. Old garments taken apart were used as patterns for new.

Hand-me-downs served well. Time and again, women remade the clothes they had brought with them as immigrants, resewing them into dresses that followed the fashions they saw in magazines from England or the United States.

Clothes were not the only job the seamstress had to tackle. She also needed curtains and rugs to adorn her new home. "I should be sorry to do such stiff sewing [making curtains] in the depth of winter," wrote Anne Langton, "from what I recall of my finger-ends last year in hard frost. My hands are not given to chap much, but just the end of my thumb and forefinger used to crack, and get deeper and deeper for two or three weeks, It is surprising how much annoyance so small a thing can give."[12]

Every housewife had a rag bag filled with worn-out clothes and bits and pieces of cloth. "I asked the wife of the resident-minister of P., what she was going to do with a basket of faded, ragged clothes, old red-flannel shirts, and pieces of all sorts and sizes;

some old, some new, some linen and cotton, others woollen," Parr Traill recounted. "I am going to tear and cut them up for making a rag carpet,' she replied, 'they are not good enough to give away to anyone.'. . . . I assure you these rag-carpets make by no means a despicable appearance, on the rough floors of a Canadian farmer's house."[13] Bits and pieces of cloth were also used in quilts when housewives gathered for quilting bees.

Ingenuity also came into play. Contemporary accounts refer to women making clothing from deerskins, blankets from hair from the tanner's vat, and cloth from a hemp-like weed.

⤙ The Laundress ⤚

Happy the town housewife with a little money, for she could take her dirty wash to a commercial laundry or have a washerwoman come in. Somewhat content the housewife who had some sort of indoor plumbing, be it only a pipe that ran from the well or the stream to the kitchen. But for most, as in the French regime, laundry was still hard, dirty work.

Some backwoods families had a wash house behind the main cabin for this unwelcome chore. Many used the main hearth to heat their water and boiled the dirty clothes of the household in the kitchen. Soap was for sale in town, but country dwellers or poor people must still make their own soap by boiling potash to produce lye and mixing it with fat rendered from pigs, sheep, and cows. Parr Traill gave long and detailed directions on how to make various kinds of soap, including, much to the relief of the housewife, "labour-saving soap." Unfortunately, this kind of laundry soap required that the housewife already have on hand bar soap or soft soap, as well as washing soda, rosin, spirits of turpentine, and salt.

Using the soap was not as simple as dumping detergent into a washing machine:

> When required for use, melt a piece in a pint of soft water, and stir into it as much warm soft water as will be sufficient to soak the clothes, which may be done over night—the white clothes by themselves: pound them a little,

NO. 217: TO MAKE BOILED SOAP

For a barrel take thirty-five pounds of scraps or other grease that is made daily in a family, put half the quantity into a five pound kettle, a pailful of strong lie, boil it thoroughly with a moderate fire or it will run over then keep adding strong lie until full, put it in a barrel and add weak lie—then take the other half of the grease and proceed as before.

NO. 234: TO TAKE GREASE SPOTS OUT OF CLOTHES

Rub on spirits turpentine, then take alcohol and rub with a sponge, it will leave the cloth unsoiled.

NO. 250: WASHING COTTONS AND LINEN

Never wash muslins or any kind of white cotton goods, with linen; for the latter deposits or discharges a gum and colouring material every time it is washed, which discolours and dyes the cotton—wash them by themselves.

— *The Cook Not Mad.*

and wring out; lay on a clean board, and put them into your boiler with a piece of soap dissolved; let them boil for half an hour; take them out into a clean Indian basket, set across two bars, over your tub; while the liquor drains off, wring the clothes into another tub of clean water; then wring again in blue water.[14]

Every housewife knew ways of removing stains from fabric. To extract grease from a silk or cotton dress, for example, *The Cook Not Mad* recommended grating a raw potato in clean water, then sieving the liquid to remove larger particles and letting it stand until the fine white particles of potato fell to the bottom. The clear liquid at the top, bottled, could be applied to the grease spot with a sponge; the garment should then be washed in clear water several times. Even with care, the writer warned, some delicate colours would still show a slight water mark.[15]

Clean wet laundry was pinned on whatever lines had been rigged near the house. As was noted more than once, a little ironing went a long way in the backwoods. For what must be ironed, the housewife used a variety of flat irons, heated before the fire or on the stove.

❧ THE NURSE ❧

The patient sweated and shook, shivered and burrowed into the covers, then vomited and sweated again. Bones ached and teeth chattered. The illness might last for weeks; months later, the fevers and chills recurred. In the nineteenth century, they called it the ague and believed it arose from the soil when it was first broken or from unhealthy swamps. They were not so far wrong: ague is a type of malaria, caused by mosquitoes that carry the disease, and mosquitoes breed in swamps and damp clearings. But even before the clearing began, traveller Pehr Kalm noted that "intermitting fevers of all kinds . . . are very common . . . between Lake Erie and Lake Huron"[16] and many subsequent travellers mentioned the disease. Many workers on the construction of the Rideau Canal between the Ottawa River and Lake Ontario ca. 1830 died from the ague, as did their wives and children.

This [ague] is the most prevalent disorder: sometimes it proves fatal, but not generally so by any means. It leaves, however, dregs of various kinds behind it, which often end in dropsies, consumptions, &c. Those who have had it once will most likely have a touch of it every year. A moist, hot summer fosters it very much; and when we fairly take it, we are rendered useless for any active business for many months. The sulphate of Quinine, a preparation from bark, is what the doctors administer for the cure of this wearisome distemper: it seems to be a very potent medicine, but being very dear, poor people are at a loss to procure it. The Indians are never troubled with any thing of the sort. There is a kind of ague, too, the patient does not shake with, termed the Dumb Ague: this is very difficult to cure, and mostly affects those advanced in years. The Lake Fever prevails at Kingston, York, and other towns and villages on the borders of the great lakes. It is often fatal, and the nature of it as yet seems not well understood.

— John MacTaggart, *Three Years in Canada*, Vol. II, p. 18.

A name also used for colds or influenza, the ague was one of a litany of maladies the housewife faced in her role as family nurse. Rheumatism was rampant and accidents frequent. Medicine had progressed little in several centuries. Backwoods housewives still relied on herbal remedies and nostrums of uncertain content bought from itinerant peddlers.

Some were useful; some were not. Though it was known fairly early that quinine could help with the ague, even Catherine Parr Traill recommended calomel—mercurous chloride that had a strong cathartic effect and was long thought to be a cure for many diseases and conditions—as well as Epsom salts and quinine.

The successful housewife-nurse grew many medicinal plants in her garden. Rose petals, hips, and leaves were used for many purposes: a soothing lotion, a sore-throat gargle, a wound-healing salve. Even constipation and palsy were held to be susceptible to rose conserve. Garlic was said to cure baldness, hot onion poultices were recommended for earache, and mashed clover blossoms took the sting out of bee stings.

A salve made from black alder, lard, resin, and beeswax was recommended for burns; a poultice made of crushed plantain leaves with the stems and ribs removed was applied to almost anything, including lame feet. The more bitter the medicine the more frequently it was prescribed.

Every ethnic group had its own remedies. German immigrants liked betony, bugloss, feverfew, horehound, and licorice, among other plants. They thought rubbing a freshly cut potato over a wart would make it disappear; the British preferred celandine juice. Parr Traill suggests marigolds as the all-purpose plant, good for treating cuts, bruises, burns, and gangrene, as well as for colouring cheese, butter, and wool.

A housewife was expected to "do for" her neighbours should the need arise. With all the transportation problems of the early settlements, the doctor usually arrived after the crisis was over—or when it was too late, something that didn't help doctors' reputations. Any woman who got a name for her nursing skills, especially as a midwife, could expect to find her less skillful—or poorer—neighbours at her door, asking for help.

At nine o'clock one night, as she felt symptoms of impending childbirth, Mary O'Brien and her husband, Edward, sent for the

SAL VOLATILE
An excellent cure for stings. Rub the part stung with it.

WATER GRUEL
Put a pint of water on the fire. Mix in a basin a spoonful of oatmeal with little water; when the water boils, stir in the oatmeal. Let it boil three or four times, but be careful it does not boil over. Strain through a sieve; salt, put in a piece of butter; stir it about with a spoon till the butter is all melted and it is fine and smooth. Sugar, a spoonful of wine, etc. may occasionally be added.

— Martha Field cookbook: ca 1842–1858.

The idyllic, virtuous, and prosperous family in Upper Canada, gathered round the fire, listening to father and mother, while a servant or daughter does the ironing—this drawing decorated the Upper Canada Christian Almanac in 1833. (Library and Archives Canada C-117836)

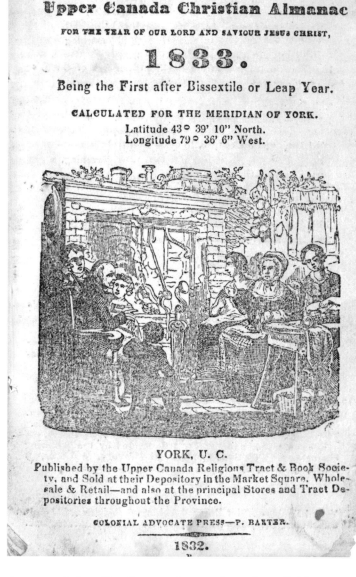

THE
Upper Canada Christian Almanac
FOR THE YEAR OF OUR LORD AND SAVIOUR JESUS CHRIST,
1833.
Being the First after Bissextile or Leap Year.

CALCULATED FOR THE MERIDIAN OF YORK.
Latitude 43° 39' 10" North.
Longitude 79° 36' 6" West.

YORK, U. C.
Published by the Upper Canada Religious Tract & Book Society, and Sold at their Depository in the Market Square, Wholesale & Retail—and also at the principal Stores and Tract Depositories throughout the Province.

COLONIAL ADVOCATE PRESS—F. BAXTER.

1832.

doctor and the wife of an employee—the only available woman in the area who could speak English. The woman arrived, the doctor did not, and O'Brien prepared herself and her room. Very rapidly, a daughter arrived into her father's hands. The doctor arrived in time to congratulate the new parents, eat supper, and go to bed.

Less than a month after her own baby was born, O'Brien attended another birth. "I was sent for to the assistance of one of our labourers' wives at the wharf. . . . I arrived just in time to do the needful for a fine little girl. This is the second time I have cheated the doctor within four weeks . . . the said doctor arrived just after the work was done to look very foolish and go home with me to dine. . . . Doctors have no chance at such work here. We make so light of it."[17]

⥤ THE MOTHER ⥢

"After dinner I went to Mama's room to get out of their way and from thence I did not very immediately return, for a few minutes made me the mother of another son," wrote Mary O'Brien in 1832. "The nurse had not arrived, but Mama was so completely taken by surprise that she had no time to be alarmed . . . ."[18]

In her diary, O'Brien spent more time describing gathering cedar and everlastings for a flower pot than she did describing giving birth, for the sensibilities of the age prevented her from going into detail. She was lucky: none of her six experiences of childbirth caused her more than minimum discomfort. She also recovered quickly. The day after this birth, she was pleased to learn that the nurse needed to go elsewhere, so she had nothing to do but look at the baby ("which is pretty tolerably ugly"), write in her journal, and wait for her husband to come home from a journey. Three days later, she stayed up most of the day, cut out a frock, and ate a dinner of boiled mutton. Two weeks later, "I have been all day superintending not only the household duties but the labours of seven or eight men, besides nursing my babies."[19]

There was no room or time in the backwoods for creating a fuss over giving birth. The household chores didn't go away because a woman was pregnant or newly delivered of a baby. With the other children and the house to look after, a mother was always on call. Though Upper Canada families were, in general, smaller than in New France and Acadia, the absence of birth control often produced four, five, or six children. Little wonder that many a chronicler describes a mother of 30 as looking as if she were 60.

Nov. 28, 1831: I have been making bacon and, since that, constructing a pair of trousers for baby, which seem to amuse him very much, out of the sleeves of an old flannel waistcoat.

— Mary O'Brien, *The Journals of Mary O'Brien*, 1828–1838, p. 170.

No. 266. To expel nameless intruders from children's heads.

Steep larkspur seed in water, rub the liquor a few times into the child's hair, and the business of destruction is done. This is an effectual remedy. Does it not make your head itch?

— *The Cook Not Mad.*

Clutching her swaddled child, urged on by her husband, the new immigrant arrives in the backwoods with her young children. (Jefferys II-244)

~~~~~~~~~~~~~~~~~~~~~~~~~~~~~~~~

TWO VIEWS OF WIFEDOM

When I was married to Mr. M., not having much previous acquaintance with his temper and disposition, I expected to receive the greatest marks of attention, kindness, and indulgence from him. But I soon found that, being his wife, I was bound by law to yield obedience to the requirements of my husband; and when he enforced obedience, and showed marks of resentment if his wishes were not met, I was tempted with anger, and felt a spirit of resentment arise in my heart, and retaliating expressions come into my mind; but I had sufficient self-possession to refrain from speaking in an unbecoming manner.

— Diary of Mary Coy Morris Bradley, New Brunswick, as quoted in Margaret Conrad, ed., *The Neglected Majority*, *Essays in Canadian Women's History*, Vol. 2, p. 45.

continued on next page

Though diaries suggest mothers of the era clearly loved their children, they tended to take them for granted, much as they had childbirth. As soon as the little ones were old enough, they were taught to do simple chores around the house or left to look after their younger siblings. The younger children dressed themselves, fed the chickens, and did whatever other chores they could; older sons worked with their fathers in the fields or woods, while older daughters were responsible for the spinning of wool, among other chores. Mother taught her daughters how to cook, sew, knit, and prepare food.

Since there were very few schools in the region, mother often doubled as teacher. If she could read and write, it was up to her to pass these skills on to her children. Sometimes, a woman who was literate gathered a number of children from neighbouring farms into her house each day for lessons in reading, writing, and simple arithmetic. Mothers were also responsible for their children's religious education.

ᚋ THE WIFE ᚋ

Writer, art critic, and fierce feminist Anna Jameson knew how to deal with an unsatisfactory marriage in pioneer country. She joined her husband in Upper Canada for a brief nine months in 1837, then fled back to England to resume her writing career. But Jameson was possessed of more fire, independence, and money—though she was by no means well-off—than most women who found themselves trapped and in the backwoods. Jameson herself, in her account of her Canadian travels, tells of a number of such women, as do other writers, who on their travels discover women who have been driven mad by the combination of too many children, too much work and isolation, and too little money.

Jameson to some extent blamed the men for the unhappiness of wives. She has a long conversation with a well-established farmer who wants a wife, but he wants someone cultivated and refined, someone who fulfills his "preconceived notions of feminine elegance and refinement," someone whom he envisions bending over a harp and singing. He had no time for the "daughters of the bush," even though he was well aware that the woman he sought would be unhappy in the backwoods. The women who came from England, he noted, were fine in the first and even the second year, but the third was fatal, for women could not leave their domestic ties behind so easily as the men. "The women, poor souls, sit and sew, and think." And he reels off a list of women who, once healthy and happy, are now prematurely old and care-worn.[20] As Jameson later notes, women whose families were close by and whose roots were in Canada did far better than upper-class immigrants. Without the close-knit social system and families of the French colonies, many women experienced the sad effects of isolation and loneliness.

TWO VIEWS OF WIFEDOM
(continued)

The women of Upper Canada pride themselves on being good housewifes; and as few servants are to be met with in the country, they have ample opportunity for the exercise of their talents in the performance of domestic duties. But they are so particularly careful of themselves, that they compel their poor hen-pecked husbands to do the greatest part of their work. A Canadian is, in fact, a slave to his wife in the most extensive sense of that term. He is obliged to answer all her calls, to obey all her commands, and to execute all her commissions without a murmur. No West Indian slave-driver issues his mandates to the sable sons of Africa in a more authoritative tone, than a Canadian fair one to him who is at once her Lord and Servant.

— Edward Allen Talbot, *Five Years' Residence in Canada*, p. 49.

The man is stalwart, the wife fearful—perhaps a true representation of a couple living in the backwoods in 1830. (Jefferys, II-245)

Yet many others thrived on the life, pitching in to help with tasks that might have been considered in the man's realm and revelling in their marriages and their challenges. They particularly valued the chance to make something of their lives and improve prospects for their children. Even those whose standard of living dropped when they came to Canada write about their satisfaction with pioneer life, notwithstanding the hard work and deprivation.

Mary O'Brien writes about a family that comes to shear some sheep: once the man has caught the sheep and tied its legs together, the women, more dexterous, remove the fleece in just a quarter of an hour. There are various accounts of widows left with 10 or more children who take over the running of the household and farm and do it well. Pioneer historian Edwin Guillet recounts a number of stories of the "uphill, both ways, in the snow" variety, where wives took over transporting heavy supplies—one of whom was said to have taken a tub of butter 65 kilometres through the bush to the town of York, where she traded it for a heavy logging chain she carried back to her family clearing. Almost every woman who wrote about the backwoods included tales of other women who cleared land and logged trees in tandem with their husbands.

Yet women were legally assumed to be helpless, unable to provide their own food, clothing, and housing. If they married badly, they must live with their decision. Sarah Welch Hill, living in

Upper Canada in the 1840s, wrote repeatedly in her diary about Mr. Hill's temper:

> Mr. Hill had been very angry that the flour was gone, I felt very ill . . . violent Palpitation of the heart. . . . Mr Hill's temper very bad indeed, I think no wife's can be more tried in that respect. . . . Mr Hill's temper very bad & his language very abusive. . . . Mr Hill swore dreadfully said he would kick me & my servants out of doors that he would not live with me if it were not for the children. . . . We all do our utmost to please him. . . . not getting us with this insolent treatment he kicked me several times. Very poorly all day.[21]

Mr. Hill continued to abuse Mrs. Hill verbally and physically, telling her what a sexual inconvenience it was to him when she was pregnant, and swearing to leave her bed if she ever became pregnant again. Mrs. Hill continued to be poorly, seeing no way out in an age when a wife rarely left her husband—and, since she had signed her rights over to him, having no other means of support. Her escape was unexpected: her husband died, leaving her with two young children.

Given the lack of travelling parsons, it was not completely unusual for a couple to live together without being married, repairing the lack when a minister finally showed up in the area. And not all women were inclined to give their husbands their proper due: "A woman from the States, in the true spirit of independence, left a church in this province, unmarried, from her refusal to say 'obey.' She had previously determined never to give the solemn promise required, and preferred living with her intended spouse, unshackled by the yoke of matrimony. She now has three children, and lives happily with her mate."[22]

My Harp is not neglected, for I assure you I am not like some women satisfied with gaining the affections of the man I marry, but I wish to retain them as long as I can, for ever if possible, and I am convinced that did the generality of wives think the same and act to that effect, there would be fewer neglected ones.

— Lucy Peel, *Love Strong as Death*, p. 84.

THE TRUE DESTINY OF WOMEN:

The Victorian Housewife

Word of grace to women: word that makes her the earthly providence of her family, that wins gratitude and attachment from those at home, and a good report from those who are without. Success in housekeeping adds credit to the women of intellect, and lustre to a woman's accomplishments. It is a knowledge which it is as discreditable for any woman to be without as for a man not to know how to make a living, or how to defend himself when attacked. . . . No matter how talented a woman may be, or how useful in the church or society, if she is an indifferent housekeeper it is fatal to her influence, a foil to her brilliancy and a blemish in her garments.

—The Home Cook Book

꙰

Baking powder and gelatin, cast-iron wood stoves and hand-cranked washing machines, earth closets and running water, the discovery of bacteria and germs: the second half of the nineteenth century brought something of a revolution into the lives of Canadian housewives. Yet this Victorian age also brought rising expectations for women, who were held to be the sustainers of the family, the country, and the empire.

Canada became a country between the middle and the end of the nineteenth century. Ontario, Quebec, Nova Scotia, and New Brunswick joined together in 1867, and Manitoba entered Confederation in 1870, British Columbia in 1871, and Prince Edward Island in 1873. The North-West Territories, containing what would become in 1905 Alberta, Saskatchewan, and a large addition to Manitoba, were turned over to Canada in 1870; the Yukon was carved out of the region in 1898. Canada's population grew by almost 50 percent between 1871 and 1891; in 1871, just one Canadian in five lived in a town or city, while in 1901, it was close to two in five. A transcontinental railway was built from east coast to west. The industrial revolution continued, with more and more goods being produced in city factories, and fewer and fewer in homes in the countryside.

The housewife had no excuse for not knowing just how she should behave in this new country. From the 1850s on, a torrent of books poured forth in Canada, the United States, and Britain, detailing how everything in the house should be done and how the mistress of the house should do it. Household skills that a previous generation took for granted were now carefully delineated in astonishing detail in 600-page books.

Decorated and ornate, the Victorian room must be well kept by the housewife; it was a reflection of her taste and her skills. A Mrs. Piers displays her music room, herself, and her children in Montreal in 1895. (Glenbow Archives, NA-1459-58)

The Home Cook Book and a number of other Canadian books took their inspiration from what would become the standard household reference work: *Mrs Beeton's Book of Household Management*, published in England in 1861. An exhaustive tome dictating every moment of the housewife's life, from how and when to receive guests to how to cook every piece of a cow's carcass, how to bind a wound, and how to buy a house, Isabella Beeton's book became an instant classic. Beeton was in no doubt about the role of the woman of the house:

> As with the commander of an army, or the leader of any enterprise, so is it with the mistress of a house. Her spirit will be seen through the whole establishment; and just in proportion as she performs her duties intelligently and thoroughly, so will her domestics follow in her path. Of all those acquirements, which more particularly belong to the feminine character, there are none which take a

Mrs. Beeton, like other righteous Victorians, looked to the Bible to define her rightful role:

Strength, and honour are her clothing; and she shall rejoice in time to come. She openeth her mouth with wisdom; and in her tongue is the law of kindness. She looketh well to the ways of her household; and eateth not the bread of idleness. Her children arise up, and call her blessed; her husband also, and he praiseth her.

— Proverbs, xxxi. 25–28.

higher rank, in our estimation, than such as enter into a knowledge of household duties; for on these are perpetually dependent the happiness, comfort, and well-being of a family.[1]

The word housewife—which seems to have come into common usage in the 1880s—was rarely seen without an accompanying adjective fraught with expectations: in the columns of newspapers and the pages of books, she was the frugal housewife, the careful housewife, the patient housewife, the faithful housewife.

Though the instructions in many of these books were intended for upper-class women, they were considered equally important for the growing middle class. This century saw the true emergence of that class, neither mired in poverty, nor living in manors; not growing and raising their own food, but living and working in towns and cities, renting or owning modest or somewhat better houses. The men of the family worked in the new industries that were growing up, or in professions, or in shops and other services. The women stayed home and cared for house and family. Many yearned for servants, but the egalitarian atmosphere of Canada meant that servants were hard to find, and those that were found were often unsatisfactory.

In the cities, few housewives milked their own cows, churned their own butter, or made their own cheese. Few sheared sheep or spun yarn and wove cloth. Instead, they went to market, to the general store or, as the century progressed, to the warehouse stores such as Eaton's and Simpson's that were the forerunners of twentieth-century department stores. Even rural women were increasingly likely to buy provisions on a trip to town or from a peddler who brought wares to their farm by boat or by road. Canadian housewives were well on their way to being consumers instead of producers.

The products they bought were many and novel, from appliances that were designed to make cooking and cleaning easier, to packaged food products intended to save time and increase reliability. Even those who lived in relative poverty could afford pots and pans from the second-hand store.

Mrs. Beeton had much advice for the housewife, but even she couldn't avoid one of the greatest terrors women faced before the 1880s: death in childbirth. She died just a few years after her book

Housewives in British Columbia had a better chance than other Canadian women of finding servants; they were able to hire Chinese men who immigrated to Canada in gold-rush and railway-building times:

What a charming Chinaman we have got. I don't know when we have had things so comfortable as since he came. He is clean, orderly & industrious, bakes & cooks to our hearts content—and (what we most feared about) washes the clothes quite as well as Sarah [the previous house help] at her best.... God, I'm sure, sends such Chinamen, as all good things comes from Him, & I'm sure we daily thank Him for His gift.

— Sarah Crease to Henry Crease, Victoria, 14 May 1866, as quoted in Katherine Bridge, *Henry & Self*, p. 93.

Bread-making remained a central activity for the Victorian housewife; here, a New Brunswick woman demonstrates her skills. (Provincial Archives of New Brunswick P430/16)

was published, at the age of 28. Though the Victorian housewife saw much change, she still had just one foot in the modern world.

⚡ THE COOK ⚡

"Went to the market," wrote Charlottetown resident Margaret Gray Lord frequently in her diaries for 1876 and 1890.² She, like most other urban housewives in the Victorian era, bought her kitchen ingredients rather than producing them. As towns and cities grew, so did their markets, from the "shambles"—the row of open stalls where products, especially meat, were sold—to covered buildings with permanent stalls. Meat, poultry, fish, vegetables, and flour and other staples entered the house from the market or the shop— or from the bread man, the milk man, or the vegetable peddler— not from the farm garden and field. Nonetheless, any housewife with a backyard still planted a garden, and harvested its vegetables and fruits as the season warranted. Pickling, preserving, canning, and jam-making were still among her tasks.

Thursday 19 [October] Mrs. Marstin and Emma Maria spun four skeins warp making in all twelve skeins spun. Lucy Ann and Joseph went upon the hill to dig potatoes, Wilfred, Eliza, Fanny and Mrs Carter put the pota- toes down in the cellar there was 20 bushels it began to rain as soon as we had nicely begun but we finished them it rained all day. Eliza put one of her toes out of joint, she put it in again, and I bandaged it up with the white of an egg.

— Eliza Carter's *Diary of Autumn*, 1865, Judith Baxter, and Beth Quigley, eds., *Life and Times: Recollections of Eliza Cox Carter*, p. 50.

Outside the towns, the housewife still performed most chores by hand. A woman in Long Branch, Ontario, churns butter in 1893. (W.B. Bayley, Library and Archives Canada/PA-126654)

BEWARE OF FRUIT SKINS
Fruit skins carry germs and are no more intended for human sustenance than potato skins, melon rinds and pea pods. The bloom of the peach is a luxuriant growth of microbes, that of the grape only less so; and when these skins are taken into the stomach they find more favorable conditions for their lively and rapid development which cause the decay of the fruit before it is possible to digest it. This is the reason many people think they cannot eat raw fruit.

— The *Halifax Herald*, June 6, 1895.

It is difficult, isn't it, to get up something different and yet dainty and not too expensive for breakfast, dinner and luncheon every day? This everlasting cookery becomes very burdensome to the housekeeper after a while, and in fact I have known more than one little woman to sit down and have a good cry over the difficulty of providing something 'nice and different' every day.

— Kathleen Blake Coleman, "Woman's Kingdom," the *Toronto Mail*, October 17, 1891.

Display and price were in no way regulated, and there were dangers and difficulties in this routine of buying food from someone you didn't know. The housewife must keep a sharp eye out lest she be cheated or fooled. The new packaged food was suspect: producers resisted any attempt to regulate their wares and the housewife could not be sure of the contents.

Lord never mentions visiting a store, but many urban dwellers bought their staple foods at the general store in the early days, then at larger shops as the century progressed. By the 1890s, butchers and grocers were advertising in the daily papers. MacWillie Bros Grocers told Toronto in 1897: "Going to be busy to-morrow, closed Thursday, Dominion Day. Busy housewives will want MacWillie's Delicious Cooked Ham, Cooked Ox Tongue, Scotch Beef Hams, special 22¢," continuing with specials on cakes, ham patties, shrimps, olives, and cookies. On the same page, Donald's suggested to housewives that, should they wonder if good hams, bacon, butter, or eggs were to be had anywhere, "Why not try Donald's?"[3]

The invention of the steam engine revolutionized transport, and steamships brought more exotic foods and spices from other lands to the store counter. English families who came to Canada from other corners of the empire cooked curries, and a Chinese cook might introduce delicacies from his part of the world to the Canadian table.

The urban housewife could store her purchases in an icebox, a wooden box lined with metal that held ice in an upper section to keep food cool in the lower section. But most housewives still depended on cold cellars and bought their meat and other perishable provisions day by day.

By the 1870s the convenience offered by the cast-iron stove had triumphed over affection for the hearth, and most housewives cooked the family's meals on top of the stove or in the oven. Women still had to feed the fire with wood or coal, but even the task of keeping the fire going was made much easier by the invention of the wooden safety match in 1855. By the 1890s, gas ranges were available.

Other innovations made the housewife's kitchen chores easier and the results more predictable. Baking powder, on the scene from mid-century, put an end to the heavy, flat cakes that had been the norm. Packaged yeast made bread-making much less nerve-wracking. Packaged and sheet gelatin made jellies and shapes ever easier and more popular. Advances in tinning technology meant that more canned salmon and other foods were available, a special boon to the poorer housewife. Packaged biscuits and teas, bottled soft drinks and beers, and a multitude of other products appeared on store shelves.

What did the middle-class housewife place on the Victorian table? *The Home Cook Book* suggests breakfasts that would have fed a farmer heavily engaged in outdoor work; husbands were to head for the office with beefsteak and potatoes à la crème, or broiled chicken, scrambled eggs, and fried oysters, or fish, ham and eggs, under their belts. Dinners for guests included three or four courses and dessert: soup, at least two solid courses of fish, fowl, and flesh, plus puddings and pies, fruit and nuts. Oysters—now

DON'T
Find fault with the cook if the pastry does not exactly suit you. Nor with your wife either—perhaps she is not to

BLAME
It may be the lard she is using for shortening. Lard is indigestible, you know. But if you would always have

YOUR
Cakes, pies, rolls, AND bread palatable and perfectly digestible, order the new shortening "COTTOLENE" for your

WIFE
Sold in 3 and 5 pound pails by all grocers.

— advertisement in the Toronto *Globe*, September 12, 1894.

A good housewife goes to her herb garden, instead of a spice shop, for seasonings and thus preserves the health of her family while saving her purse.

— Toronto *Globe*, June 9, 1887.

available anywhere refrigerated railway cars could go—appeared frequently, as did roast turkey, roast beef, and boiled fish.

The Victorian ethic demanded that women do more for their neighbours and for the underprivileged. In diaries of the time, women frequently report preparing food for invalids outside their own family and taking part in that staple of female fundraising, the bake sale.

RECIPES

LOBSTER SALAD

Take a good-sized lobster and one head of lettuce. Chop the lobster and some of the lettuce, reserving the best leaves for garnishing the dish. For dressing use two table-spoonsful of mustard, one tablespoonful each of sugar and salt, with a little pepper. Add a cup of diluted vinegar and two well beaten eggs. Cook, stirring constantly, until it thickens, then add two large tablespoonsful of melted butter. When perfectly cool, mix part of the dressing with lobster and lettuce, pour the rest over. Garnish with two hard boiled eggs and one lemon cut in slices.

—*Halifax Herald*, June 10, 1895.

GINGER BEER

Mrs. James Scrimger

Ten gallons water, six pounds white sugar, six ounces crushed ginger, two ounces cream tartar, one ounce tartaric or citric acid, one yeast cake. Boil ginger for two hours, dissolve sugar when hot, put yeast and acids luke warm to stand over night. Bottle next day.

—Margaret Taylor and Frances McNaught, *The Early Canadian Galt Cook Book*, p. 380.

Martha Field and her sister Fanny Simpson kept a recipe book in the nineteenth century; it is now in the National Archives of Canada. Among the recipes from the Victorian era:

TO CURE GREEN BEANS

¼ lb salt-petre, 1 lb bay Salt, 1 lb coarse sugar, 3lbs common salt, 2 gallons of water, to be simmered about a quarter of an hour and skimmed. The beans must not be rubbed but put into the brine & cover'd with it. Let them lie about a month then smoke them as usual. This is for two hours. N.B. it is a good plan to put a plate with a stone on it to keep them in the brine.

DANDELION TEA

Dig up two ounces of the fresh dandelion root. Wash and slice them. Boil them in two pints of water reduced to one. This quantity may be consumed in a couple of days drank alone or mixed with a little sherry.

ORANGE JELLY

Mix together two pints of spring water, one pound of lump sugar, two ounces of isinglass, the rind of two lemons. Let it stand all night. Then put it on the fire and boil it half an hour, drain it through a fine sieve, or muslin, and add a pint of orange wine with the juice of three lemons. N.B. If half the quantity is sufficient for a small dish, sherry or any other white wine will do.

RECIPES

I made Spanish cream and jelly for Mrs. Carruther [who was laid up with an ulcerated jaw].... Had to make another shape of jelly for Mrs. Carruthers as I upset the one I made. Also made whipped cream and salad.

— Margaret Gray Lord, *One Woman's Charlottetown*, February 26/27, 1890, p. 120.

SPANISH CREAM
Mrs. J.H. Brown
Boil one ounce of gelatine in one pint of new milk until dissolved; add four eggs well beaten and half a pound of sugar; stir it over the fire until the eggs thicken; take it off the fire and add a full wine-glass of peach water; and when cool pour it into moulds; serve with cream.

GELATINE
Mrs. J.H. Mead
Take a good packet of gelatine, the juice and rinds of three lemons, soak for one hour in a pint of cold water; then add three pints of boiling water, two pounds of white sugar, one pint of wine; strain into moulds and set out to cool.

— *The Home Cook Book*, pp. 223, 252.

EVE'S PUDDING
If you want a good pudding, mind what you are taught;
Take eggs, six in number, when bought for a groat;
The fruit with which Eve her husband did cozen,
Well pared, and well chopped, at least half a dozen;
Six ounces of bread, let Moll eat the crust,
And crumble the rest as fine as the dust;
Six ounces of currants, from the stem you must sort,
Lest you break out your teeth, and spoil all the sport;
Six ounces of sugar won't make it too sweet,
Some salt and some nutmeg will make it complete;
Three hours let it boil without any flutter,
But Adam won't like it without wine and butter.

— *The Home Cook Book*, p. 166.

The availability of exotic spices made pickles more interesting:

INDIA PICKLE
Mrs. George Simpson
Take three quarts vinegar, quarter pound mustard, half ounce black pepper, one ounce cloves, one ounce allspice, one ounce turmeric, one ounce ginger, one ounce cayenne pepper, handful salt, same of sugar; boil for twenty minutes. When cold put in the vegetables and cover closely; if the liquid should become thin, boil again and add more mustard in three weeks after making.

— *The Home Cook Book*, p. 128.

BROILING
Meat to be broiled is better after hanging a day or two; it then may be sprinkled with pepper and salt, or allowed to lie an hour or two in oil and vinegar, or other marinade, after sprinkling. In any case a good clear fire is necessary, charcoal being the best; a good substitute may be made of wood, all the flames to be burned out and the clear embers left. Failing this, of course the ordinary coal fire may be used, or gas. Make the broiler very hot, rub it over with a little fat, put on the meat and turn constantly, cook according to size, a beef steak of one pound will take about ten minutes, but the thickness of the meat must be taken into consideration. When done, rub over with a little butter, and serve at once.

— Amy G. Richards, *Cookery*, p. 88.

Husband, wife, child, servant, flowers, sideboard, gas lamp, needlework, tea sets, pictures, hangings, bread, food, ornate dining room—all so Victorian…but is that a cat perched on the table in early 1890s Regina? And a hog's head in the background? Even the supposedly staid Victorians had their amusements. (Glenbow Archives ND-37-5)

THE MODEL HOUSEWIFE

In the first place she is the most thoroughly cheerful and happy-looking woman you will meet in a day's travel; and although she is thirty-five years old she does not look thirty. This is because she never allows the petty cares of housekeeping to worry and plow lines across her face. She does one thing at a time, never making the error of undertaking a dozen duties at once.

Good judgment: The model housewife keeps a scrupulously neat home, but in no room is comfort sacrificed for the sake of appearance. She has neither too much furniture nor bric-a-brac. She dresses her children neatly but plainly.

— Prof. B.G. Jefferis and J.L. Nichols, *The Household Guide*, p. 328.

❧ THE HOUSEKEEPER ❧

Two steps forward, one step back. The Victorian age saw a variety of inventions and discoveries that made the housewife's life easier. Coupled with the advances, though, were rising expectations: books and articles on household matters left no doubt that a woman would be judged on how well she kept her house.

A poem published in the Toronto *Globe* in 1889 laid out the criteria:

A GOOD HOUSEWIFE
I can tell her
By her cellar,
Cleanly shelves and whitened wall;
I can guess her
By her dresser,
By the back staircase and hall,
And with pleasure
Take her measure
By the way she keeps her brooms.
And by peeping
At the "keeping"

Whatever the era, the work went on, especially for the wife of the working man. An 1871 illustration in Montreal's *L'Opinion Publique*: "You're complaining," says the housewife, "about your ten hours of work; here I've been working for fourteen hours today, and I'm not even done yet." (Bibliothèque Nationale de Québec, *NO 3057*, *L'Opinion Publique*, Vol. 2, no. 44, pp. 532)

Of her back and unseen rooms;
By her kitchen's air of neatness,
By its general completeness
Where in cleanliness and sweetness
The rose of order blooms.[4]

The "rose of order" was much valued by those who wrote household compendia. Women should work according to a schedule: every day had its assigned task. Most writers agreed that women should do the washing on Monday, but opinions varied about what must be done on every other day of the week. Some said iron on Tuesday, some said bake, but however the housewife ordered her days, she must set a day aside each for washing, ironing, baking, cleaning, and mending—and perhaps a second day for baking. Sunday, of course, was not a working day, except for cooking.

The growing number of middle-class housewives followed the lead of their upper-class sisters, crowding their parlours and living rooms with knick-knacks and decorations, covering every surface and inch of wall space. Such decorations had, of course, to be regularly dusted, perhaps with a feather duster, patented in 1876 in the United States by a woman who used turkey feathers, and vastly improved when ostrich feathers, with their dust-catching barbs, were used.

41 TO POLISH MAHOGANY
Take a quarter of an oz of the finest white soap grate it small and put it into a earthenware vessel with a pint of water hold it over the fire until the soap is dissolved then add the same quantity of white wax cut into small pieces and three oz of common wax as soon as the whole is mixed it is ready for use then dip your flannel into your varnish and rub it on your furniture when it has stood a quarter of an hour use your hard brush then polish it with some clean flannel this will produce a polish like a mirror.

— "Eliza Carter's Recipe and Remedy Book," Judith Baxter and Beth Quigley, eds. *Life and Times: Recollections of Eliza Cox Carter*, p. 85.

Carpets covered the floors, and they must be cleaned. The industrious housewife might sprinkle salt over the carpet, then sweep it well; sponge it with water and ammonia; do the same with a weak solution of soda or alum and water; or use the oldest method, hanging it outside and beating it with a carpet beater.

Professor B.G. Jefferis, author of *The Household Guide* published in Toronto in 1894, was responsible for all the above solutions and added another: "Fresh green grass dampened a little and spread upon the carpet and then swept up will brighten and beautify a carpet. It is much better than tea leaves, for it will leave no stains." Jefferis also detailed instructions for sponging carpets, a job that should be done once a week. He took note of the carpet sweeper, introduced in the 1880s: "A carpet-sweeper is indispensable to every well-regulated household, particularly when one has been sewing to such an extent as to litter the floor."[5]

Moving from hearth to iron range made the cook's life easier but didn't help the housekeeper. The fireplace, still used for heating, must be cleaned, the ashes removed, and new firewood brought in. Looking after the iron range could be just as complex. Each morning, the housewife must remove the previous day's soot and ashes and lay a new fire of wood or coal ready for lighting. She must clean the outside surfaces, then polish them with a flannel cloth laden with stove polish. To prevent rust, the housewife from time to time rubbed her stove with fat, then polished it. The stove once lit, she could proceed with cooking breakfast. If she planned to bake that day, she must keep a careful eye on the fire, making sure the adjoining oven was at a temperature suitable for her bread or cakes. Sweeping the floor, doing the dishes, wiping down the oilcloth (first commercially produced at mid-century) that covered the kitchen table, were all part of her daily kitchen routine.

Tending to the bedroom in Victorian days was no simple matter. Backwoods mattresses in the early days of settlement were often filled with corn husks, but the Victorian housewife aspired to feather beds. A feather bed needed frequent airing, the mattresses hung out in the shade and taken in before nightfall. Bedrooms suffered, too, from the universal use of chamber pots: the smell of urine was not uncommon.

In 1849, Nova Scotia-born geologist Abraham Gesner invented a process to distill kerosene from petroleum, and houses

Readers of the Toronto *Globe* on Feb. 8, 1862, are encouraged to buy the latest innovations:

No good housewife would be without a box of Crawford's patent fire lighters. They prevent dirt, unnecessary labour and are expeditious. A fair trial only asked to ensure their constant use. For sale at all grocery and drug stores, 25 cents a box of six dozen.

Pure kerosene coal oil. We beg to inform our customers that we are prepared to supply them with the above. Justly celebrated coal oil. Wholesale or retail at the very latest market rates. Bryson Bros. Wholesale and Retail Oil and Lamp Store.

To prevent crust in Tea-Kettles—Keep an oyster shell in your tea-kettle. By attracting the stony particles to itself, it will prevent the formation of a crust.

To Clean Knives—Cut a small potato in two; dip one half in the brick-dust, and run the knives, and rust and stain will disappear like magic from their surfaces.

After a stove has been blackened, it can be kept looking very well for a long time by rubbing it with paper every morning.

— *Home and Health and Compendium of Useful Knowledge*, p. 291.

NINETY-NINE CENT PARLORS

The advocates of the "cheap and pretty" system of furnishing houses are becoming tired of the unsubstantial things which cost little and the prettiness which has turned out to be not really pretty after all, but only novel for a short time and afterwards tiresome for a long time. There is either coarseness of texture or lack of stamina in the very inexpensive teaspoon, for example, and the same is true of every other necessity of a house. Now, as coarseness of texture is something that the good housewife of the present day "can't abide," it follows that the countless "things of beauty," falsely so-called, the directions for making which abound in every household magazine, are marked by constitutional fragility, which quickly transforms them into things of ugliness.

— "Woman's World," Toronto *Globe*, Nov. 10, 1887.

Mrs. H.W. Beecher makes a morality play out of evil dust versus innocent duster:

The descent from careless surface-dusting to real slovenliness is so gradual that the latter state becomes the established fact before the mistress has recognized the evil; and then, though she may deplore it, she is unconscious that it arises from any remissness on her part. No doubt every morning she goes through the pantomime of dusting. With a pretty feather-brush she flirts from chair to bookcase or table, and gracefully passes it over the top surfaces, but never thinks to look farther; while day after day the dust is slyly secreting itself in every crevice where it is secure from the gentle approaches of that innocent dusting-brush…. The daily attention that should be given to dust—which no care can prevent from entering, but which at first rests on the furniture so lightly that it is removed with ease—consumes not half the time that a careless and less methodical mode of working, or pretending to work, will do.

— *All Around the House—or, How to Make Homes Happy*, p. 14.

brightened considerably. Easier to use, almost odour-free, easier to store, never spoiling the way whale oil could, kerosene became the choice of most housewives for lighting their houses, and glass lamps fuelled by kerosene were soon found in every room. The housewife no longer had to make her own candles, but she did have to wash the glass chimneys and trim wicks in glass lamps so that they burned cleanly.

Twice a year, spring and fall, housewives across the nation gave their houses a thorough cleaning. If they were in doubt as to what this entailed, the ever-present household guides included checklists of chores, even prescribing what the well-trained housewife should wear for this mammoth task. Margaret Gray Lord outlined the process, undertaken in her case with the help of servants and children:

> Friday, November 7: The girls cleaned the double windows and William got up the hall stove. . . . Thursday, November 13: We cleaned the spare room and boy's room today. . . . Friday, November 14: Busy housecleaning all day almost all done up stairs. I did the attic....Wednesday, November 19: We house cleaned the drawing room had a nice day for the furniture out-side. Thursday, November 20: We did the dining room and hall. . . . Friday, November 21: we house cleaned the nursery and pantry—big job always the latter. . . . I put down stair oil cloth the first I ever used. Made pies for tomorrow and Sunday. Saturday, November 22: Such a day. Cleaned the range flews and all; then finished kitchen and back kitchen and all done but I am done myself. Just going to take a hot bath and wash my head!

↬ THE SEAMSTRESS ↫

By late in the nineteenth century, the housewife—especially one who lived in a town or city—could easily buy ready-made clothing. The frugal housewife, however, conscious of both her budget and her obligations, was more likely to sew much of her own and her family's clothing. Gone, though, were the obligations to card, spin,

The invention of the mechanical sewing machine made life much easier for the seamstress. The "Little Wanzer," made in Hamilton and simple enough for a child to operate, was advertised on this carte-de-visite. Four thousand Little Wanzers, powered by a hand-turned wheel, sold in 1867, the first year they were made; half a million were manufactured over the next decade. (Library and Archives Canada PA-125318)

The sewing-machine is doubtless a great help to the weary, a great blessing to the heavily-laden mother and housekeeper—or it should be; but all have need of caution, lest they make this gift a curse. Let us look back to the time when sewing-machines were unknown, and compare the amount of cloth, time, and stitches necessary to make the most elaborately fashionable dress with that which is piled on the ordinary dress of the period. Look at the ruffles, puffs, flounces, etc., that mothers put on even a little girl's dress....Think of putting one hundred yards of ruffling on one dress! And any lady knows that is but a small estimate of the number required for some stylish dresses....If not very careful, there is danger of many becoming devotees of fashion, who [but for this]....would have made better mothers and happier homes.

— Mrs. W.H. Beecher, *All Around the House—or, How to Make Homes Happy*, pp. 64–65.

Entitled "The New Year's Gifts from the Manitoba cousin," this drawing from Montreal's *L'Opinion Publique* of January 1876 shows mothers and children gathering around hand-crafted items sent from Manitoba to Montreal. (Library and Archives Canada C-107646)

and weave wool, to break flax, or to spin hemp. Every general store, every department store, overwhelmed her with a choice of fabrics and notions.

She was aided in her task by the invention of the mechanical sewing machine, foot-powered via a treadle that she pushed rhythmically. Thousands of sewing machines, from the industry-leading Singers and a raft of other competitors, were sold to families across Canada from the 1850s on.

By the mid-1880s, the production of new synthetic dyes meant that fabrics were available in a kaleidoscope of colours and patterns. Mills in Canada, the United States, and overseas turned out a vast variety of fabrics, from woollens to silks to cottons to novelty cloths. Seamstresses no longer had to carefully unpick an old garment to make a pattern for a new one. In the 1870s, the Butterick Company began selling its tissue-paper patterns, in a range of sizes for men, women, and children, throughout Canada, and competitors soon followed suit.

If all this made life much easier for the Victorian seamstress, then fashion made it more difficult. Victorian fashions, especially for women and children, involved much use of ruffles, laces, braids, and fringes. Even the armchairs and chesterfields were ornately adorned.

Most housewives knew, at a minimum, how to knit, crochet, and embroider. With enough light to see by in the evenings and, presumably, time on their hands, housewives also turned to an array of fancy sewing and craft techniques, often undertaken at sewing circles and displayed in competitive fairs and exhibitions. An 1898 exhibition in Toronto listed classes for types of lace made into things such as cuffs and vests; Berlin wool work; hand sewing ("One can hardly fancy that anyone can still be found to undertake such a piece of work as that of making a gentleman's white shirt by hand, yet nonetheless. . . ."); machine work; flannel shirts, nightgowns, by hand and machine; embroidered pocket handkerchiefs; knitted shawls; woollen crochet for baby; silk and cotton crochet; table centrepieces; silk patchwork quilts; crazy patchwork quilts; decorated pillow shams; toilet sets; photograph frames in embroidered linen; handkerchief cases; veil cases; various embroidery classes including Danish, Roman, and Mexican; country work such as homemade flannels, carpets and rugs; rag carpets in very intricate patterns; and homemade counterpanes.[7]

A woman with sufficient time and money might also sew for the poor. The poor, meanwhile, were discovering they could make a little money sewing in their homes for garment manufacturers. In Montreal, in particular, the garment trade depended on the low-paid labour of hundreds of housewives, paid by the piece for their work.

⁘ THE LAUNDRESS ⁘

The chore of laundry improved somewhat as the nineteenth century advanced, especially in towns and for the middle and upper class. Washing powders, city water systems, and basic washing machines all helped relieve the washday blues. It was possible for even the middle class to send laundry out: a housewife might rely on the poorhouse laundry, the prison laundry, or the Chinese

Among the sale items available from Eaton's dress goods and fabrics department according to an advertisement in the January 31, 1895, Toronto *Globe*:

42-in. French Hopsacking, in light and dark shades. 20¢; regular 35¢.

42 in. German novelty cloth, in Fancy Checks, 50¢; regular 1$.

22-in. printed Pongee silk, dark shades, 15¢, regular 35¢.

22-in. Faconne Glace silk, extra heavy, 25¢, regular 75¢.

40-in. Twill Serge Cloths, 5¢, regular 10¢.

27-in. Ginghams, assorted patterns; special 5¢ yard.

Wide Imitation Fur, in black, navy and brown, 5¢ yard; regular 20¢.

Black Silk Spools, 50 yards, 2 for 5¢; regular 5¢ each.

41-inch pillow cotton, 11½¢; regular 14¢ yard.

23-in Canadian flannelette, good assortment, 5¢ yard; regular 6¢.

Embroidery Silks, 1¢ a skein; regular, 3¢, 4¢ and 5¢ a skein.

Canadian Fingering wool, 40¢ lb.; regular 65¢.

TO WASH WOOLLEN BLANKETS

Mrs. J.A. Packard

Dissolve soap enough to make a good suds in boiling water, add a tablespoon of aqua ammonia; when scalding hot, turn over your blankets. If convenient, use a pounder or any way to work thoroughly through the suds without rubbing on a board. Rinse well in hot water. There is usually soap enough from the first suds to make the second soft; if not, add a little soap and ammonia; and after being put through the wringer, let two persons, standing opposite, pull them into shape; dry in the sun. White flannels may be washed in the same way without shrinking.

— *The Home Cook Book*, p. 360.

Gillet's Powdered Lye. 99 per cent. Purest, Strongest, Best. Ready for use in any quantity. For making soap, softening water, disinfecting, and a hundred other uses. A can equals 20 pounds sal soda.

— Toronto *Globe*, May 29, 1888.

laundry. If you were poor, of course, your laundry day wouldn't be much different than it had been fifty years earlier.

Growing towns demanded new ways to deliver water. An 1854 editorial in the Toronto *Globe* opined that, "It is no longer possible for the housewife to supply her weekly wash-tub with a hogshead from the bay for a reasonable sum. The distance is too great, and the unconscionable carter is not content with the York Shilling which was once his regular fee, but demands his quarter dollar or his eighteen pence. This falls very heavily on the poor, who are often compelled to a want of cleanliness for their want of means." The writer argued that piped water had become a necessity, if not into every home, then certainly within reach of same, and called for the establishment of hydrants throughout the city.[8]

Cities in Quebec, the Maritimes, and the west were equally determined to build waterworks. In Victoria, British Columbia, for example, the city council determined in 1873 to establish a water system to replace the previous bucket delivery (25¢ a bucket in 1858, $1 for 20 buckets in the 1870s—a fairly hefty price). The housewife might still have to go to the hydrant for water if her house did not have pipes, but that was a great deal simpler than getting it from the river, lake, or well. And heating water on the stove was simpler than heating it over the fire. Many stoves included a tank that kept water hot for use at any time of the day.

Though inventors worked to solve the problems posed by agitation, motors, immersion in water, wringing, and draining, washing-machine technology was slow to catch up to other innovations. By the 1890s, hand-powered machines included a tub for agitation and a wringer that did the worst job of the laundress: wringing out clothes, first from wash water, then from several rinses. Most women, though, still used the scrub board and a tub of boiling water to do their wash.

Women could buy commercial laundry powders now, but many still made their own soap. They no longer had to produce lye from wood ashes, however, instead buying commercially produced lye from the stores, as well as washing soda, used to soften water or boost the cleaning power of soap.

British and American publications were often reprinted in Canada with a new title page. The May 1892 issue of *The Girl's Own Paper*, an English magazine reprinted in Toronto, contained a long

Ironing was a hot and heavy task: Mrs. Margaret Hyde wraps her flat iron handle in a cloth to protect her hands and works on a board laid across a table on an outdoor porch in Ottawa in 1893, with her "small things" drying behind her. (May Ballantyne, Library and Archives Canada PA-131939)

HINTS FOR THE LAUNDRY
To Prevent Colors from Fading

Dissolve one ounce of sugar of lead in one bucket of water. Put the dress into water and let it stay about half an hour; then wring it out and let it dry before washing. Hay water cleanses and stiffens brown or buff linen. One large spoon of beef's gall to two buckets of suds, improves calicos and prevents their fading. Make starch for black calicos of coffee water to prevent any whitish appearance. Glue is good for stiffening caalicoes. Never let your calicoes freeze while drying. To prevent calico from fading while washing, infuse three gills of salt into four quarts of water; put the calico in while hot and leave in till cold. In this way the colors are rendered permanent and will not fade by subsequent washings.

— *Mother Hubbard's Cupboard*, p. 95.

article on the proper way to do laundry. The article looked down its English nose at the "continental habit" of doing the wash once every three or six months, thus requiring many clothes and household linens. But the writer saw no need, either, for a weekly wash; once every two or three weeks should be sufficient. "The Art of Washing" assumed a servant or washerwoman, but still advised a cold dinner on wash day. Gather the clothes on Monday, sort and mend those that need mending, soak the personal linen, the table linen, and the household linen separately. Sort out the coloured clothes to be washed separately. The three main tasks of laundry—soaking, scrubbing, and boiling—must always be done in exactly that order. A very good rinsing was essential, to get the grease and soap out. The writer explains the mysteries of "blueing" for linens and the water temperature for each of three rinses. Drying the clothes indoors or outdoors, wringers, mangles, bar soap, washing soda, borax, paraffin, ammonia—all are explained in detail for the anxious mistress of the house.[9]

Irons remained much the same, though the Victorian liking for ruffles and pleats increased the work. Flatirons, heated now on the stove top, were used to iron out wrinkles and shape ruffles. Produced in various shapes and sizes, irons could be used to nip into corners and slide along seams. In the 1880s, sadirons appeared: pointed at both ends, they had a removable handle. A number could be heated on the stove at the same time. When one iron cooled, the ironer removed the handle and used it to pick up a hot iron.

⊰ THE NURSE ⊱

Louis Pasteur's enormously important discovery in the 1880s that bacteria existed and were responsible for many illnesses and deaths, plus the later discovery of germs and realization of their role in causing disease, slowly revolutionized the world of medicine. It did not, however, immediately change a great deal for the Victorian housewife in Canada. At home, salves and potions, home remedies and gentle care, were still the order of the day. Now, though, the urban housewife was more likely to buy the basic ingredients of her mixtures—or get them ready-mixed—from the druggist rather than plucking them from her garden. The apothecary made much use of his metal or marble mortar and pestle, grinding herbs and chemicals and mixing them with various liquids. Alcohol and opium were among the most used elements of such medicines.

Ipecac, best known for causing vomiting, was frequently used to treat a cold or the flu; this extract from the root of an Amazonian shrub used in small doses made the patient spit or sweat. Castor oil was often administered to children as an all-round health-improver, and beef tea was considered the very best thing to restore the strength of an invalid.

PATENT SOAP

Five pounds hard soap, one quart lye, one-fourth ounce pearl-ash; place on the fire and stir well until the soap is dissolved; add one-half pint spirits of turpentine, one gill spirits hartshorn, and stir well. It is then fit for use. The finest muslin may be put to soak in this suds, and if left for a time will become beautifully white. A small portion of soap put into a little hot water, and a flannel cloth will save hard labour in cleaning paint. One who has tried it thinks it worth the price of the book.

— *Mother Hubbard's Cupboard*, p. 101.

WHAT EVERY HOUSEWIFE REQUIRES HACK & CO.'S CELEBRATED WASHING SOAP
No Washboard or Rubbing Required with this Soap

We, the undersigned, do hereby certify that we have used W.B. HACK & CO.'S WASHING COMPOUND SOAP, and have found it to be the best article for washing and family uses, also for toilet purposes or washing paint, that has ever come under our notice and we have much pleasure in recommending it to the public. [signed: nine women]

— Toronto *Globe*, April 16, 1869.

The housewife had to know how to treat wounds and bruises, as well as minor illnesses. Her care was probably as good as that of a doctor, for even with Pasteur's discoveries, neither the housewife nor the doctor knew much about the cause of sickness. Arthritis, rheumatism, chilblains, colds, flus, and fevers continued to plague the Canadian populace, and time was perhaps the best cure for all non-fatal diseases.

The quacks of the age hustled tonics, pills, powders, and balms that were said to cure almost all ailments known to man—and especially woman. Their makers often invented quotes to substantiate their claims; one such suggested, in 1894:

> A well-known lady and mother of six says, "I seriously and confidently recommend Paine's Celery Compound to all mothers who wish to keep up their health and strength during the very hot weather of summertime. I use this

By the 1890s, germs had entered the general vocabulary, a fact quickly picked up on by the makers of various medicines. Consumption was an early name for tuberculosis:

If you want to preserve apples, don't cause a break in the skin. The germs of decay thrive rapidly there. So the germs of consumption find good soil for work when the lining of the throat and lungs is bruised, made raw, or injured by colds and coughs. Scott's Emulsion, with hydrophosphites, will heal inflamed mucus membranes. The time to take it is before serious damage has been done. A 50-cent bottle is enough for an ordinary cold.

— Toronto *Globe*, Oct. 20, 1896.

To restore from Stroke of Lightning.— Shower with cold water for two hours; if the patient does not show signs of life, put salt in the water, and continue to shower an hour longer.

— *The Home Cook Book*, p. 378.

The good housewife, when she is giving her house its spring renovating, should bear in mind that the dear inmates of her house are more precious than many houses and that their systems need cleansing by purifying the blood, regulating the stomach and bowels to prevent and cure the diseases arising from spring malaria and miasma; and she must know that there is nothing that will do it so perfectly and surely as Hop Bitters, the purest and best of medicines.

— Toronto *Globe*, March 19, 1881.

Grandmother's Salve for Everything. —Two pounds of rosin and half a teacup of mutton tallow after it is hard, half as much beeswax, and half an ounce of camphor gum; put all together into an old kettle, and let it dissolve and just come to a boil, stirring with a stick; then take half a pail of warm water, just the chill off, pour it in and stir it carefully until you can get your hands around it. Two persons must each take half and pull like candy until quite white and brittle; put a little grease on your hands to prevent sticking and keep them wet at all times. Wet the table, roll out the salve, and cut it with a knife. Keep it in a cool place. — Mrs. Gardner

— *The Home Cook Book*, p. 371.

medicine every day and feel healthy and strong, and have no difficulty getting through my household work and cares, which are never very light. Since I have used the compound I do not find it necessary to go off to the country for two or three months to gain health. In every dose of Paine's Celery Compound I find a supply of strength."[10]

Carter's Little Liver Pills were said to cure sick headache, dyspepsia, indigestion, dizziness, nausea, drowsiness, bad taste in the mouth, coated tongue, pain in the side, and torpid liver. One of many advertisements for tonics, blood purifiers, and a raft of other cures recommended Holloway's Ointment, "good for diseases of the skin, sores, wounds, bad breasts, bad legs, blood to the head, apoplexy, rheumatism, gout, stiff joints, glandular swellings, bronchitis, mumps, sore throat and diphtheria."[11]

❧ THE MOTHER ❧

The stern paterfamilias is the stuff of Victorian legend: the man whose word was law and whose need for quiet in the home meant that children should be seen and not heard. But what of the mother? Victorian convention dictated that the home was the basic building block of the British Empire and that becoming and being a mother fulfilled a woman's role in life. Motherhood was a patriotic duty. The mother's task was to make sure that she raised her children to be obedient, upright, and dutiful.

Did the Canadian mother follow the rules? It depended. In upper-class families of British origin, home, Empire, and decorum were the rule. The wife must be industrious, self-sacrificing, and respectable; her children should be modest, obedient, and accomplished in those arts and skills most needed according to their gender. By 1870, children were, by law, to go to school; there, they learned reading, writing and arithmetic. Further schooling of this sort was regarded as unnecessary for girls. Instead, they needed to learn domestic skills from their mothers or from ladies' academies, and to be schooled in embroidery, music, and the arts. Girls played with dolls and tea sets; boys played with toy guns.

Well-off mothers often doted on their children, especially their sons. A fashion column in the 1892 *Globe* advised:

> It is in light cotton that the summer boy of this year will bloom in perfection. . . . Immense trousers and a sailor blouse of white drilling striped with hair lines of red, or blue, or pink; large loose rolling sailor collar of the plain color. . . . Add to this dress black legs, a straw hat atop wind-swept curls. . . . In a less neglige [informal] moment the elegant youngster who was born with a golden spoon, will be suited thus. Coat, trousers and vest of white cotton Bedford cord. The coat is double breasted. . . . [12]

But that was the stuff of the wealthy. The poor, in city and country, needed their children to start chores early in life, and go out to work when barely in their teens. A hard-worked mother with six children and little money had no time to coddle her children, though she might love them dearly.

The spate of newly published books and newspaper columns had much to say on the rearing of children. Be sure to bathe them daily, admonished one, appending a long description of how baby should be bathed; leave behind the era of the Saturday night bath. Do not let a child sleep with its parents, advised another; it will not be as healthy as if laid in its own well-aired bed alone. Do not overcuddle a child; leave it to stretch and play on the bed or roll about on the floor on a rug.

Yet for all the advice stillborn children were not unusual, and infant deaths were high. In 1889, the infant son of Adelaide Hunter Hoodless, herself the youngest of twelve children, died from drinking impure milk. Her outrage led her to champion reform in many areas of mothers' lives. In the years to come, she would be a driving force in the Women's Institute, the YWCA, and other women's organizations, telling women that they were not paying enough attention to the health of their children, campaigning vigorously for mandatory pasteurization of milk. That victory lay far in the future, however; for the Victorians, high infant mortality was simply a fact of life.

Do reflect that a pert child is an abomination; train your child to be respectful and to hold their tongues in the presences of their superiors.

Do sing to the little ones; the memory of a nursery song will cling to them through life.

Do attend to them yourself; a go-between betwixt mother and child is like a middle-man in business, who gets the largest share of the profits.

Do maintain a respectful tone to their father before them; if he is not all you wish, still make them respect him; he is always their father, and disrespect to them is a reflection upon yourself.

Do bear in mind that you are largely responsible for your child's inherited character, and have patience with faults and failures.

Do talk hopefully to your children of life and its possibilities; you have no right to depress them because you have suffered.

Do, if you have lost a child, remember that for the one that is gone there is no more to do; for those remaining, everything: hide your grief for their sakes.

Do impress upon them from early infancy that actions have results, and that they cannot escape consequences even by being sorry when they have acted wrongly.

— Toronto *Globe*, January 26, 1884.

⚭ THE WIFE ⚭

The wife was the queen of the domestic sphere, but she reigned according to societal dictates. "In [woman's] hands rests the power to uplift man from moral degradation," wrote one guide author.

> True, men whose nobler powers are blunted and whose appetites are in control may be able to defeat much of woman's work. And yet where there is any manhood left, there will be something at least to recognize and encourage the work of the faithful housewife. . . . The only fountain in the wilderness of life, where man drinks of water totally unmixed with bitter ingredients, is that which gushes for him in the calm and shady recess of domestic life.[13]

Such expectations called for occasional dissimulation from many a husband and wife. The wife was expected to close her eyes to the smoking, drinking, and carousing that her husband might enjoy. The husband was expected, in his turn, to enjoy for at least some part of the day the domestic harmonies of which he was master.

94 FOR SORE HEADS
Creosite ointment a little to be applied every night.

126 POISONOUS RASH
Simmer Lilac flowers in cream for poisonous rash.

128 EAR ACHE
Tobacco & roasted onion drop one drop into the ear.

140 SHINGLES
1 dram of sugar of lead to one pint of water, dress them with it 3 or 4 times a day plaster with lard and keep the bowels open

160 PILES
Apply warm treacle, or a tobacco leaf steeped in water twenty-four hours, or varnish which perfectly cures both the blind and bleeding piles.

218 CROUP
Take the white of an egg stir it thoroughly into a small quantity of sweetened water and give it in repeated doses until a cure is effected, if one egg is not sufficient a second or even a third may be used M.C., March 12th 1872

— "Eliza Carter's Recipe and Remedy Book," Judith Baxter, and Beth Quigley, eds., *Life and Times: Recollections of Eliza Cox Carter*, pp. 90 ff.

Legally handed over from her father to her husband, the wife was to obey in all matters. Once she was married, she no longer existed as a legal person, and could not own land or other property. Though the house was her domain, she furnished it and kept it according to his purse. Whether she looked after his pay cheque or used the money he carefully doled out to her, she had only the money he gave her. While widows, spinsters over a certain age, and the wives of the poor might need to make money outside the home by sewing, cleaning, or looking after other people's children, or inside by taking in boarders, a woman of a certain standing did not work for money.

If she did earn money, it legally belonged to her husband. By the 1890s, the question of whether a woman should have an allowance of her own, rather than begging for money for personal needs and wants, was much discussed. You would find as many women as men arguing that the lordship of men over women was natural and right. And you would find many of both genders agreeing that the woman should have a voice in where and how money was spent.

Yet the union of husband and wife was seen as a partnership. "He is not her judge or master, but her other self," wrote Mrs.

Room for the children: once more we repeat it. What a dismal place this would be without them—with only selfish, proud, vain, business men, or worse yet, flaunting, gadding, gossiping women to people it and no children to delight, perfume, melodize and make things merry.

— Toronto *Globe*, September 19, 1887.

The Ritalin of the day, soothing syrups often contained opium derivatives. An advertisement in the *Halifax Evening Mail*, June 6, 1895 told mothers:

For Over Fifty Years, Mrs. Winslow's soothing syrup has been used for children teething. It soothes the child, softens the gums, allays all pain, cures wind colic, and is the best remedy for diarrhea. Twenty-five cents a bottle. Sold by all druggists throughout the world.

Here's an excellent receipt for obliterating Old Sol's summer work in the shape of freckles: —Dissolve one ounce of honey in half a pint of warm water. Squeeze into this the juice of two lemons and strain through a flannel bag. Add to this two ounces of brandy and one drachm bitter almonds. Shake thoroughly and apply with a camel's hair brush. Oh! Girls, if you only knew the 'vanities' the men write about.

— newspaper columnist Kit Coleman, "Woman's Kingdom," Toronto *Mail*, September 26, 1891.

A teacher in Vancouver explains to Alice Barrett in 1891 why she has remained single:

Mary said so many people wondered why she had never married—how she managed to withstand the opportunities and importunities of a new country, where so many men are walking around unattached.... Mary said she had so long earned her own money, and spent it as she pleased, not having to give account to anyone, that she could not bear the idea of having someone else give it to her, & she added, "To tell the truth, I don't care to give up a sixty dollar school for a forty dollar man."

— Jo Fraser Jones, *Hobnobbing with a Countess*, p. 44.

H.W. Beecher in her book of advice to women. "Being one, it is wiser to bear the frets and vexations of life together. Let both confide in the other. He will give her strength and courage, and her quick, instinctive penetration will often help him see things in a truer light than he would have alone."[14]

Sometimes, her body might betray her, and she might falter. Then the patent medicine men were ready, even eager, to help her out. "The way out of woman's troubles is with Doctor Pierre's Favorite Prescription," read one 1893 advertisement.

Safely and certainly, every delicate weakness, derangement, and disease peculiar to the sex is permanently cured. Out of all the medicines for women, the 'Favorite Prescription' is the only one that's guaranteed to do what is claimed for it. In all 'female complaints' and irregularities, periodical pains, displacements, internal inflammation or ulceration, bearing-down sensations and kindred ailments, if it ever fails to benefit or cure you, you have your money back.[15]

Part of this advertisement, as with many others, contains the Victorian euphemism for birth control: female irregularities might well mean pregnancy. Though birth control was rarely discussed outside the company of female friends—and often not even there—family size in most areas of Canada was dropping, and it must be presumed that women were finding some ways other than abstinence of not having children.

Only depraved women, it was said, experienced any enjoyment in sex; "lie back and think of England" is a Victorian phrase. But presumably fashions had nothing to do with sex—though much to do with attracting a mate and keeping him. The fashionable lady taking tea or strolling the stores had a waist that averaged 18 inches, whether naturally or confined by corsets and stays. Kerosene had replaced whale oil in lamps, but nothing was the equal of whalebone for corsets.

The worst moment in a woman's life was the death of a husband. The rules of deportment stated that widows wear black for two years, then come partly out of mourning to wear white, grey, or purple for the third year. Unless the husband left a good estate, widows were in a double bind: they had children, but were unable to earn the means to support them except in menial, low-paying jobs, and were still expected to keep up the house.

◇◇◇

A Model Housewife....Agreeable and Sympathetic: This very sensible woman is a loving wife and agreeable companion to her husband. She knows how to save time and thus finds opportunity to read, and is able to discuss topics of interest with her husband in the evening by the fireside. She is a gentle mother to her little ones, and when she says 'no' she keeps her word. She is never impatient with the baby when he is sleepy and clings to her skirts. Instead of spanking him, she takes the tired form to her arms and rocks it to sleep.

— Prof. B.G. Jefferis, *The Household Guide*, p. 329.

· 4 ·

DUST AND ITS DANGERS:

Into the New Century

The object of this Institute shall be, to promote that knowledge of Household Science which shall lead to improvement in household architecture with special attention to home sanitation, to a better understanding of the economic and hygienic value of foods and fuels and to a more scientific care of children with a view of raising the general standard of health of our people.

—*from the minute book of the Stoney Creek Women's Institute, 1897*

～

The ideal woman in 1900 had a pouter pigeon silhouette, with looming bosom, tight-laced waist, and sweeping skirts. Check again in 1918: the dresses are still long—though not as long—but the silhouette has changed radically, is softer and more natural, a hint of the flapper fashions to come in the 1920s.

Like fashions, women who kept house between 1895 and 1918 were leaving one world and entering another. Canada's population grew rapidly in those years, from five million to eight million. Though rural dwellers still outnumbered urban folk, the gap narrowed as towns and cities expanded. By the end of the period, many urban housewives had access to the electricity, running water, and indoor plumbing that radically changed home life, though most rural housewives could only hope for the day when they too could leave behind much of their hard manual labour.

Many women, urban and rural, were beginning to question the Victorian assumption that women's sole sphere was the home. "A woman's place is in the home; and out of it whenever she is called to guard those she loves and to improve conditions for them,"[1] famously declared feminist Nellie McClung, who, with many others, argued that women must act publicly to improve the conditions of women's lives. It was the housewife's duty, she declared, to fight alcoholism, abuse, and poverty.

With the growing cities and industrialization came urban poverty. Industrial wages were often low and, unlike their farm counterparts, urban housewives could not grow much food and families had to pay rent. A report on slum conditions in Toronto in 1913 revealed a husband, wife, two children, and three boarders living in a half basement. The health department had closed the premises

once, but so great was the need for accommodation that new rent-ers had soon appeared. "Found mother and five children, young-est three months, huddled together in one bed, shivering with cold, covered with one ragged quilt," said the same report. "Father intoxicated, trying to light the kitchen fire. Water pipes frozen." The children were taken into care and kept "until the father showed signs of reformation and obtained work."[2]

Across the country, women came together to fight poverty, high child mortality, isolation, abuse, and other ills. Some declared war on alcohol, which they saw as a destroyer of families, and

At the turn of the century, women were laced into pouter pigeon silhouettes, left. By 1910, a bridesmaid in Alberta dressed very differently, right. (*Ladies Home Journal*, June 1905; Glenbow Archives, NA-217-22)

fought for temperance and prohibition. From church auxiliaries to political groups, they discussed matters domestic and political. The National Council of Women, formed in 1893, aimed to improve conditions of life for women, families, and communities. The women of the Stoney Creek region in southern Ontario created the world's first Women's Institute in 1897; it was quickly followed by other chapters formed to help educate and inform rural women.

Women still fought to be regarded as persons in their own right. Many women and their organizations campaigned for the right to vote. Undeterred by opposition, male and female, that suggested that voting would destroy womanliness, that women did not have the right sort of brains to vote, or that voting would coarsen women by throwing them into the political fray, individuals and organizations marched into the battle, declaring that voting women would have the means to improve social conditions. Rights campaigner Nellie McClung gave some arguments the sarcastic treatment they deserved:

Alice Barrett Parke writes of life on a ranch in British Columbia's Spallumcheen Valley, where she kept house for her brother in the 1890s, until she married and continued her domestic chores as a wife:

Mr. Hays was here this morning, so I had the men to dinner. I had intended ironing this morning, but I had to churn, attend to the bread, cook beets, carrots & potatoes, boil a shank and cut the meat up for hash—& just as I thought I'd have a minute's breathing space Mr. Hays ran over a hen in the meadow, cutting its legs half off, so Harry cut its head off & brought it in—& I had that to pick & clean. I roasted it for tea. I was glad when dinner was over & now the bread is all baked too, so I think I'll take a little rest, although I really want to write some letters.

— Jo Fraser Jones, ed., *Hobnobbing with a Countess*, p. 36.

Rebecca Chase Kinsman Ells describes a day in the life of a woman whose husband has left their Nova Scotia home at the turn of the century to seek gold in the Klondike. Ells and her 18-year-old son, Manning, with the help of various hired women, ran the farm, sold butter and eggs, and looked after the daily routine:

Wed. Aug. 28th
This has been a busy day though I have not accomplished much. This morning churned and dressed butter 11 3/4 pounds. Did up the other work, baked lamb for dinner, then went down to Mrs. Len Cogswells to help her some as she had an "At Home" to night—came home just 12 made up the fire and sat down to dinner quarter to one—thought I was pretty smart—after washing the dishes went down again and helped some more— then came home did the night chores got the Boys supper and Manning and I went to the "At Home." Had just a delightful time, saw a lot of my friends and it is just a perfect night. Think I will have one next summer if I live.

— Margaret Conrad, Toni Laidlaw, and Donna Smyth, eds., *No Place Like Home, Diaries and Letters of Nova Scotia Women 1772–1938*, p. 219.

Father comes home, tired, weary, footsore, toe-nails ingrowing, caused by undarned stockings, and finds the fire out, house cold and empty, save for his half-dozen children, all crying.

"Where is your mother?" the poor man asks in broken tones. For a moment the sobs are hushed while little Ellie replies: "Out voting!"

Father bursts into tears.[3]

When women gained the vote in Manitoba in 1916, they opened a door that would not be closed again. By 1918, they had the right to vote in most Canadian provinces and in federal elections; in Quebec, they had to wait until 1941.

Women's Institutes and women's clubs were a godsend to isolated rural women. For 25 cents a year, members heard presentations on such topics as proper food for children, how to be happy though married, home decoration by girls, how to cook vegetables, how to make coffee according to new methods, butter making, housekeeping vs. homemaking, dust and its dangers, sanitary hints for housekeepers, woman's duties and possibilities, and physiology readings on such topics as the spine and ribs.

"Often filled with perplexity I find myself facing the same situation, then the suggestions given in our meetings come flooding back," wrote one woman, who against her will, was talked into an executive position with a prairie club, then found it introduced her to some 40 other women whom she had previously regarded with a degree of distrust. The women took suggestion books to their meetings, and wrote down all manner of household hints: how to bone a chicken, how to make jelly, how to conquer various sewing problems. "Club life has filled life with bright spots for me. No dreaded sense of isolation now—life is too busy and too taken up with studying, planning and working for each other."[4]

The message of many women's organizations—that housewives needed help—was underlined by the increasing cry for domestic science courses for girls. Girls are not learning the right way to do things from their mothers, said the proponents of scientific housewifery, and must be taught in school how to cook and clean and sew. A 1913 domestic science manual included a long list of kitchen and cleaning equipment the housewife would need,

Constance Kerr Sissons lived in Fort Frances, in northern Ontario, early in the twentieth century:

Thursday October 31st

Then over to our house to give some directions to painter, then to look up man to send stoves over and finally to office where I did some copying, and entered some letters in books and pasted them. Finally I went round to house again and found the man had left all the truck on the verandah. He said the workmen would not let him put it in. Very cold by this time and pitch dark…went to tea. Came home by light of Mr. B's lantern made crochet hook out of a piece of kindling and knife and sandpaper—cut out a pair of pyjamas for Harry.…The two stoves were going and the house got very hot.

— Kathryn Carter, ed., *The Small Details of Life*, p. 204.

Not all Klondikers grubbed for gold. These wives, with their husbands and families, camped on the shores of Lake Bennett in 1899, where they provided a hearty picnic. (Yukon Archives 4798)

City and town life at the turn of the century had their own forms of busyness. Caroline Alice Porter writes in her diary for Wednesday 18th September 1907, Moose Jaw:

I started to wash a down quilt today, and as soon as I got into the basement and a fire on, the bell began to ring. the meter man, a music teacher, a blind pedler, a green grocer, Annie, Mrs. Cochran, then we went over to tea at Bob. pa came in from the farm at about 5ock, this evening, nice fine day, put add in paper to rent house.

— Kathryn Carter, ed., *Small Details of Life*, pp. 249–50.

including preserving jars, mixing bowls, washboard, scrub brushes, ironing board and garbage can, for a total expenditure of $202.70, less $48.30 if you didn't include such items as the stove and cupboard.[5]

The era continued the trend of women becoming consumers, rather than producers. Though women in the city still made their families' clothing, cooked, cleaned, and did the traditional domestic chores, sometimes even keeping a few chickens, they were likely to work with store-bought materials, utensils, and machines.

As cities grew larger and more numerous, so did newspapers and magazines, buoyed by advertising for consumer products. Farm housewives bought from Eaton's catalogues and got their goods via mail order. City dwellers went downtown on the streetcar to buy from Eaton's, Simpson's, and a growing number of other stores that geared their advertising to women—and their insecurities. "Happy is the woman," lectured a T. Eaton & Co. advertisement in 1905, "who is blessed with good managing ability. The problem of keeping the household machinery in smooth running order upon a certain weekly expenditure, and laying away, besides, a certain amount for future needs is one that requires considerable thought."[6]

At the turn of the century, advertisements for new miracle foods could share a page with "A Timely Talk about Corsets," advertising side steels and heavy boning and insisting that every new dress deserved a new corset. By 1917, modern and scientific had definitely taken over. An issue of *Maclean's* magazine that year displayed ads for cocoa, a coal-fired warm air generator, under-arm hair remover, peerless water systems, knitted underclothing, removable collars, and electric irons and toasters. "Put an end to broiling hot kitchens and summer drudgery. Shut up the range—and do your cooking and ironing the easy pleasant way, with 'Canadian Beauty' electric appliances," suggested the ads, and recommended hot water heaters, coffee percolators, and a toaster-stove-grill that boiled, fried, broiled, and toasted.[7]

⤳ THE COOK ⤳

The frugal housewife, the careful housewife, the thrifty housewife: the homemaker was repeatedly lectured about the best way to deal with increasing choice from a multitude of stores and markets. "We all know that to live we must have food, but we do not all real-ize that we must eat the right kinds of food to be at our best and to work efficiently," advised an insurance company cookbook in 1918. "The average housewife today finds that it takes a great deal of thought and care to make wise choices of food. . . . Many house-wives have increased the cost of their food supply through lack of thought in buying."[8]

The housewife needed to look carefully at advertisements designed to part her from her husband's hard-earned cash by telling her how modern and wise she would be to buy their food products. Promoters of Malta-Vita, a prepared breakfast cereal, for example, crowed in 1902: "What a boon Malta-Vita would have been to our mothers! What a saving of time, thought and energy Malta-Vita is to the modern housewife! What a boon to human-ity is offered by the makers of this delicious food, who have placed within easy reach of the public at an economical price, a food which will remove one-half the troubles of the race!"[9] As was

"Sama" reports on the first annual meeting of the National Council of Women:

We are going to try to get our chil-dren taught to use their hands as well as their brains in the public schools, so that the girls at least may have some idea of how to cook and do housework in a scientific manner.... [We will do that] by trying to get every woman in the country to see the need of it, talk it up, create public sentiment, and the rest is sure to follow.

— *Our First Annual Meeting*, National Council of Women of Canada, Toronto, 1894, p. 11.

Butcher's advertisement in the August 5, 1905, Toronto *Globe*:

Most of us remember when the aver-age dinner in the country was associ-ated, by reputation at least, with salt pork, and when the city cook had no alternative but to go in for a large roast for the dinner table. In the one case there was a monotony to which the modern palate could scarcely be reconciled, and in the other there were bother and expense, which now happily are often avoided. What would the housewife do to-day, say, in the hot weather without some-thing like Clark's boiled tongue? How many scorchings in the hot kitchen are saved by this ready-to-use line of cold meats?

Patterned linoleum, patterned wallpaper, patterned flour sack, shiny cast-iron stove, baking ingredients and utensils all laid out—a Toronto housewife demonstrates a model kitchen in the first decade of the 20th century. (Arthur Beales, Library and Archives Canada PA-800211)

The tomato is made so much of these days that it seems to blush redder and redder with a modesty vastly becoming to it. The canning, preserving, drying, the making of catsup, chili sauce, chutney, goes merrily on, for, no matter how many items the careful housewife may strike from her list of table luxuries, the toothsome tomato will not be among them.

TOMATO PRESERVE

Ten pounds ripe tomatoes unsliced, ten of sugar, 4 lemons shredded, 2 ounces citron shredded. Mix all together and cook slowly until very thick. To allow to boil hard mars the beautiful color. Green tomatoes can be used instead of ripe ones if desired.

— Toronto *Globe*, August 22, 1918.

customary at the time, the advertisement ran in the news columns, in the same type as articles on fires and court cases.

Some new food inventions captured the housewife's imagination and became staples in her repertoire. Invented in the 1880s, a flavoured, sweetened gelatin dessert made no inroads until the company that manufactured it hired salesmen to travel the United States and Canada and advertised heavily, including displaying recipes for the new wonder product. "Jell-O is the dainty dessert that can be made in a minute," promised a 1905 booklet. "It is all so easy that the woman who cannot boil potatoes—if there is such a woman—can make a Jell-O dessert. The fruit flavours of Jell-O are delightful and are an agreeable change from the second-hand perfume kind of flavor that is so noticeable in the common dessert preparations."[10] Available in lemon, orange, strawberry, raspberry, cherry, peach and chocolate, the dessert cost 10 cents a package.

By the turn of the century, most housewives used cast-iron stoves fired by wood or coal for cooking; some had electric or gas ranges. Cooks still favoured long and slow over quick and crisp. According to conventional wisdom, vegetables needed to be thoroughly boiled. The *Galt Cook Book* of 1898 suggested half an hour for green peas, an hour for young carrots, and an hour and a half for string beans. Not much had changed 15 years later: a Vancouver bride's book of 1913 suggested one to two hours for string

RECIPES

By the 1910s, many women's groups, from church auxiliaries to women's institutes, were publishing cookbooks to raise money for their organizations. *The Economical Cook Book*, written by the Ottawa Ladies Hebrew Benevolent Society in 1915, included recipes for chicken soup and matzo balls:

CHICKEN SOUP

3 to 4 lb. chicken
3 to 4 qts. water
1 tablespoon salt
1 onion
1 carrot
2 stalks celery
1/4 teaspoon pepper

Select an old hen. Singe, clean and joint; then salt and let stand several hours. Put on to boil in cold water and let come to boil quickly. Skim thoroughly if you want a clear soup. Let simmer slowly two to three hours, add the vegetables, boil one hour longer, strain, remove fat and add seasoning. Serve hot with dumplings or any of the soup garnishings.

MATZO BALLS-NO. I

1 tablespoon poultry fat or butter
1/8 teaspoon salt
Matzos or cracker meal
3 eggs
1/2 cup grated almonds

Beat the yolks very light, add seasoning and the almonds and enough matzo meal to make stiff batter, then add the beaten whites. Drop by teaspoon in deep hot fat, fry light brown; place in oven to keep warm and put in soup just before sending to the table.
— pp. 43, 46.

Maclean's of August, 1917, contained the first "Women and their Work" section. In it, Mrs. Elizabeth Atwood gives long and detailed directions for preserving and canning in the war days of sugar shortages:

In these days when sugar is so expensive, it is encouraging to know that most canning and preserving recipes call for far too much sugar. Practically every variety of fruit will keep just as well if less sugar is used.

PRESERVING GRAPES

6 quarts of grapes
1 1/2 pints of sugar
1 gill of water

Squeeze the pulp of the grapes out of the skins. Cook the pulp five minutes and then run through a sieve that is fine enough to hold back the seeds. Put the water, skins, and pulp into the preserving kettle and heat slowly to the boiling point. Skim the fruit and then add the sugar. Boil fifteen minutes.

PLUM PRESERVE

4 quarts greengages
2 quarts of sugar
1 pint of water

Prick the fruit and put it in a preserving kettle. Cover generously with cold water. Heat to the boiling point and boil gently for five minutes. Drain well.

Put the sugar and water in a preserving kettle and stir over the fire until the sugar is dissolved. Boil five minutes, skimming well. Put the drained greengages in this syrup and cook gently for twenty minutes. Put in sterilized jars.

Other plums may be preserved in the same manner. The skins should be removed from white plums.

Madame Dandurand describes fête days in Quebec:

In the large kitchens, where swarm the whole family, feasts and prospective joys are prepared. While on the stove, encumbered with simmering pots, the odorous doughnut is fried under the superintendence of the mother, others knead pie crust into innumerable tarts, season the stews or pluck the fowls that will shortly be put in the store to freeze.

— *Women of Canada: Their Life and Work*, p. 29.

beans, and almost as long for spinach, tomatoes, cauliflower, and onions. Fish should be boiled for at least 30 minutes—though, to give cookbook authors credit, they decried overcooked fish equally with undercooked. "An underdone fish is disgusting," wrote the editors of the *Galt Cook Book*, "while an overdone one is tasteless and mostly tough."[11] The editors also warned that a fish put to boil in cold water enriched only the water, not the diner.

Housewives were becoming a little more cosmopolitan. Amid the traditional recipes for a nice relish or baked squash, the reader might come upon a recipe for *frijoles conpuestos*. In general, housewives still stuck to the tried and true—though paying attention to new rules of diet, "scientifically composed," that suggested the proper proportions of such things as carbohydrates and protein.

RECIPES

BEAUTY SALAD
Dissolve a package of Raspberry Jell-O in a pint of boiling water and fill individual moulds or cups one-fourth full. Let harden. Coarsely chop three bananas, sprinkle with lemon juice, and add half a cup of English walnut meats coarsely chopped. Put the mixture in the moulds and pour on the rest of the Jell-O when it is a cold liquid. At serving time arrange on lettuce with slices of bananas sprinkled with nutmeats around the turned-out Jell-O. Serve with salad dressing. This makes nine individual servings.

— Jell-O booklet, 1905.

Women wrote down the recipes conveyed in lectures at the Women's Institute and similar organizations, and clipped recipes from newspapers. Mary A.B. Campbell, who lived in Perth, Ontario, from about 1887 to 1913, collected the following notes from demonstration lectures and newspapers:

APPETIZING DISH
Mix equal quantities of bean or pea pulp & chopped almonds, salt and pepper to taste. Break 4 soda biscuits into pieces with fork after pouring boiling water on these, add $\frac{1}{4}$ c. cream. Put $\frac{1}{2}$ bean mixture in bottom of bake dish, on this spread the biscuits then other half bean mixture, &

over this pour another $\frac{1}{4}$ cup cream. If milk is used add a little melted butter. Bake this mixture $\frac{3}{4}$ hr. turn out when cold, cut in slices for serving.

SWISS CHARD
Swiss chard that has provided greens throughout the summer months will continue to yield during the winter if the roots are dug up and removed to the basement. A fair amount of light and a temperature of 45 to 55 degrees will give good production. If placed on an earthern floor the chard will not need any further soil. If placed on a cement floor a small quantity of soil around the roots is necessary.

Log cabin or mansion, every home needed to be kept clean. Taken before World War I somewhere in Ontario, this photograph suggests a woman's work went on regardless of her age. (A.W. Barton, Ontario Archives, C 121-1-0-8-2)

◇✕✕◇✕✕◇✕✕✕◇✕✕✕◇✕✕✕◇✕✕✕◇✕✕✕◇✕✕◇

SWEEPING

Apparatus

Damp pieces of newspaper, sawdust or washed tea-leaves, a broom, a dustpan, dustcap and gloves.

Directions

1. Open window at top, shut all doors and drawers.

2. If possible, put away small articles, and cover big furniture with dust sheets.

3. Sprinkle the damp newspaper or other material over the floor.

4. Begin to sweep that part furthest from the door. Keep the broom nearly perpendicular; sweep from the corners towards the centre; take up the dirt into the dustpan frequently.

5. Leave the room shut up with window open for fifteen minutes, or longer, for dust to settle.

6. Burn the dirt and paper and wash dustpan; also broom if necessary. Replace everything.

— Annie B. Juniper, *Girls' Home Manual of Cookery, Home Management, Home Nursing and Laundry*, p. 130.

❧ THE HOUSEKEEPER ❧

Though electricity was no longer a novelty in 1900, few houses were hooked up to electrical power. By 1918, a high proportion of housewives in towns and cities could plug in electric lights and electrical appliances. In 1900, advertisements were for coal furnaces and better washtubs. In 1913, ads in a book for Vancouver brides featured incandescent light bulbs and electric toasters. By the end of World War I, almost every city house in Canada had running water and most had indoor bathrooms with toilet, sink, and bath. The urban housewife's tasks were changing accordingly. In the country, though, housewives still relied on kerosene lamps, wells—or streams and lakes—and the outdoor privy.

The housekeeper's task in the city, it seemed, had never been easier. Yet rising expectations and larger houses kept cleaning tasks at the centre of the housewife's life. Cleanliness was still next to godliness in many a commentator's mind, and godliness was still important in twentieth-century Canada.

Girls taking domestic science courses were provided with books that detailed how to do every household task. A manual produced

---

Friday, November 1, 1901:
I took up carpet in our room, swept it, washed oil cloth—, shook all carpet and Turkish rug out side , then spent afternoon and part of Evening sweeping H.'s office and laying carpet (which I carried over in installments), dusted and arranged and oh what a job it all was—came home after it was all done a little while after supper, did some writing, attended to fires polished shoes and dusted.

Friday, January 3, 1902:
A great day changing stoves. Took down Queen and put up Bank Stove. Clear cold day, Afternoon—two men came to put hot-air shaft into my bedroom. Lots of dirt and muss to clear, went out shopping to Hudson's Bay Stores…

Saturday, January 4, 1902:
The new stove smokes, I discovered pipes were coming apart in Henry's room.…I did usual work, made three pies and pastry cakes, went up town swept and dusted Harry's office got mail indexed in letter book.

Monday, January 6, 1902:
A great day cleaning…brought in piles of wood made kindling, mended darning bag etc., washed oilcloth, swept all upstairs, oiled all stained floors, shook rugs, changed bed linen, and put up pictures, tidied and arranged little sewing room. Went to office, finished indexing and bookkeeping as far as marked, bought oilcloth, came home and did Harry's washstand, made curtain for it.

Saturday, May 3, 1902:
It rained very hard and I couldn't get waterman, so H. brought a pail from River, and I have 14 saucepans out to catch water (we have no eaves.). H. gathered water from vacant lot for baths.…I wasted a great deal of day wandering around with pails etc.

— Constance Kerr Sissons, diary, Fort Frances, Ontario, in Kathryn Carter, *The Small Details of Life*, pp. 204–5.

The real French Canadian housekeeper,—redoubtable enemy of microbes,—not content with brushing the furniture, rubs the table underneath as well as on top. The rich are not the only ones to cultivate this perfection in housekeeping. At any time, through the half open door of a thatched cottage, the passer-by may catch a glimpse of a well arranged interior; neat rag carpets drawn in a straight line over the floor, yellow with recent scrubbings; brightly polished iron stove, and opposite to that, standing in rigid solemnity, the "lit de parade," or best bedstead.

Cleanliness is the luxury of the poor as well as of the middle class. All pleasurable and serious occasions are prepared for by a grand scrubbing from top to bottom…The greater the event, the more thorough the overhauling. One little corner neglected causes as much remorse as a sin unconfessed.

— *Women of Canada: Their Life and Work*, 1900, p. 23.

in British Columbia in 1913 included instructions on almost everything, including sweeping, mopping, scrubbing, and dusting, with the correct tools or apparatus and directions for each. White cheesecloth dusters were highly recommended for dusting, "as they quickly show the dirt and are easily washed and dried."[12] They should be slightly dampened in the steam from a kettle, then used to dust first the small articles, then the furniture, then the chairs and table, and last the window sills, ledges, doors, and baseboard. Dusters must be careful to wipe the dust up, not merely flick it on from place to place.

A 1913 book of hints, probably produced by Gillett's Perfumed Lye, told the housekeeper how to clean lamp chimneys, marble sinks, and a multiplicity of other items. And household diaries of the time frequently refer to the work of housekeeping, with or without the assistance of a maid.

By the end of the era, however, making soap and sweeping floors had taken a back seat to more modern ways of tackling housecleaning. A 1917 advertisement for a new vacuum cleaner that plugged into a socket on the light fixture trumpeted, "The OHIO gets into every corner, under and behind the furniture and makes short work of dirt and dust. . . . The OHIO gives the house-wife a new lease on her time, enables her to have the housework finished in half the usual time without that grimy tired feeling. Let us send you full particulars of the OHIO Easy-Payment plan."[13]

❧ THE SEAMSTRESS ❧

"For the woman who would combine style with economy, this is a splendid book,"[14] the Butterick sewing patterns company declared of its pattern book for winter, 1908. By the turn of the century, the home seamstress had a wide choice of patterns in a bewildering variety of sizes for almost every garment she might want to make.

Butterick even put out its own magazine, *The Delineator*, acclaiming it as the "leading women's magazine," $1.00 a year for fourteen issues in Canada, with a coupon for a free dressmaking pattern in each issue. Doctors, fashion designers, and well-known authors and personalities, such as Rudyard Kipling, composer Oscar Hammerstein, and arctic explorer Lieut. Robert Peary, all

---

HOUSEHOLD HINTS

Lamp chimneys should not be washed, as this makes the glass brittle, but if held for a moment over a steaming tea-kettle and then polished with a soft dry cloth, the result will be all that could be desired.

When marble and other marble-lined articles are neglected, until yellow stains have been allowed to appear on them, muriatic acid has to be used to remove them. Shut the water from the basin, and dry the marble well. Tie a rag to the end of a small stick, dip it into the acid, and with it touch the stain, and immediately the spot will disappear. Put water into the basin at once upon disappearance of the stain, and then scrub the basin with soap and water. When applying the acid, be careful not to get it on the metal about the basin, as it will destroy the plating. Do not get it on the hands, nor drop it on your shoes, nor get it on your clothing, as it will destroy them.

Also things to remember:
Save refuse grease and make soap of it with Gillett's perfumed Lye, full directions on each package.

— *Gillett's Pure Flake Lye*, household hint book, 1913.

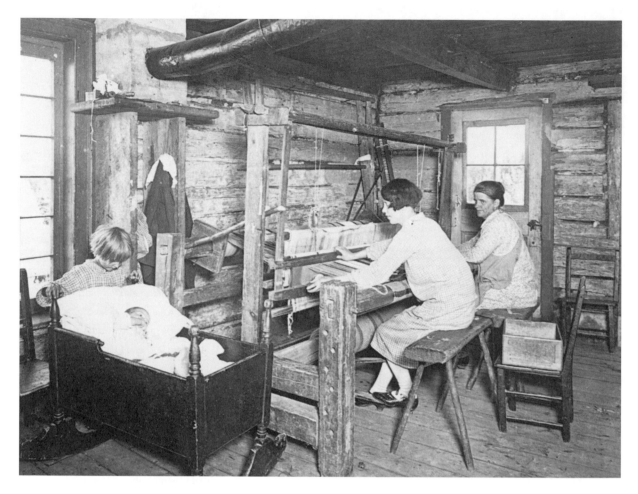

Though few housewives early in the 20th century wove their own cloth, some made extra money by weaving in their homes. These housewives work on their looms in Cap à L'Aigle, Quebec, in 1910, with their children nearby. (Edith M. Small, Library and Archives Canada PA-040744)

wrote for the magazine. "*The Delineator* [is] first in the field of litera-ture. Its Contributors to Departments, all recognized authorities, make *The Delineator* first in its practical value to the Home."[15]

Fashion illustrations filled the women's pages of the news-papers. The *Montreal Gazette* ran a weekly page called "In Woman's Realm" around the turn of the century, filled mostly with descrip-tions of the latest in clothing styles. "A crepoline [a fine, stiff-ened type of silk gauze] possibility is shown in the production of a serviceable street suit in prune color. Very simply, the skirt, bolero fronts, collar and cuffs are relieved by a treatment in braids of two tones, which, by the way, is a favorite trimming," enthused the fashion writer in October of 1900. Women were encouraged to continue their fine sewing as well; the *Gazette* women's page, for example, frequently carried advertisements for embroidery silks.

I have a lot of outdoor work and managing to do, and I wonder if anyone would care to hear about my overall dress which I use for that purpose.

First, I get six yards of blue denim-overall cloth—I paid 20 cents a yard for mine. I shrink the cloth by dipping first in hot, then cold water then back into the hot again and hang it in the wind until it is almost dry, when I press it all out and it is ready for cutting. In this way I avoid having it shrink after it is made up and the necessary letting down of hems. I take great care to have mine fit perfectly and to have it sufficiently full without any bulkiness. I wear no aprons with it, and it is surprising how easy it is to wash, and I always starch mine, tho I do not always have time to iron it. I have two large pockets in front, which are handy to carry various articles and tools around in.

Instead of making buttonholes and using buttons I use the Wilson hook and eye. They're so strong and so flat, and one can change dresses easily when you come from the outdoor to the indoor work. I make mine into a one-piece dress with three-gore skirt and sailor collar. It seems so suitable for resisting the winds and it does not tear easily. One dress lasts me almost two seasons, Then, too, I wear a Dutch cap most all the time, which keeps my hair from flying about, and I find them very comfortable on the head no matter how you have the hair done up, owing to the elastic band in the back.

— MDK to the *Grain Growers' Guide*, July 19, 1916, as quoted in Barbara E. Kelcey and Angela E. Davis eds., *A Great Movement Underway*, p. 153.

Fashion provided a prime example of the development of new roles and fewer restrictions for women. The Rational Dress movement that began in the Victorian era continued into the twentieth century. In addition to less voluminous skirts and more practical clothing, the aim of the English Rational Dress Society was to have no woman wear more than seven pounds (three kilograms) of underwear. The *Gazette* included a column on the triumph of short skirts—though still long by twenty-first century measure—and listed the reasons women used to justify them: they didn't get wet trailing along rainy streets; they were very convenient in getting on and off streetcars; they were much more comfortable and cool in a theatre on a hot evening. The writer suggested that, though "normally minded women" were horrified by the actions of their sisters, they were won over if they wanted to bicycle or play golf. It was just a short step from wearing shorter skirts for sports to wearing them in the city.

The seamstress might try her hand at these shorter skirts, but complete conversion would have to wait another decade or two. Even by 1908, women continued to wear extremely restraining corsets, with "rustproof boning thruout,"[16] and the average width of the summer skirts in the pattern books was six to eight yards at

Many of our older citizens will remember when nearly every article of clothing had to be made either by the tailor or in the home. Forty years ago the housewife had to knit the stockings, cut and make the underclothing, as well as nearly every garment worn by the husband and child. Today all that is changed. Every article of clothing known to our civilization is offered ready made, and in such variety of style and sizes as to fit and suit the most fastidious.

— Toronto *Globe*, June 28, 1902.

Fancy work was a skill prized by many a housewife. Two women in Cranbrook, BC, knit and embroider at home in 1912. (Mary Peck, Library and Archives Canada C-045390)

the lower edge, with eight yards of fabric required for the dress skirt, another three and a half yards for the bodice.

Department stores carried an enormous variety of fabrics, available both through the big-city stores and catalogue sales. Cotton foulards, mercerized sateens, coloured muslins, French taffeta, water and dress silks, corded skirting and calico: all were available to the busy seamstress.

So central still was the idea of sewing to the housewife's job description that the sewing kit a soldier carried during the Boer War was called a housewife: "a remarkably useful domestic outfit, [that] contains needles, thread, scissors, pins, safety pins, buttons, thimble and other indispensables."[17]

~+ THE LAUNDRESS +~

Try Pearline for washing blankets. It saves at every point. Coarse things are easily washed by delicate women. Fine things safely washed by strong women, No care necessary. By saving most of the rubbing Pearline saves most of the wear.

Washing is hard work under any circumstances, why should you make it harder by using poor soap? Sunlight soap cuts the work in half. It does part of the work itself, you don't have to scrub or boil the clothes. The Sunlight way is the easy way as well as the nest and least injurious to clothes and hands.

— advertisements for laundry soaps, 1905.

"The best washer at the best price," shouted one advertisement for a washing machine. "We have used one for fifteen years and prefer your Washer to others," read a testimonial from a Hamilton woman ordering a new washer at the reduced price of $7.50. "The greatest labor-saving machine ever invented," declared another, accompanied by illustrations of one exhausted woman, her hands

Sometimes the housewife got a little help: a husband uses the washtub and hand wringer in Quatsino Sound, BC, in the early 1900s. (Vancouver Public Library 71662)

plunged into a tub of steaming water, and another relaxed and reading a book, her laundry already hanging on the line at 9 a.m.[18] A 1917 advertisement in the Winnipeg Free Press offered a high-grade $6.50 machine for just $4.95, but the machine shown looks primitive indeed.

In truth, washing machines, developed in the mid-nineteenth century and made somewhat popular at the turn of the century, still meant hard work. The hand-cranked machines required that the operator move paddles by means of a lever and feed clothes through a wringer also turned by hand. The first electric-powered machine, a metal tub that oscillated, was first sold in Canada around 1910. It left much to be desired, and was bought by few customers. Like

TO CLEAN AN IRON HEATED ON A STOVE

1. Rub on powdered bath brick; dust this off, do edges carefully.

2. Rub beeswax carefully over iron.

3. Polish on a clean rag.

4. Test for heat on clean paper before using.

If an iron becomes coated with starch, scrape off with a blunt knife and clean as above.

—Annie B. Juniper, *Girls' Home Manual of Cookery*, p. 177.

Hanging out the laundry, rain or shine, warm or freezing cold, was a weekly chore. In 1903, an Ottawa woman pins the wash to a clothesline beside her backyard water pump. (Photograph attributed to James Ballantyne, Library and Archives Canada PA-133487)

its predecessors, it had to be filled with hot water and emptied by hand, and clothes still had to be fed into a wringer.

Girls taking domestic science in British Columbia in 1913 had the process of laundering clothes and household linens laid out for them in nitpicking detail. For example, washing clothes with paraffin or kerosene, a new method for getting out dirt and stains, should follow this routine:

1. Put clothes, dry and dirty, into wash boiler half full of boiling water, containing:
   One tablespoonful paraffin or kerosene.
   One tablespoonful washing soda.
   Half pound of shaved soap.
2. Boil clothes quickly for one hour.

3. Remove clothes with stick and rinse in three hot waters; the first two waters should contain one tablespoonful soda solution. It may be necessary to rub bands and very dirty parts in first water.

4. Dry in the open air.[19]

That same tome contained a long description of how to deal with a weekly family wash. On Monday, the housekeeper should make sure she had the appropriate softened water, soap, and starch, then sort the clothes, remove stains (instructions for various methods included), mend holes, and put white clothes to soak. The book told how to sort the wash into various categories: woollens, table linen, face towels, fine white things, bed and body linen, coarse towels and kitchen towels, and coloured cottons. On Tuesday, she should heat water and wash the clothes, starching where necessary. When the wash was done, she should clean the utensils and the wash house, then fold slightly dampened clothes for ironing or mangling. The clean clothes could be mangled and hung to air Tuesday night or mangled on Wednesday. Wednesday was the day to iron and air clothes.

The invention of the electric iron had slightly improved the job of ironing. But the irons did not have thermostats, so they were, invariably, too hot when plugged in, too cold when unplugged. And they were heavy: some weighed two kilograms. The book gave detailed instructions for the ironing of everything: what order to do it in, how to fold it, general rules for ironing, and even how to iron a handkerchief, a job that took a remarkable amount of turning and folding.

⤙ The Nurse ⤚

The Countess of Aberdeen, wife of Canada's Governor General, was convinced much could be done to help the housewife with her nursing duties. At the annual meeting of the National Council of Women in 1896, many of the members "told pathetic stories of cases where young mothers and children had died, whilst husbands and fathers were traveling many weary miles for the medical and nursing aid which might have saved them," she wrote.

COUGH MIXTURE
Mrs. Howie

One pound of honey, five cents worth of peppermint, five cents worth of laudanum, five cents worth of paregoric, five cents worth of anise, half cupful of whiskey; melt the honey and put into a bottle, add the ingredients, shake well, Teaspoonful whenever the cough is troublesome.

CURE FOR CUTS AND BRUISES
Mrs. Addison

Cut fingers and bruises of all kinds if wrapped in a cloth wet in alum water heal with a rapidity that is truly wonderful.

— Margaret Taylor and Frances McNaught, *The Early Canadian Galt Cook Book*, p. 42.

Her determination to help resulted in the formation of the Victorian Order of Nurses, a service that sent visiting nurses to homes that were far distant from doctors, or where there was no money for medical care. "In the towns they will go to those who cannot now afford the care of trained nurses and often die for lack of it," she declared. "On the prairies, in the forests, in mining districts—everywhere throughout the country—they will go hither and thither amongst our brave pioneers and bring help to these heroic people who are building up the future of this beautiful country amidst many hardships and privations."[20]

Such innovation made it possible for increasing numbers of housewives to consult medical professionals. The housewife and mother, however, remained responsible for the day-to-day health of her family. Though medical treatment had advanced much over the previous century, self-help manuals still prescribed dubious cures, both old and new. A 1913 manual for new brides suggested that 30 drops of laudanum would treat cholera, recommended warm water or a lobelia emetic for convulsions in children, and prescribed a mixture of potash, dilute nitro-muriatic acid, tincture of aconite, spirits of nitrate, tincture of henbane, and glycerine for colds and fever.

THE TREATMENT OF COMMON AILMENTS

Cold in the Head. This is infectious. Patient should sleep alone. Patient should go to bed, take a bowl of bread and milk, then steam head as follows, sitting up in bed. Into a jug of boiling water put a few drops of eucalyptus oil, hold head over jug, cover head and jug with a thick towel to keep in steam, then inhale as long as possible. The steam and oil will break up the cold. Patient should dry face and rub vaseline on bridge and sides of nose and also grease nostrils. Great care should be taken to keep body warm and to have room well ventilated. Instead of handkerchiefs, use cheesecloth and burn.

Rheumatic Pains generally affect joints, and are a dull ache. Rub part affected with a good liniment. Take a tablespoonful of Epsom salts one day, after which take half-teaspoonful in half cup boiling water, before breakfast (sip it slowly) every morning for a month. This keeps the bowels open each day, and the poison is removed from the blood.

Linseed Poultice. Pour one cup boiling water, more if a big poultice is required, into a hot bowl. Sift in linseed meal with left hand and stir with right, mix well and when it cuts dry add a little olive or castor oil. Spread at once on warm cotton wool, fold over the edges, place between hot plates and take immediately to patient.

Bread Poultice. Prepare as for linseed poultice, using crumbled bread.

— Annie B. Juniper, *Girls' Home Manual of Cookery*, pp. 150–51.

Many advertisements promised cures for children's ailments. Advertisers of patent medicines had mothers in their sights. "It strikes terror to a mother's heart to have her child wake up at night with a croupy cough," read one advertisement for Dr. Wood's Norway Pine Syrup. Castoria, for infants and children, cured diarrhea, constipation, and flatulence, relieved teething troubles, regulated the stomach and bowels, and was indeed the children's panacea and the mother's friend.

The advertisements in newspaper and magazine suggested a virtual epidemic of complaints such as indigestion, bad backs, and lingering colds, all of which—and much more—could be cured by electric belts, kidney pills, restorative tonics. Some offered your money back if not satisfied; some suggested you need not even pay unless you were content.

Every book for housewives or future housewives, though, still recommended herbs, plants, and common household substances for the various ills that might beset members of the household. Every housewife still needed to know the best recipes for potions and poultices, bandages and liniments, to succour their husbands and children. Newer recipes, however, continued the trend begun in Victorian times, calling more for substances that could be bought in the store or at the druggist's than for garden herbs and wild plants.

❧ THE MOTHER ❧

The beginnings of the twentieth century brought changes to the role of the housewife as mother: not a revolution, but an evolution. Columns of information on rearing children vied with the age-old motherly wisdom, as an emphasis on scientific methods and efficiency touched motherhood. Inspired by the growing sense that they could improve family life only by public battles, some housewives took timid steps into public discussion of the minefield of birth control and abortion.

Motherhood was still considered women's highest calling. "Motherhood then is the permanent function, its magnitude no mortal mind can conceive," declared a 1900 publication for mothers. "Every mother should not only desire to know but should know

The Countess of Aberdeen, wife of the governor-general and president of the National Council of Women, speaks to the council's first annual meeting in 1894:

We come together as women who are more or less alive to the high duties and opportunities which are ours in virtue of our being women …And how can we best describe this woman's mission in a word? Can we not best describe it as "mothering," in one sense or another? We are not all called to be the mothers of little children, but every woman is called on to "mother" in some way or another. And it is impossible to over-look what a great work of "mothering" in a special sense is committed to the women of Canada.

— *Our First Annual Meeting*, p. 5.

how to mould the plastic nature of her infant, so as to maintain a healthy mind in a healthy body. To possess both herself is the first essential."[21]

She must listen to professionals, not her mother or the neighbours, to provide accurate information about childcare. Dr. Helen MacMurchy, reporting to the Ontario government in 1910, sought ways to cut the high rate of infant death. Believing that the gradual switch in the nineteenth century from the breast or the wet nurse to bottle-feeding endangered children through poor nutrition and tainted milk, she urged mothers to breast-feed their babies. "Because the mother-in-law, or the sister-in-law, or the nurse, or the neighbour, or some other meddling busybody, has told her not to" was not sufficient reason to switch to cow's milk before the age of nine months, she wrote. She also suggested the government should pay the mother of a baby a pension if she would otherwise have to go out to work. MacMurchy deplored inadequate labelling of preparations for children, such as a popular soothing syrup that contained opium, and railed against labelling that suggested a baby food was a perfect substitute for mother's milk.[22]

Mothers were expected to mould their children into obedient, respectful, and hard-working citizens. If words and example didn't work, then spanking would. Some families went by the "just wait till your father gets home" model, but, in others, mother was the disciplinarian. "Mother was the spanker and we were really scared of her," wrote Anne Anderson, daughter of a Scottish father and Cree mother in Alberta. "Dad never laid a hand on us but he lectured us and made us understand." But, she stressed, "We truly had a happy home environment. We were lucky children indeed."[23]

Canadian authorities wanted to teach new immigrants how to mother in the Canadian way. In Toronto, for example, the Department of Public Health hired nurses who could speak other languages, such as Italian, Russian, and Ukrainian to visit new mothers, and translated some of its pamphlets on child care into other languages. But the visiting nurses were not always successful in their tasks. Some immigrant mothers, for example, thought children should be wrapped in many layers of clothing, while the nurses tried to persuade them the child should be lightly clothed and get fresh air.

Schools had taken over the job of teaching children the basic skills of reading, writing, and arithmetic—though children in rural areas were often unable to get to school in winter, and children of poverty-stricken parents left school young to earn money for the family. Even the skills of sewing and cooking were no longer mother's sole purview: domestic science classes were increasingly common. But mother still supervised her child's learning, and many mothers taught their daughters how to cook, sew, and clean by example.

Many a commentator opined that women—and it was always the women who were to be responsible for this—should limit their families to the number of children they could afford to support. "Fewer and better children are desired by right-minded parents," wrote doctor Alice B. Stockham in her 1893 book *Tokology*. "The world is groaning under the curse of chance parenthood. It is due to posterity that procreation be brought under the control of reason and conscience."

Stockham was insistent that Canadian women should know about contraception. "It has been feared that a knowledge of means to prevent conception would, if generally diffused, be abused by women; that they would to so great an extent escape motherhood, as to bring about social disaster," she continued. ". . . [But] with this natural desire for children, we believe few women would abuse the knowledge or privilege of controlling conception." [24]

But when it came to actually describing methods of contraception, Stockham got less definite, no doubt influenced both by legislation enacted in 1892 that made publishing details of contraception illegal and by her own beliefs about what was and was not acceptable. She was also battling against the catch phrase "race suicide": the Victorian and post-Victorian suggestion that if British Protestants didn't breed, they would quickly be outnumbered by other nationalities, religions, and races that did.

She recommended, first of all, continence. If that didn't work, she suggested the rhythm method, paying attention to the "physiological laws of ovulation"—though, unfortunately for those who used this method, the wisdom of the time dictated that conception couldn't take place in the last two weeks of a woman's cycle. She strongly disapproved of withdrawal before ejaculation. She accurately declared that douches could not be relied upon, nor could

Coming home I met Mrs. Weir hurrying along. She is a poor woman who lives back of us. I had heard her baby was sick, & stopped to ask her about it. She was crying and said she feared he was going to die. The Doctor had been there three times today, & was going to bring in another doctor. Poor woman!

— Alice Barrett Parke, in Jo Fraser Jones, *Hobnobbing with a Countess*, p. 74.

the current theory that a woman could avoid conception by "avoiding the last thrill of passion herself, during coition." "Sedular absorption"—no ejaculation—might just work.[25]

⤜ THE WIFE ⤛

"The salvation of the human race demands that women shall retain their humility, simplicity, and faith, and should teach men by self-denial and kindness to curb the animal part of their natures and become more noble and human," wrote one man who, without a scrap of irony, signed himself "Woman's Friend" in an 1891 letter to Kit Coleman, "Woman's Kingdom" editor and columnist at the *Toronto Mail*. This correspondent suggested such nobility of spirit would only be injured by women having their own money.

But Coleman would have none of it. "For the sake of a few," she sweetly asked, "would you deprive all women of such a common right as a monthly or yearly allowance? Many and many a wife does more than the work of a hired servant girl." The masterful man was all very well, but "the woman can be man's equal, her foot by his foot, her hand in his," no slave, no master.[26]

This type of heated exchange was not unusual at the turn of the century and beyond. Men and women could be found on both sides of the campaign for women's suffrage and the battle for rights for women. Yet even those who felt most strongly about these rights usually did so in the context of women in the home. Campaigners repeatedly pledged that women would become better wives and mothers if they could take a larger part in discussions of social and moral issues.

To do so, they needed to be regarded as more than just attractive appendages of their husbands. By 1910, most provinces had taken some hesitant steps into the world of equality. Ontario had passed a Married Women's Property Act in 1884; by 1910, a number of other provinces had followed suit, allowing wives to keep control over their own property and any wages they earned. By 1911, several provinces had passed laws to help women who had been abandoned by their husbands. And in some provinces, women could now petition the court for support from the father of their illegitimate children. Provinces also guaranteed some rights of inheritance for wives, and denied a husband the right to sell or mortgage property without his wife's consent.

Now that most urban men worked for wages, it was the house-wife's job to spend those wages wisely. "The home bread winner hands over the result of his daily toil to the housewife, and it's her duty to get from it all the good obtainable," noted a 1905 advertise-ment that suggested Eaton's was the store that could be trusted with the household money.[27] Wives were still expected to run their homes in a way that demonstrated their success as wives and hostesses.

Advertisers sympathized with the health problems caused by the hard work that housewives undertook. Patent medicine suppliers paid much attention to "women's problems," sometimes skirting the issues with flowery language, sometimes being very direct. Every cure was a cure for everything. "I am a woman," Mrs. M. Summers told readers of the *Halifax Herald* in 1903. "I know woman's suffer-ings. I have found the cure. . . . I know my home treatment is a safe and sure cure for Leuchorrœa or Whitish discharges, Ulceration, Displacement or Falling of the Womb, Profuse, Scanty or Painful Periods, Uterine or Ovarian Tumors or Growths, also pains in the head, back and bowels, bearing down feelings, nervousness, creep-ing feeling up the spine, melancholy, desire to cry, hot flashes, weariness, kidney and bladder troubles where caused by weaknesses peculiar to our sex."[28] Some of these remedies used code phrases for causing abortions: restoration of periods, curing female irreg-ularities, female treatments. If an ad recommended that its pills or potion not be used by women who suspected they might be preg-nant, it was, in fact an invitation to do just the opposite.

Alice B. Stockham, M.D., frowns upon withdrawal as a means of contraception:

The act is incomplete and unnatural, and is followed by results similar to and as disastrous as those consequent upon masturbation. In the male it may result in impotence, in the female in sterility. In both sexes, many nervous symptoms are produced, such as headache, defective vision, dyspepsia, insomnia, loss of memory, etc. Very many cases of uterine diseases can be attributed solely to this practice.

— *Tokology*, p. 325.

Help the war effort on the home front by being thrifty and industrious: in this poster from World War I, grandma encourages mother to preserve fruit and vegetables, thus ensuring that nothing edible is scrapped. (Library and Archives Canada C-095282)

꘎꘎

The Housewife and the First World War

꘎꘎

Soldiers and sailors, airmen and ambulance drivers—and house-wives. Canada's housewives made many a contribution on the home front during the war of 1914-1918.

Governments asked them for many sacrifices. The greatest was of their husbands and sons. It was their patriotic duty, said posters and advertisements, to save their country by convincing their men to go to war, or at least by not opposing them if they wanted to enlist.

They were also asked to make sacrifices and changes at home. By 1914, the prairie wheat-growing lands had suffered through two years of drought and wheat reserves were low. As farm men enlisted in the armed forces, women across the country were asked to help the war effort by substituting other grains for wheat. Various pub-lications listed the ratios: 1 ⅜ cups of barley, ⅞ of a cup of buck-wheat, or 1 ½ cups of rolled oats could replace each cup of wheat flour in a recipe. Canadian housewives were also encouraged to cut back on butter, beef, and pork, so that more could be sent to Brit-ain in its time of need. "We are saving you; YOU save FOOD," read one poster; "Fish and Vegetable Meals will save wheat, meat & Fats for our soldiers and allies," proclaimed another.

"Are YOU breaking the law?" asked an ominous poster with the shadow of a policeman with his nightstick on the window blind. "Patriotic Canadians will not hoard food." The man and woman with their hoarded bags of sugar and flour look suitably fearful.

Housewives were also encouraged to save every penny they could and to invest them in Victory Bonds, with the money used to help finance the war effort. Housewives were asked to join the 50,000 club, "50,000 members by Thursday night," and beg an extra 25¢ a week from their husbands—"or, better still, save the amount from your table luxuries."[29] The $1 a month thus saved would go to help the dependents of those fighting overseas.

Included in the Christmas packages Niagara women sent to soldiers over-seas: one pair of socks, one pound of fruit cake, three pounds of peach, pear, or plum jam; chocolates, gum, a pencil, writing paper, envelopes, handkerchief, toothbrush, toothpaste, cigarettes (just three), tobacco, adhe-sive plaster, OXO, soap, candle, play-ing cards, shoelaces, and a Christmas card from the folks at home.

But saving should not mean being inhospitable, a columnist in the *Globe*'s page for the homemaker lectured in 1917. Surface hospitality, the kind that laid out all manner of foods to impress the guests, was one type; more important was whole-hearted hospitality, which welcomed the guest and said, "We are happier because you are with us."[30]

The nation was told it should never forget the sacrifices of Mrs. Tommy Atkins. (In Britain, soldiers were known as "Tommies" and "Tommy Atkins" became a generic term for a soldier.) But housewives whose husbands were at the front subsisted on a minuscule allowance—16 cents a day for each housewife, four cents a day extra for each child.

Women's homely skills were in great demand during World War I. Women's Institutes, as well as other formal and less formal women's groups, worked hard to collect and make clothing, knit socks, make jam, and raise money for the troops and allies overseas. The Niagara Women's Institute, for example, in one of many collections, amassed 247 articles of women's clothing, including coats, waistcoats, stockings, nightdresses, and shirtwaists; 87 articles of men's clothing, including coats, socks, overcoats, shirts and suits; and a vast array of children's clothing and blankets and sheets, all to be bailed and shipped overseas. The members also crated up jam, honey, pickles, and canned fruit. They sent Christmas boxes overseas to Niagara-area soldiers. Their efforts were echoed by every Women's Institute in the land.

From BC to Saskatchewan to Quebec, members of the Imperial Order of the Daughters of the Empire, an organization dedicated to furthering the bonds of the British crown and its colonies, knitted thousands of pairs of socks for overseas servicemen, and added in sweaters, mittens, scarves, wristlets, caps, helmets, wristlets, and cholera belts—wide waistbands of flannel or wool believed to guard against cholera and gastrointestinal ailments.

"It is interesting to find that far from having become lost, the homely art of knitting is still a much prized accomplishment of Canadian women," wrote a member of the IODE. "Articles often bear attached to them such human documents as: 'These were knitted by an old lady of 90 years'; 'I can no longer see to knit, but I can knit by feeling'; 'Canadian ou Canadienne, c'est la même chose, n'est-ce pas?'"[31]

Some women blamed the capitalist system for the ills of women. Mary Nicolaeff wrote to the *Grain Growers' Guide*, September 22, 1915, condemning the system and dependency in marriage:

A modern, well-educated man, wants a wife-comrade, but not a wife-servant. Why to marry if we have to be a servant? According to the custom of Canada, you cannot get a divorce, you have to "serve a merciless master until you die." To improve his humour you have to look in his eyes, as a devoted serf, and kiss him (oh, the horror!) when your heart is crying from its depth....a sweatshop (you call it home!); long hours of work, low wages, good enough to get food and some rags to cover the body. No right to the wealth you have produced with your hard work. All products of your work belong to the master you see!....I fight [my husband, who is a good man]. I never obey his will, I obey the rightness only. He respects in my person a self-respecting human being and is sure that I will rather die than be a servant of the man who pretends to be my husband. This is not my opinion only, but the opinion of all our Russian intellectual women.

— as quoted in Barbara E. Kelcey and Angela E. Davis, eds., *A Great Movement Underway*, pp. 140–41.

•5•

SOD HUTS AND CATALOGUE CLOTHES:

Settling the Prairies

1903, January 2	*Wash and churn 6 lbs of butter. Hens are laying two eggs a day.*
February 21	*Seward, Ethan and Otto go to Regina. I wash and do the chores at night. I am alone all night.*
March 11	*Unpleasant day. The house is now enclosed and the roof on, the men move the furniture from the hay stack and store it in the house. I finish my center piece—wash and iron it.*
September 7	*I wash, am alone at night. Not a custom of mine, but decided to leave clothes on line all night.*
September 9	*Harvesting—I drive the binder, Seward stooks.*
September 28	*Begin cutting flax, mosquitoes awful.*
October 6	*We plow out potatoes, I pick them up.*
November 24	*Very cold—rise early—frosted my feet while milking. Am still alone.*
January 21	*John does chores, I bake bread, beans, pies, roast meat, make doughnuts.*
February 1	*Blizzard all day—have to shovel drifts to get into my hen house.*
February 16	*Worst blizzard of the season. The first day I have been unable to feed my chickens. When I got up this morning, snow was drifted half way across the room.*

—from Mrs. St. John's Diary, Saskatchewan, 1904

꧁꧂

The "house" for the prairie housewife in the early homestead years could be a tent, a dugout in a hill, a log shanty insulated with prairie wool and chinked with mud, a sod hut thatched with straw. Wind whistled through the cracks between the boards of wooden houses and snow drifted in through ill-fitting doors. Wildfires raced through dry prairie grass, and freezing cold, mosquitoes, grasshoppers, and even the occasional tornado tested the homesteading family. Ellen Munson, who settled with her family near Norquay, Saskatchewan, later recalled what she saw when she emerged from the cellar where she had taken refuge as a tornado funnelled through:

> A terrible noise was heard even long after it had passed us leaving pieces of our house and furniture scattered for many miles. . . . Neighbours . . . had seen the whole house lifted off the earth as a little whirl-wind would pick up some light dry sticks. The house had been lifted over a hundred feet straight up in the air and then came down with a crash a few yards north of where it originally stood. . . . A large piece of our kitchen range was found a mile away . . . groceries of all kinds were strewn all over the ground. . . . dead chickens all over the ground. . . . There was of course no such thing as insurance.[1]

Such were the trials for the men and women who arrived in their thousands to the west in the late nineteenth and early twentieth century, utterly transforming the land. In 1881, the Canadian prairie was still mostly a wild land. A few thousand white settlers clustered in settlements in Manitoba or ranched in the shadow

Rough and drafty, sod or board or mud, the house was home, and settlers were proud of their homes. This housewife in the Huns Valley of Manitoba dressed her family in their best for a photograph. (Glenbow Archives, NA-3080-1)

Families should first husband their finances to the greatest extent possible, only buying for the first year or two those articles they cannot possibly do without, and don't pay anybody for anything you can do yourself. Be sure your land is high and dry before you spend a dollar on it. On arrival, get your garden planted with the necessary vegetable seeds, look after your garden well, have your cellar frost-proof, get a few little pigs from your neighbours, and buy nothing that you can raise; buy a cow and feed her well, and if you don't get along well in Manitoba you won't do so anywhere else, I'll assure you.

— Mrs. A. Bethune, of Archibald, Southern Manitoba, in *What Women Say of the Canadian North-West*.

Lend a helping hand to the men, not supposing it is out of a woman's sphere, as the first year brings lots of extra work on the men.... Bring a few simple medicines with you, or procure them in the town, before going in the country on your farm.

— Mrs. W. Cooper of Treherne, Manitoba, in *What Women Say of the Canadian North-West*.

of the Rockies, but native people and Métis greatly outnumbered them and few farms or fences divided the landscape.

Over the next forty years, the population of Canada west of Ontario and east of the Rockies grew more than fifteen-fold, from some 120,000 to almost two million. The newcomers came from Ontario, the United States, Britain, continental Europe. Some swelled the population of the cities and towns, but the greatest number came to homestead and farm on the prairies. Once marked mainly by rivers and coulees, the central plains were sliced into square homestead blocks and traversed by railways.

Homesteaders were lured west by lavish government advertisements and private colonization schemes that promised paradise. "Free farms for the millions," they trumpeted, pledging that immigrants would find rich virgin soil and endless opportunity. The advertisements exaggerated: though homesteaders could indeed stake large tracts of land for their own, the winters were long, cold, and dismal; building houses was not simple on the treeless prairie; and the hard work, isolation, and poverty of the early years made life in the west less than Nirvana.

More men came west than women, but single men rarely stayed long and, as elsewhere, the housewife was the mainstay of settlement. Women have been called the reluctant pioneers of the west, leaving their extended families and friends in Ontario or Europe to settle distant from any neighbours. Some women hated the west

Though life might be hard, the West allowed housewives a fair degree of freedom. These women are fishing from a buggy in York Lake, Saskatchewan, in the early 1900s. (Glenbow Archives NA-2878-57)

These thrifty women sew without machines, spin, knit, and make their own baskets and linen. They reap in the harvest fields, too, and, if need be, can take a hand at the plough....Much has been made of the fact that the Dukhobor women perform the arduous work of harnessing themselves to the plough, but this is entirely at their own suggestion.

...It was when only a few draught horses were available, and these were needed to haul logs from a distance so that homes might be built before the rigours of winter set in, that the women volunteered, with true Spartan fortitude, to break up the land.

I went into one of the houses to see the process of making linseed oil. The flax had been chopped, and the women were kneading the meal in troughs. The meal was then heated in a large shallow pan, and then subjected to great pressure under a jack-screw. The refuse, after the oil is extracted, is given to cows, but the children, too, licked it up greedily. The Dukhobors use this oil for various purposes, but mainly for cooking.

— Emily Murphy, *Janey Canuck in the West*, pp. 58–59.

and never came to terms with it. Some persuaded their husbands to leave. Most were deeply affected by the isolation. A few were delighted at first sight and ever after by the wild, open land, with its swathes of wildflowers, endless sky, and sense of freedom. Most of those who stayed learned to love their new home, taking a deep sense of satisfaction from the hard work they put in to ensure their family's future.

The prairie housewife still did laundry in a tub with water heated on the stove, made bread, doctored her own children, and sewed the family's clothes, as well as doing a variety of farm chores. But times had changed: if she had the cash, she could buy tinned food from the far-distant store or fabrics from the Eaton's catalogue. And she could garner advice on raising children, getting along with her husband, and cooking food from weekly papers intended for the farm wife—the *Nor-West Farmer, Grain Growers' Guide, Family Herald* and *Weekly Star*, and a variety of other publications.

Some settlers came in groups, like the 2,500 Barr colonists collected in England by two Anglican clergymen and brought, with much trial and more error, to Saskatchewan to homestead. Some came with others from the same region. Minister of the Interior in charge of immigration, Clifford Sifton, encouraged immigration from central and eastern Europe—"men in sheepskin coats" who would be better able to withstand the toil and trouble that establishing a farm on the prairies might bring. Ukrainians, Doukhobors, Hungarians, Romanians, Hutterites, Croats, Serbs, Poles, and Slovakians were among the immigrants to the west.

The Ukrainians sought land and freedom; the pacifist Doukhobors sought freedom to follow their religion and communal way of life. Both continued their customs of food and clothing; vegetarian borscht and intricate needlework on flour sacks became part of the prairie housewife tradition. Both Ukrainians and Doukhobors were known throughout the districts where they settled for working hard. "Do not eat for three days but be cheerful," runs an old Ukrainian proverb; the housewives who came to the prairies from that region were used to difficult times.

The Doukhobors fled imperial Russia, seeking the freedom to live communally, not be drafted into any army, and educate their children in their own way. Settling first in southern Saskatchewan, they raised eyebrows among their more individualistic neighbours, but many looked on them with approval. "The Dukhobor woman is a housewife," wrote Emily Ferguson Murphy, a crusader for women's rights and later a judge. "She does not believe that her home is a jail, and that her babies are the turnkeys. Like Solomon's 'virtuous woman,' she 'seeketh wool and flax, and worketh willingly with her hands.' On the other hand, she is a housewife only. She is not expected, as our women are, to be a combination of Mary, Martha, Magdalen, Bridget, and the Queen of Sheba."[2]

↤ THE COOK ↦

Many prairie housewives started farm life by cooking bannock and beans. It wasn't unusual, though, for them to progress to roast beef and peach pie within a few years—provided the house got built, the garden didn't freeze, and the crop sold for a decent price. For all the hardship of the early years in the west, almost every prairie and western housewife's account of pioneer life includes a list of food to salivate over. And you didn't have to belong to the family to be fed: with distances long and weather often severe, a traveller could knock on any rural door and be welcomed in for a meal and a bed.

Years after her Ukrainian family came to Canada, Mary Adaowska recounted the early years in Canada, including months spent living in a rough cabin with another family and in a dugout cave in a riverbank:

Came winter, our cow stopped giving milk. Aside from bread, there was nothing to eat at home. Was one to gnaw the walls? One time I happened to notice tears rolling down mother's cheeks as she sipped something from a small pot. We children began to weep with her. "Mother, why are you crying? Won't you let us taste what you're eating?"

Mother divided her gruel among us. She tried to say something, but all she could manage was "My chil-"; further words died on her lips. Only a moan of anguish escaped from her breast. We learned afterwards that, late in the fall, mother had visited the garden of our former host and painstakingly raked the ground for potatoes that had been too small to be worth picking at potato-digging time. She had found a few tiny ones, no larger than hazel nuts. From these potatoes she had made a gruel that tasted like potato soup and it was this gruel that we children shared.

— Henry Piniuta, ed., *Land of Pain, Land of Promise: First Person Accounts by Ukrainian Pioneers 1891–1914*, p. 53.

With luck and planning, families first arrived on their land in spring, in time to turn enough sod to plant a garden with salad and root vegetables and plough a few furrows to plant potatoes. Women and children picked wild fruit, such as Saskatoon berries, strawberries, and cranberries, to eat fresh or make into jam. Especially in the early years, before the prairies were crowded with settlers, game was plentiful, though one common rhyme expressed some settlers' feelings: "Rabbit hot and rabbit cold / Rabbit young and rabbit old / Rabbit tender and rabbit tough / Thank you, but I've had enough." Trout and other fish caught year-round provided a welcome addition to the diet.

The way we canned fruit in 1896 (if we had plenty of jars) was to put hay in the bottom of a wash boiler we had. On this we put our jars filled with fruit, sugar and water. We used Mason jars and old rubbers and metal caps. We filled up the boiler with water to the caps and then boiled them for two hours. Let cool and stored in cellar. We canned wild gooseberries, saskatoons, raspberries, made preserves of strawberries, currants, and blueberries, jelly and jam of cranberries. Preserved rhubarb out of our own gardens.

— Mrs. John Irwin Jameson papers, Provincial Archives of Alberta, Acc. 75. 182, as quoted in Beth Light and Joy Parr eds., *Canadian Women on the Move, 1867–1920,* p. 175.

It was 1890 before mother saw her first can of salmon—good red salmon, two tins for twenty-five cents! When they received a barrel of apples from the east, they thought themselves well off indeed. Dried fruits could be bought in town. Their own wheat was taken to the mill in Wolseley to be ground into flour for their own use.... The barn was not warm enough to keep calves, so there was no milk during the winter. Consequently, in the fall, the milk was poured into pans and frozen, to be kept in the milkhouse and thawed out during the winter as it was needed, Butter was also packed away in the same manner.

— Mrs. H. McCorkindale, and Mrs. Jean Thomas, "Homesteading at Indian Head," p. 68.

Gertrude Quelch came to Manitoba with her family in the early 1880s and later homesteaded near Brandon with her husband.

After I married I lived some 30 miles east of Winnipeg. The land was no good for grain being low and marshy but there was unlimited hay, so we kept stock and sold butter and eggs. I traded pounds and pounds of butter at 10c a pound, and eggs 10c per dozen in the summer and 20c to 25c was considered a good price in the winter.... Our garden furnished us with an abundance of every kind of vegetable even cucumbers and watermelons. We had our own milk, butter and eggs, but many times we found ourselves hard-pressed for bodily needs, but there always seemed a way out.

— Gertrude Quelch fonds.

There were a few scattered bachelors who used to bring me a 100-lb sack of flour to make into bread for them for which I received $1.00, sometimes $1.25. It was a common sight to see some lone bachelor come with a sack and carry it home on his shoulder full of bread loaves.

— Saskatchewan Homesteading Experiences Collection.

One of the toughest jobs for the cook-housewife was keeping the harvest crews fed. This woman has brought lunch—and her child—to a crew in the Foremost area of Alberta in 1917. (Glenbow Archives NA-2604-30)

Most farm women raised chickens and kept a cow, to provide eggs and milk. Like their counterparts in backwoods Ontario, they soon learned how to preserve eggs for the winter months when the hens wouldn't lay, how to make butter from the cream skimmed off the milk, and how to keep frozen milk for the times when the cow wouldn't give milk. The first crop of wheat was eagerly awaited, for the farmer could take it to a mill in a nearby town to produce flour.

As time progressed, farmers were able to provide their own meat by raising and butchering cattle and pigs. In the co-operative spirit of the times, some arranged beef rings, where each farmer in turn killed a cow, and provided a basket of steaks, mince, roasts, slices of liver, and stewing beef to each family in the ring.

Almost every prairie housewife planted a garden, often with seeds ordered from the Eaton's catalogue, with essentials such as cauliflower, cabbage, tomatoes, onions, cucumbers, peas, and beans—and flowers essential for her spirit, petunias, poppies, and sweet William. She and her children dug and planted, thinned and weeded, watered and mulched. Their reward was vegetables to eat fresh in the summer and fall, canned and pickled through the winter.

Yet there was much the farmer's wife could not grow or raise. Depending on their distance from town, farmers made a six-monthly or monthly trip to the store—or to a neighbouring town—to buy staples, such as flour, sugar, tea, oats, baking soda and baking powder, and extras, such as canned meat and fish, dried apples and peaches, and canned tomatoes. "We use a great deal of tinned

[On the way to Lloydminster] I drove the covered wagon which contained a bed for the smaller children to sleep on the way, a cupboard in the back for supplies, and here on this same bed, bread for the multitude was rising while we traveled on our way, to be baked at night after we unloaded our cook stove.

— Mrs. H.C.C., Saskatchewan Homesteading Experiences Collection.

1902, June 6—Plant first garden—radishes onions, lettuce, peas, beans, cucumbers, sweet corn, cannas, and sweet peas.

June 28—Our first experience with Canadian cut worms—took most of our garden last night.

August 29—Frost ruins what the cutworms left of our garden and flowers.

— from Mrs. St. John's "Diary," pp. 26–27.

Settlers in the West often used pioneer skills half-forgotten back East or in the country they came from. The work done by Doukhobor women fascinated travelling photographers: the women worked extremely hard at physical tasks such as pulling the plough when their colonies had no draught animals, building roads, and, here, in 1899 in Saskatchewan, winnowing—separating the grain from the chaff. (Library and Archives Canada, C-008891)

◇◇◇◇◇◇◇◇◇◇◇◇◇◇◇◇◇◇◇◇◇◇◇◇◇◇◇◇◇

We have no outside larder or anywhere to keep our meat and butter, so have instituted a lovely one by putting all our things down the well, which is nearly dry and is under the kitchen floor. In winter there is never any need of a larder, as the meat is frozen so hard that it has to be twelve hours in the kitchen before they can attempt to cook it. Our food is very good and we have the best of all receipts, ravenous appetites for every meal. Our breakfast consists of porridge, bacon, and any cold meat, jam, and any quantity of excellent butter and bread. Dinner, a hot joint and a pudding of some sort, finishing up with coffee. Supper, much the same. We have coffee for every meal, and, as the pot is always on the hob, anybody can have a cup when they like.

—Mrs. Cecil Hall, *A Lady's Life on a Farm in Manitoba*, p. 53.

corned beef; and very good it is, it makes into such excellent hashes and curries and is good for breakfast," noted Mrs. Cecil Hall of her time in Manitoba.[3]

A woman who lived on a ranch near Lacombe, Alberta, in 1903 reported years later on the food that the family brought to the ranch to last them six months: 1,000 pounds of flour; 160 pounds of rolled oats; 10 pounds of black tea; 5 pounds of coffee; 10 pounds of cocoa; 25 pounds of rice; 25 pounds of beans; cases of dried apples, peaches, apricots, pears and prunes; cases of canned corn, tomatoes and salmon; 5 pounds of currants; 10 pounds of raisins; 3 pounds of candied peel; and 5 pounds of coconut. Even so, they ran out of sugar, coal oil and cattle salt, and the farmer had to travel through a blizzard to a trading post 25 miles away to replenish supplies.[4]

Bread and potatoes, salt pork and fish, rabbit stew and cakes, and all the miscellany of homestead food were cooked on or in the cookstove, which also served to keep the pioneer house warm in winter. Those who didn't bring a stove with them purchased one the moment they could afford it. Prairie newspapers contained dozens of advertisements for different types of stove, from the simplest $12 one with no water reservoir, to an $80 marvel with oven, shelf, six holes, reservoir, and shiny name plate.

RECIPES

SELF-RISING DUMPLINGS

To two cupfuls of flour, 1 teaspoon of salt, and an egg mixed with milk or water. I put them in potato soup or beef soup and always have a dish full with sauerkraut. When the mixture has set, say one hour, and dinner is about ready to serve, I cut them off with a sharp knife into some boiling water and dip the knife into the water occasionally to keep them from sticking to it.

HOME MADE BEER OR HOP ALE

I take 13 packages of hops and tie them in a cheesecloth sack, also 2 cups of cornmeal in another and put them in a large kettle of water and boil about half an hour. Then I take out the bags and set the water off to cool; when lukewarm I put a yeast cake in and let it stand for 4 hours, when it will be ready to bottle. About 5 gallons of water is required, and by adding 2 tablespoons of ginger, or four or five lemons, a most delicious wholesome drink will be the result. A member also asks for directions to make sauerkraut. Cut or chop the cabbage fine, then into your keg or barrel put a generous layer of the cabbage, and then sparingly of salt, use just enough salt to season the whole thing right, by sprinkling it on the layers as it goes in, and mash it down tight. Keep mashing or pounding till the brine is drawn out of the cabbage, and covers the whole, then put a heavy weight on it with a clean flour sack beneath it, spread over the cabbage to keep out the dirt and flies and set away. If kept in a warm place it ought to be sour in two weeks.

— *Free Press Prairie Farmer*, July 2, 1912, as quoted in Norah L. Lewis, ed., *Dear Editor and Friends*, pp. 98–99.

BANNOCK

By the turn of the century, various commercial companies were publishing cookbooks to help along their customers. Flour and baking powder producers were prominent among the publishers. This Five Roses recipe for bannock is far fancier than most bannock recipes, which were simple compendia of flour, fat, baking soda, salt, and milk, cooked in a frying pan on the stovetop, or on the stovetop itself.

1 ½ pounds Five Roses flour
½ pound butter or lard
½ pound raisins
½ pound currants
1 ounce candied peel
1 cup sugar
1 teaspoon carbonate of soda
1 teaspoon cream of tartar
Pinch of salt
Buttermilk

Rub the shortening into the flour, add other ingredients, and mix with buttermilk to make a nice light dough. Bake in moderate oven about 1 hour.

— *Five Roses Cook Book: Bread Pastry Etc.*, p. 40.

Prairie housewives couldn't always get the supplies they wanted, so they developed substitutes. This vinegar pie recipe was used instead of lemon pie. The housewife might have made the vinegar herself, beginning with a "starter" from a neighbour and brewed it from sugar and water.

1 egg
1 tablespoon (heaping) Five Roses flour
1 cup sugar
1 ½ tablespoons sharp vinegar
1 cup cold water
Nutmeg to taste.

Beat the egg, flour and sugar together. Add the vinegar and cold water. Flavor with nutmeg and bake with 2 crusts.

— *Five Roses Cook Book: Bread Pastry Etc.*, p. 85.

At harvest time, travelling crews moved from farm to farm, helping each farmer harvest his wheat. The housewife cooking for them rose before dawn and stayed up till after midnight preparing and cooking vast amounts of food. "Jane and I had them 16 meals," American immigrant to Alberta Rachel Weber wrote to her in-laws in 1911, describing feeding a threshing crew. "It took nearly ¼ beef and a whole hog to feed the brutes besides 20# butter, 60 loaves of bread, 30 pies, 8 bu. potatoes, nearly a square yard of cake etc. It's no easy job to feed 25 hungry men but we got on fine."[5]

Prairie hospitality was expected and duly famed. Even if she had very little, a housewife always served the best food she had to guests invited for dinner or a dance. She shared the family meals with travellers who needed food and shelter in a storm or on a long trip from an outlying homestead to the store or town. Weber noted the menus for dinners she gave for visitors and dinners she ate at the houses of distant neighbours. Her menu for one such dinner included both home-produced and store-bought foods: "Bouillon and croutons; chow chow, escalloped potatoes, fried chicken, radishes, onions; banana salad on lettuce leaves, lemonade, wafers, orange jello, cream puffs, sour cream cake."[6]

THE HOUSEKEEPER (AND THE FARMER)

"I do all the chores, feed from twelve to fifteen hogs, milk seven to twelve cows all the year round, cut nearly all the wood, carry it in and fill the water pail," wrote one Saskatchewan woman who signed herself Broken-Hearted Wife. "I have to work in the harvest and hay field as long as there is anything to do—and I also do all the stacking." Not surprisingly, she added, "I have not had a happy day since the first year of my marriage."[7]

Broken-Hearted was unusual: few wives had so many outside chores. It was quite usual, though, for women to drive the stoneboat while the men and children picked stones, to help with

Alice Rendell was one of the original Barr colonists from Britain, who settled without adequate preparation near Lloydminster, Saskatchewan, in 1903–4. The Rendell house was considerably better accommodation than the tents and shanties many of the other colonists lived in.

One great drawback here is lack of water. We dug one well without success and have now started another. They have got down 20 feet but no luck as yet. Every drop of water I use for cooking and washing is melted snow and lovely water it is too, but of course it means a lot of labour carting it and melting it down....Our bungalow has kept beautifully warm, it is heated throughout by pipes connected with the kitchen stove and a heating stove in the hall. The rooms are all pretty well of an even temperature.

— Alice Rendell fonds, Library and Archives Canada.

the haying, to drive the team to town, and to bring wood indoors. Looking after the chickens and milking the cows was almost always woman's or child's work. When women were widowed, or when their husbands went to town for supplies, or spent months working in town or on the railroad, women and their children had to do all the work, inside and out.

A family of Romanian immigrants lived in a burdey—a dugout with a cone of poles covered with sod as a roof—while the men of the family went off to earn money for winter supplies. The women cut and sawed logs, put up the walls, got help from a neighbour to build a roof, used a linen pillow case for a window, then wove willows together for the walls and roof of a porch over the door. They used local white clay to plaster their walls and made a door from batts of

A pioneer housewife often ended up cooking for an extended family and hired men. This settler's wife in Manitoba ca. 1880 works with her wood stove to feed the men and children. (Library and Archives Canada C-082968)

East, centre, or west, floors and verandahs must be swept. A daughter of the house does the job in 1913 Calgary. (Glenbow Archives NA-5610-21)

Facing page: Women put their skills to work in many ways, including, here, laying the carpet in the pulpit of the Presbyterian church in south Edmonton in 1898. (Glenbow Archives NA-614-16)

One night it was 20 below the wind came blowing through the cracks and blew the snow on the floor, we could get no lime so the house isn't plastered up. The floor was awful cold my feet were like ice, when all my work was done I opened the oven door and shoved my feet in as far as I could get and even then I shivered, we have no coal yet....I stuffed up all the cracks with paper and rags, and the last two days John plastered the outside with mud....

— Eliza Wilson letters, Glenbow Archives, November 20, 1902.

sedge, a willow frame for the chimney, and a clay bake oven. The top of the oven served as a bed for the children on cold nights.[8]

Indoors, prairie homesteaders swept and dusted, washed wooden floors or sprinkled and swept dirt floors, and polished the stove. With dust or snow sifting in through the walls and windows, women who brought along their fancy napkins and tablecloths left them in the trunk, for they were easily dirtied by people who worked outside all day, and washing them was a heavy chore. Instead, they bought white oilcloth to cover the table, for it could easily be wiped down day after day and still look clean.

In winter, one of the housewife's most important tasks, shared with her husband, was keeping the fire going in the stove through-

A prairie farm woman improves her kitchen, which she finds gloomy and dull:

I went and got a roll of cream building paper, containing 400 square feet, and costing one dollar in these parts; also a package of alabastrine, cream colour, at fifty cents, and two boxes of tacks and some grey floor paint. I did the ceiling with the alabastrine, as the shingle nails were too thick for the paper, laid it on good and thick until it looked creamy and nice. Then did the studding on the walls with the alabastrine, then tacked the cream building paper between the studding on the walls. By this time the room looked nice and clean and light. The floor got a couple of coats of paint, the windows little white cheese-cloth curtains—no blinds. My range showed up nice and black and nicely, and I felt proud as could be.

But I did not like the raw look along the border, so I fared up to the attic, where lay a pile of Saturday Evening Posts, You know what nice cover designs they have. Well I cut out a lot of these carefully—little girls skipping, boy unwillingly washing his feet, boys making snowmen, etc.—and these I pasted at regular intervals in a sort of frieze all around the room. The same colours are almost always used in these covers, so it is quite harmonious.

— from Wolf-Willow to the *Grain Growers' Guide*, August 16, 1916, as quoted in Barbara E. Kelcey and Angela E. Davis, eds., *A Great Movement Underway*, p. 153.

Even in rough country far from town, women didn't neglect their fine sewing. Mrs. Luella Goddard works at her embroidery on the ranch near Cochrane, Alberta. (Glenbow Archives NA-2084-30)

~~~~~~

One day a bachelor rancher brought a sack of clothes remarking that they had no use for them "they were some the boss left behind last summer." On opening I found pants, overcoat and two swallow-tailed coats of evening dress of the finest French broadcloth. All of these made serviceable garments, but my eldest boys had overalls of broadcloth, strange to state; never before, I venture to state, were overalls made of swallow-tail coats. They stood the wear too. It is strange when one gets down to simple life, how many things can be eliminated of what we call necessities. Our children went barefoot most of the time from spring till fall.

— Mrs. H.C.C., Alberta, 1902, in Saskatchewan Homesteading Experiences Collection.

~~~~~~

We both of us feel much like our old nurse when we are doing our mendings, cutting up one set of old rags to patch another; but thanks to ammonia and hot irons, we flatter ourselves that we make them look almost respectable again.

— Mrs. Cecil Hall, *A Lady's Life on a Farm in Manitoba*, p. 56.

out the day, and starting it up again in the morning. They usually let it go out at night, for only by staying awake could they preserve the coals.

There were other household chores. Shirley Keyes Thompson and her husband moved into a shack built by a predecessor:

Our mattress was a straw-filled tick with two depressions in it. . . . We were awakened again and again. . . . the narrowness of the bed was such that if one turned over, the other must turn also. Finally, such restless rest was beyond endurance and so one night we lit the oil lamps. Our tormentors were quite visible: countless numbers of them on the sheets and on the walls coming and going. . . . We killed all we could of the tough-shelled bugs but many of them escaped. . . . The unplastered walls of lath covered with building paper of a sickening blue offered plenty of hideouts. Over and over

I washed and sprayed and powdered the cracks and joists. Fresh wall paper with poison in the paste helped to seal off ancestors. However, against the hatching progeny we were almost helpless.[9]

She recounts that they used every device they could—fumigation and "liquid poison for those who drank and powder for those who ate." In the end, Timothy Eaton came to the rescue: the bedbug annihilator from Eaton's turned the buggy tide. And Thompson learned not to judge: the woman who had lived in the shack before her had done her best. "She was just another prairie wife struggling to make a home. If this gallant soul failed to reach standards of cleanliness, there were extenuating circumstances. The prairie homemaker fought against great odds."[10]

Mrs. Carl Tellanius came to a Saskatchewan homestead from Scandinavia during the first decade of the twentieth century:

The woman on the prairies had to be able to do anything! I used to spin all my own wool, and knit my family's sweaters, and their stockings, and their mitts and all that. We canned all the vegetables and fruit and we canned the meat too. I patched till my fingers were sore and tried to make things different by remodelling all the time. We just kept using and using things over and over again, for one thing or another, until they…weren't any good for anything, except maybe a floor cloth or a duster. Even then when a floor cloth was all falling apart, we used to dry it out and roll it up into little balls and use it in the fire, or stuff it up cracks in the wall of the barn. Nothing was wasted. We couldn't afford to waste anything.

— http://collections.ic.gc.ca/heirloom_series/volume1/chapter5/164-169.htm.

Often a whole bolt of calico was bought by one family and all the sewing was done by hand until a sewing machine could be acquired. On Sundays the mothers and the girls would come in dresses all alike and the boys would even have shirts from the same bolt of calico….Flannelette and flour sacks were sewn into underwear. Naturally, when the cold weather came, warmer clothing was worn. Wool goods by the yard were bought from the general store if it could be afforded. Old clothing was used to its last shred; it was made over into the very common hand-me-downs. Mother sheared, washed, carded, spun, and knitted mittens and socks for her own flock, her husband, and herself.

— Elvira Backstrom, "Pioneer Parents," p. 16.

⤷ THE SEAMSTRESS ↞⤶

Western farm housewives sewed up a storm and mended and remade clothes, but few, outside communities such as the Doukhobors, wove their own cloth, though some carded and spun wool from their sheep for knitting. Like their counterparts in the city, they bought their cloth ready-made, from the general store, the mail-order catalogue, or town.

They cut out and sewed up by hand or ran up on their treadle sewing machine calico, bed ticking, and woollens, by the yard or by the bolt. If they couldn't afford new cloth, they just made do, turning bed linens side to middle, darning socks, and mending clothes, never discarding a piece of cloth until it was completely worn through.

For all the extra chores that an oldest child had to do, at least he or she got the best of the clothes that were handed down from child to child. Everyone had, worn though it might be, at least one good outfit for church and special occasions. It shouldn't be too fancy, though: nothing ruined a housewife's reputation faster than "swank."

Housewives still treasured skills such as the practical—knitting and crocheting—and the ornamental—quilting and embroidery. Immigrants brought their needlework traditions with them. Though they might have only flour sacks, the Ukrainians, for example, still created the fine and intricate embroidered patterns known as *rushniki*.

⤷ THE LAUNDRESS ↞⤶

Like many another family that headed into the Canadian west, the Winters were a little short on pioneer skills—not surprisingly, since they came from England and Mr. Winter was a writer. Laundry posed a major problem after they arrived on a Manitoba homestead in the 1880s. Daughter Gertrude Quelch recalled:

> Our first venture was getting our clothes washed, of which we had collected a goodly store. The boys drew the water

Monday night I would sort over the soiled clothing, fill up my tubs, and set the white things to soak. While the family were eating breakfast, around six o'clock on Tuesday morning, I would set the wash water in two large galvanized iron wash-boilers, on the stove to heat. By the time the dishes were cleared away and washed, the separator scoured, the beds made and the floors swept, and the table set for dinner, it would be about nine o'clock, and I would be ready to start on the main business of the day—the washing.

Washing! What a job that always was. Usually it took me the entire day. In summer I washed outside; in winter, down in the basement. The boiling sudsy water had to be carried from the stove to wherever my tubs were set. More than once I burned myself severely, spilling water on unprotected hands.

— Kathleen Strange, *With the West in Her Eyes*, p. 220.

from a hole that had been dug by the side of a slough near the house. It was hard, but of that we were in blissful ignorance. What a mess we made of the clothes, the flannels were quite spoilt, the soap stuck to them in hard little lumps and they were sticky and horrid, and none of the clothes looked clean. How tired and disheartened we were.[11]

Many who came to the prairies after 1900 came from towns where they had had access to running water; some might even have had the new tankless water heaters. Once on the prairie, they had to revert to the old methods. At first, water came from the slough or the stream; even when the well was dug, it was often at a distance from the house, and water had to be carried in pails and barrels. To do the family laundry, women heated water on the stove—some stoves had a hot water tank tucked in behind the firebox—then used the old methods of boiling, scrubbing on the scrub board, wringing, rinsing, hanging out to dry. As soon as they could, housewives persuaded their men that they needed a hand-cranked washing machine, but even these machines could be difficult and were sometimes sent back to the store they came from.

Winter posed the greatest problem for drying clothes. Most housewives left the clothes out on the line to freeze dry, then brought them in to thaw. Ironing with irons heated on the stove

We did a big washing today and Walter and I are both tired but it seems good to have it done, just the same. They froze but I have two long pieces of "quarter round" between two chairs and I have my clothes spread before the fire to dry.

— Rachel Weber to her in-laws, February 8, 1912.

completed the job—though the heavier, rougher clothes worn by most rarely felt the touch of an iron.

❧ THE NURSE ❧

For a year after she arrived in Alberta, Mrs. H.C.C. saw no other white woman. One day, an Irish neighbour—a neighbour being anyone within a day's travelling distance—came to her door. "I shall never forget the joy of seeing a woman's face again," she told an interviewer years later. "Upon my asking her what we were going to do if we needed a Doctor, she laughed and said, 'Shure we'll have to dope each other,' which we did on more than one occasion."[12]

Though the doctor's advice was considerably more helpful in the twentieth century than it had been in the nineteenth, it wasn't much use to a woman a day's journey or more from town. Caught in a week-long blizzard, with drifts up to her door, the prairie housewife needed to nurse her own family. To do so, she used old home remedies, passed on to her by her mother, a neighbour, or the native people of the area. She also used the remedies and medicines advertised in papers and magazines and sold by stores or salesmen, or available through the mail-order catalogue.

Women exchanged remedies through the farmers' papers. "Christina" asked readers of the *Free Press Prairie Farmer* in 1912 if anyone knew the name of a root, plentiful in the woods, that the Indians used for childbirth, a use that the immigrant housewives had quickly adopted.[13] Doukhobor women harvested seneca root, learning from the Indians that, boiled into a tea, it helped greatly with colds, coughs, and asthma. Some native groups also used it to induce abortion, and perhaps the overworked housewife with a family larger than her means discovered this as well.

In her book on early prairie remedies, Sheila Kerr notes that a mother might fill a child's socks with chopped onions, to be worn overnight, to prevent a cold; cough syrups were made of vinegar and brown sugar; and poultices of flax, buttermilk, bran, stale bread, and soap were variously said to draw infection from a wound or halt the spread of blood poisoning.[14] One woman looked back on her childhood in Alberta, recalling that when she was helping to reap,

she cut her finger with a sickle, deeply enough so that the finger dangled, barely held on by the skin. Her mother spliced it back on and the wound healed, though the scar remained all her life.[15]

Some swore by a potato in the pocket as a remedy for rheumatism, some by linseed oil with vinegar and honey for colds. Some waited anxiously by the sickbed, applying poultices and plasters, praying that this child would not die, as so many did, from whooping cough or influenza. Many housewives from central Europe relied on the old woman in their district who knew how to pour wax or throw coals to relieve the aches and pains of daily life, and who knew specifics against the evil eye. Judy Schultz notes that her pioneer grandmother even went against her fierce teetotal beliefs to create a specific against "spells," by cutting a round of raw beefsteak and covering it with rum or rye whiskey, then decanting it after a day or two and administering it a spoonful at a time.[16]

Accidents were common and complete recovery rare. Her husband away in town, an Alberta farm wife went out with her

Two versions of childhood and motherhood—a well-off family in Fort McLeod, Alberta, in 1899, with a chick hatched under the table; a poor immigrant from central Europe stands barefoot with her child at Yorkton, Saskatchewan, ca. 1903. (Glenbow Archives PB-848-2; NA-2878-63)

137

Having six little girls under twelve, I am at a loss to know how to get them some good warm clothing for this bitter weather, and should be so thankful if someone would send me any warm clothing. I am handy with my needle and used to make over-clothes, so should be glad of anything.... I am so much in need of bedding.

— "Late Comer, Good Company," *Family Herald and Weekly Star*, December 12, 1900, as quoted in Norah L. Lewis, ed., *Dear Editor and Friends*, p. 26.

One woman, her hands full with her other work, hired a "little German girl" to help out with the children:

She had a cough when she came, she was getting over the whooping cough we found out when it was too late. Baby took it in about ten days and then pneumonia. I took her to the Dr. and stayed right at the Drs. House. But she died in a couple of days.... One man made a casket covered it with white cotton, lined it lovely, there was a small plot of ground donated by a farmer for burying ground. So we laid our little one away as nicely as we could.

— Saskatchewan Homesteading Experiences Collection.

children to move the bull, which had been tethered by a heavy log, to new pasture: "Dora was driving old Taurus. . . while Mother was guiding the log. Mother tripped and fell, and the log was drawn right over the left side and that side of her face. She was a terrible sight and there was no one to do a thing for her but herself. Ever since her face has been noticeably crooked, and it is a wonder she escaped with no broken bones."[17]

⊷ THE MOTHER ⊷

It's likely that pioneer prairie housewives, tried to the teeth by whining children, might have exploded, "Behave yourselves! We're doing all this for you!" Many families moved to the Canadian west and undertook the difficult life there because it promised their children a better future. Particularly difficult were the harshest winter weeks when children were confined to the small farmhouse all day long.

Though advances in medical knowledge meant that town women had a better chance of raising a child to adulthood, losing a child in childbirth or infancy was not unusual on the farm. "Only a short time ago," a 19-year-old farm wife wrote to the *Family Herald and Weekly Star*, "I lost my two babies, one a little over a year old, and the other an infant. I have never been strong since and I don't think I ever will be again. It is a trial for me to get my work done."[18] Repeatedly, women who lived on the prairie write of the death of a baby or young child. Especially in winter, there was little chance that a doctor could get to the homestead in time, and there were few neighbour women able to act as midwives. "My sweetest baby boy, that God gave to me on the 16th of December, He has also taken him from me,"[19] wrote one farm housewife in 1905.

A child born prematurely was particularly at risk. One was saved when the father was able to keep the oven of the stove just warm enough to serve as a makeshift incubator. There were no such miracles for women who had a very bad time birthing—some lived, but many died.

Articles and letters in the prairie newspapers and magazines gave farm mothers advice, much of it the same as that given mothers in town. Mothers must deny themselves much, but

Many accounts of prairie settlement note the isolation of women settlers, far from other women. This 1913 photo of the Polish wedding of Michael and Teresa Yakubic in Coleman, Alberta, shows the imbalance between men and women in the area. (Glenbow Archives NA-3091-25)

A correspondent to the *Family Herald and Weekly Star* gives her rules for bringing up baby:

I never on any account neglect their morning bath, give them plenty of fresh air, let them wear woolen shirts and bands (hand-knitted is best): in fact I keep woolen shirts on all my children the year round, and never have any trouble with bowel complaints. When they are teething and the little mouth is hot, I give a teaspoonful of cold water occasionally. I also dip my hand in cold water and gently smooth it over the little head. I give for a three months old baby one teaspoonful of fluid magnesia three times daily, one teaspoonful daily if not fretful. I am always careful about my own diet, avoiding anything sour, such as pickles. I very seldom touch coffee and drink very little tea. Cocoa or milk is much better, I never nurse my baby if I am overheated or excited in any way. I always take a certain amount of outdoor exercise every day if possible. I do not believe in any kind of soothing syrup.

— "Nil Desperadum," June 17, 1903, as quoted in Norah L. Lewis, ed., *Dear Editor and Friends*, p. 31.

"Bas," an English visitor to Alberta who married and stayed, talks about the birth of her first child in 1914:

Alvin Jocelyn is the name of the marvel & we call him Alvin. He is a proper little John Bull, so fat and rosy-cheeked, saucy blue eyes & a real little eater. He is absolutely a bottle baby & is a great credit to the cows. He is 5 ½ months old now, & weighs 17 lbs. was 7 ½ at first. His morning bath is the happiest hour of the day —Marvin [stepson] gave him a dear little bath tub & he just loves to disport himself in the water. He is a fine specimen of health & content & is always so happy & merry that I have to forgive him for not being a girl.

— "Bas" papers, as quoted in Beth Light and Joy Parr eds., *Canadian Women on the Move, 1867–1920*, p. 181.

seeing their children grow up healthy and happy would make it all worthwhile. Never rock your baby to sleep, they were told; lay him down awake and leave him there. Have a fixed time, a schedule, for everything in baby's life. Don't let them listen to adult conversations; they grow up too fast as it is. "The doctor told us that the first five days would determine her conduct," Rachel Weber wrote after the birth of her daughter in 1911. "We have laid down a few rules about picking her up, eating every 2 hours etc and we're trying to train her to be good."[20]

Yet perhaps such advice had less effect on farms and homesteads. Many children growing up on the prairie had a great deal more freedom than those living in town. Some were able to ride or walk the long distances to a one-room schoolhouse, but, in many cases, any education they got was imparted by their mother, who taught them to read and write and do arithmetic. It's no surprise that such children, writing about their experiences later in life, look back with affection on the time spent roaming the prairies, picking wild flowers, learning to ride horses, and romping with dogs and cats.

⤏ THE WIFE ⤎

"'Poor girl!' say the kind friends," wrote author and feminist Nellie McClung. "She went West and married a farmer'—and forthwith a picture of the farmer's wife rises up before their eyes: the poor faded woman, in a rusty black luster skirt sagging in the back and puckering in the seams; coat that belonged to a suit in other days. . . hair the color of last year's grass, and teeth gone in front."

But, said McClung, there was no reason to think that farmers' wives were a downtrodden class of women. "They have their troubles like other people. It rains in threshing time, and the threshers visit is prolonged until after their welcome has been worn to a frazzle! Father won't dress up. . . . Father also has a mania for buying land instead of building a new house. . . . Cows break out of pastures; hawks get the chickens; hens lay away; clothes-lines break. They have their troubles, but there are compensations."[21] Among them: plenty of room outdoors, no rent to be paid, distance from the disagreeable things in the city, opportunity to develop their own resources. If they wanted a shelf put up, they didn't ask someone else to do it; they got out the hammer and did it themselves. No gentle lady, subject to fainting fits and using her wiles to get her way, could make it as a prairie housewife.

Perhaps because they did develop those resources and learned to be independent, prairie women led campaigns on social issues. Partners in hard work in their homes with their husbands, they wanted to be partners in political life. Women in Manitoba, Saskatchewan, and Alberta all gained the right to vote in 1916, beating their counterparts in other provinces by a year, two years, six years—or, in the case of Quebec, twenty-four years.

Yet prairie marriages were still governed by "for better or worse." Though divorce was legal, a woman could divorce her husband only if she could prove both adultery and other acts such as sodomy or bestiality (men had to prove only adultery). The prairie provinces had no divorce courts, so divorce was obtainable only through an appeal to Parliament—or through a visit to

One of the worst things was the loneliness. You couldn't even see the lights of a neighbour's house. The nights were very, very long in the wintertime and, of course, there were no radios at that time. I used to sing a lot. The harder I worked, the more I sang, and every night I sang my children to sleep with a song about the lily that lived alone in the woods; and even today when they come to see me, they ask if I'll sing it again, and I always do, in the Scandinavian language.

— Mrs. Call Tellanius, http://collections.ic.gc.ca/heirloom_series/volume1/chapter5/164-169.htm.

It was quite common to hear a noise like a lot of coyotes howling, and on investigation to find out that it was several sleigh loads of folks from all over the district coming to spend the evening. They brought the eatables and all you had to provide was the tea and the coffee. They did the work. Beds were taken apart or piled on top of each other to make room for all who came. Elegance had no place in these gatherings. A good time was all we looked for.... Supper was served at midnight, then the fun began again until the dawn was breaking.

.... [At Christmas parties], we had a great time.... there was always a fiddler among the guests, and we also had an old-fashioned phonograph. Between dances, there would be songs and recitations of a comic act.... When the children got sleepy, they were put to bed, and it was funny to see them lying like herrings in a box, as we say, but they didn't mind it and were quite comfortable.... There was always some wine for the women, while the men had their jug of liquor.

— Catherine Neil, manuscript reminiscences 1905– , pp. 49, 53–54.

a neighbouring American state. Social conventions as well as legal strictures meant that most couples stayed together—though some men did walk out on their wives and children.

Some of the women who wrote to farm publications railed against the sacrifices that society or their husbands demanded. Asked one:

> Why does the average husband deny the coveted bit of praise for which his wife hungers? He gave it in abundance when they were lovers. Why not now? . . . Ask him to plant trees around the home, and you are cursed for your trouble. Ask for a pump or a closet, the same result follows. Ask for small fruit, you are told you are insane. Now, this is a really true picture of by far the greater number of farmers' homes in some vicinities, and it is the lack of all that that constitutes a real home that makes women detest the farm.[22]

As elsewhere in Canada, sex and birth control were still matters to be kept very quiet, though the Eaton's catalogue did offer a series of books on the self and sex. Targeted for various periods in a woman's life, they sold for 90 cents each. Among the vast variety of patent medicines and appliances for man, woman, and child, Eaton's advertised ladies' syringes, including the marvel Whirling Spray Syringe.[23]

Farm life was not all drudgery for the farm wife. Men and women treasured opportunities to get together, especially at dances and parties held to break the winter monotony. News was sent for twenty miles around, and on the appointed day families arrived at the door ready to celebrate. Everyone pitched in to clear the floor of furniture; the women brought food for a midnight supper. Children were put to sleep on beds and benches and no one went home till dawn the next day.

The farm wife's love for her husband and her determination to work with him for the betterment of their family shine through many a diary. Life on the homestead demanded hard work from both husband and wife, but together they could create something better for themselves and for their children. Though she might fear the journey and go reluctantly, "a woman cannot do otherwise but give in to and throw her lot in with her husband and help him to the best of her ability to make it a success."[24]

Do not worry a man with little trifles, things that annoy a woman are not always understood by a man. Meet him cheerfully, he will always appreciate your welcome, and his home made bright and pretty will be more to him than a gander away from you....Make up your mind from the start to help your husband to succeed in all his undertakings, it can be done. Trials will come, but be brave, and always loving. Love is a mighty weapon, use it at all times for good.

— *The Farmers' Advocate*, June 26, 1905, as quoted in Norah L. Lewis, eds., *Dear Editor and Friends*, p. 39.

· 6 ·

SCIENCE, THE NEW WOMAN, AND MAKING DO:

Housewives in the '20s and '30s

The housewife of today is to her home what her husband is to his office. She is a house manager. To be successful in that sphere she must apply the same principles of management to her work that her husband does to his.

—Saturday Night, *January 17, 1920*

Now I am supposed to pay $30.00 a month rent. Now when we received the little money, I had to buy coal, pay light and water Bills, buy food—where do you suppose the rent was going to come from?. . . . if we don't help those out of this struggle we will have a terrible revolution. I see it coming. . . .

— *Mrs. William Watson writes to the mayor and aldermen of Saskatoon on April 2, 1932, seeking additional help for her family.*

For housewives, as for other Canadians, the period from 1919 to 1939 was a tale of two decades. The 1920s brought hope and prosperity. The war was over, and peace would bring a better life for all. Science would revolutionize life on the home front. Now that she had the vote, the new woman would march forward, making political changes that would improve life at home and in the wider world. The 1930s denied the hope and destroyed the prosperity. As the worldwide economic depression deepened, buying a new refrigerator took second place to feeding and clothing the children. Yet from the harsh experiences of the Depression rose new women's movements whose influence would endure well beyond those troubling times.

By 1922, women throughout all of Canada except Quebec had gained the vote in municipal, provincial, and federal elections. Those who fought for female suffrage argued that voting would give women the chance to influence critical social decisions about family and home. But it was the housewife as consumer, not political advocate, who was front and centre after World War I. Manufacturers and retailers courted her through advertising; finance companies sought her business. Flip through a Canadian magazine in the 1920s, and you'll find an abundance of articles aimed at the housewife and mother, promoting efficiency and the scientific method, proclaiming progress on the home front, and touting new appliances and other goods for the home.

Some deplored the way they thought Canadian women ran their homes:

> If women organized the home as men have done the business of supporting the home, if they made the home the

Modern earphones and old ways of doing laundry—a woman in Midnapore, Alberta, does her laundry in 1922 to the sounds of a new radio station from Calgary. (Glenbow Archives NA-1319-1)

industry that men make made the shop, there will be work for all. . . . The trouble is that the home today is the poorest run, most mismanaged and most bungled of all human industries. Its possibilities haven't been touched. Many women running homes haven't even the fundamentals of house management and dietetics.[1]

New publications were happy to repair the lack. The first issue of the women's magazine *Chatelaine* appeared in March 1928. Filled with columns and articles on cookery, entertaining, interior decoration, needlework, health, art, child study and welfare, fashions,

Thrifty citizens are the backbone of Eaton's. We mean thrifty folk in the cheerful French housewife sense of the term: clever planners and wise shoppers—the real economists of private life who are good at spinning out the dollar so that when their needs and obligations are met they've enough left over to dress in their best and go places.

—Eaton's advertisement, Toronto *Globe*, March 5, 1935.

gardening, and home planning, it featured regular departments on the domestic workshop, the family purse, and beauty tips. Advertisements for sewing patterns, sanitary napkins ("What comfort there is in complete security! What peace of mind!"), deodorants, oil-burning ranges, and umbrella dryers were all aimed at the housewife. Both *Chatelaine* and the *Canadian Home Journal* contained ads for vacuum cleaners, carpet sweepers, household cleansers, and food products with articles that told housewives how to cook better, clean better, and be better wives and mothers.

Helen Campbell, director of the Chatelaine Institute, founded in 1930 to test and evaluate consumer products, told the Women's Advertising Club in Toronto how to tap into the housewife market. The homemaker must look at her family as her permanent public, she told the gathering, as people she had to please. Her most difficult task was the preparation of three meals a day.

"It doesn't take long for them to get tired of this, tired of that, and then what?" Change, novelty, variety, were essential, and the advertiser could help the homemaker achieve all three and sell the product at the same time. Women, she added, weren't interested in the mechanical end of things, in learning how the wheels went round, but wanted to know how to do their job of homemaking better. If you are selling air conditioning, for example, don't sell the technical details; instead, tell the housewife that her house will be easier to keep clean, that it will look better, and that the added humidity will be good for her complexion.[2]

If the housewife and her family could not afford the new appliances or the new automobile, there was a new solution: credit. Compared to income, appliances and cars were vastly more expensive than they are now, and few families could afford to pay cash for a washing machine or electric stove. A prize-winning essay written in 1930 lauded the credit system:

> If installment buying enables many who otherwise would have continued the daily round of monotonous labour to obtain some share in the larger life from which they are now excluded, if it pays the way to the comforts of home life. . . . if it brings comfort into the home and brightness to the lives of those who have suffered. . .who is to deny that it has atoned for its shortcomings?[3]

For some, though, such comforts were completely out of reach. The 1921 census recorded that, for the first time, more than 50 percent of Canadians were living in towns and cities. Urban working-class housewives were hard-pressed to stretch their husbands' wages to cover the basic necessities of rent, food, and clothing. Many worked part-time, at home or outside it, or took in boarders to an already crowded flat or house. A coal or wood stove in their city apartments, a treadle sewing machine—though they might have to go home to borrow mother's—were often the limits of their home appliances.

It was no use for most farm women to yearn for vacuum cleaners and electric stoves: few farms were served by electricity. Running water and flush toilets were also for the future: many rural farm wives relied on an outhouse and water from a well or other distant source.

Many of those who scrimped and saved to buy a house, appliances, or other amenities were defeated by the Depression that began in 1929. Thousands were thrown out of work or living on reduced incomes in the 1930s. With no money available to make monthly payments, the shiny new stove or vacuum cleaner might be repossessed. In the 1930s, editors were forced to temper their enthusiasm for consumer products with advice on making do and cooking inexpensively.

Inner-city families moved from small apartments to even smaller ones, looking for the cheapest rent. Women did laundry and dishes and bathed their children in the kitchen sink. Though electricity powered most apartments and houses in urban areas, many tenants could not afford to run appliances, and some, cut off for not paying their bills, stole power through illegal connections.

The unemployed and their families all across Canada suffered, but worst affected were farm families in southern Saskatchewan, southeast Alberta, and southwest Manitoba. Plummeting prices for farm crops were bad enough. Worse, though, was the horrendous drought that lasted eight years, from 1929 to 1937, and destroyed crop after crop, leaving only giant Russian thistles in the drifted dunes of sand. What the drought didn't get, the grasshoppers did.

Farm income was reduced to almost nil, and thousands of families left the Dust Bowl, heading north to homestead again, into

Then came the "Great War", and women were forced to rush into all sorts of strenuous activities quite outside their 'home sphere', yet strange to say, the bread was still baked, the pantry run on the most economical lines, and the destitute cared for as never before! The hearth fires kept burning, and the camp fires burning brightly too. Women will never be the same again—they have awakened to a sense of their responsibilities, and will not rest until they have the right to assume them!

— *Daily News*, St. John's, Newfoundland, May 25, 1920, as quoted in Beth Light and Ruth Roach Pierson, *No Easy Road*, p. 355.

the cities, or back to families that were severely stretched themselves. Canadians responded with relief trains, stocked with food and clothing bought by the federal government or contributed by individuals or groups (including housewives) in other parts of Canada. Cheese and codfish, apples and vegetables, canned milk and turnips were shipped wherever help was needed.

Men without work walked away from their families, unable to stand the pressure any longer. Housewives who had prided themselves on their ability to "make do" were reduced to taking charity, or to near-starvation. Relief coupons, handed out as a type of welfare payment in goods, were for the most basic of items, making it a challenge for the housewife to produce anything interesting or different for her family. Some housewives colluded with storekeepers, who took the coupons in exchange for items such as candles or sewing needles that were not considered necessities by those who made up the list.

Women did what they could to help. When hundreds of men boarded trains in Vancouver on a trek to Ottawa to protest unemployment and the treatment of the unemployed, they clutched packages of sandwiches made for them by the Vancouver members of the Mothers' Council. Housewives who were members of the ladies' auxiliary of the Unemployed Workers' Association fed the men when the train went through Golden, BC.

The unemployed quickly recognized women with generous hearts. All through the Depression, tramps scrawled symbols on gateposts and doorways across the country, marking houses where they could count on a gift of food or a few hours' work paid for in food or money.

The era brought other visitors to the housewife's kitchen. The Watkins Man walked door to door with his suitcase full of spices and extracts and the Fuller Brush salesman brought all manner of brushes to the door. "How Fuller Brushes take drudgery out of house-work and gives women time for other things," read one ad. This company was the brainchild of Nova Scotian Al Fuller, who took his concept of "Make it work, make it last, guarantee it no matter what" and sold it door to door across North America. The FBM became such a common sight in the 1930s that Red Skelton starred in a slapstick movie called *The Fuller Brush Man* and even poet Irving Layton did a stint as a Fuller Brush man.

Not all housewives were content to be uncomplaining consumers. As early as the end of World War I, faced with skyrocketing prices, housewives' leagues and women's associations picketed and boycotted. In the 1920s and 1930s, they also protested against legislation that would have allowed price fixing by major manufacturers. During the Depression, the Vancouver Mothers' Council in petitioned the government to provide a living wage for the unemployed. The Greater Vancouver Housewives' League protested against rising prices of such necessary products as milk and bread. Housewives in Toronto picketed kosher butchers and boycotted dairies to protest high prices.

Some women decided that what one family couldn't do alone, many families could do together. In Saskatchewan, groups of women helped found some of the country's first co-op stores and supported bulk buying. Some housewives supported the idea of community kitchens, partly to keep costs down, partly to lessen the work each housewife must do. "Why should a more or less untidy kitchen, a weary woman, and since all women are not good cooks, an oft-times badly cooked meal, constitute a home?" a speaker asked the United Women Voters in Toronto in 1919. "Wouldn't the

---

Mrs. Phoebe McCord talks about the old days in Shawville, Quebec:

I became a farm wife.... I joined the ranks of the Good Women.... A Good Woman is virtuous.... You went to the barn in the morning before your child was born. And the morning after. You were excellent at fancy work. You made quilts. You were a good, plain cook. I was a good plain cook but I could do the fancy stuff.

....A Good Woman was good with her hands. You took the front out of the overalls when they were worn out, and you took a part that you'd saved from another pair of overalls and you set them in so that the men all went to the bush with overalls that were new down the front. And everyone knew

you were good. You were a good knitter and a good mender and a good darner.... A Good Woman always put a washing out on the line whiter than her neighbours'. You made your sheets out of flour bags and you bleached them pure white.... A Good Woman knew how to prevent diaper rash. You washed diapers in rainwater until they were as soft as soft water. You always hung them outside, no matter what the weather, every single day.... With a Good Woman, cleanliness was next to Godliness. You washed three things every morning...the dishes, the baby, and the separator.... Down in the basement, the Good Woman had her supply for the family sicknesses. You have the jar of goose oil in case of croup.... A Good Woman was one

who had her own fruit and preserves and pickles.... A good Woman voted Conservative, marched her family to church, always went with them. She worked in the barn and helped with the chores.... A Good Woman always had her babies at home with the help of Grandma or whatever neighbour woman was skilled.... A Good Woman nursed her babies.... A Good Woman never mentioned if her husband drank.... She never talked about sex....

— Joan Finnigan, ed., *Some of the Stories I Told You Were True*, pp. 285–288.

Coming to Canada was a dream for many, but poverty was still the lot of countless immigrants, and hard work was required of new Canadian housewives. Immigrants look after chickens outside their Kensington area home in Toronto in 1922. (John Boyd, Library and Archives Canada PA 084811)

time be less wearisomely and more acceptably spent in attending to the dainty service of the food which would with Community Kitchen service be brought to the home?"[4] Little came of the Toronto efforts, but they were among the signs that housewives were thinking beyond the stereotyped role of consumer that manufacturers and advertisers suggested for them.

❧ THE COOK ❧

"You couldn't get anything for our home that would please me more," smiled the housewife in the Westinghouse ad at her equally smiling husband. "It's so simple—just a turn of a button and I get the exact amount of heat right where I want it." "My baking is absolutely certain now—no guesswork. The kitchen is cooler and cleaner. There's no waste to pay for either. . . . I don't have to think about dust or dirt, and there's not an odor or fume to worry about."[5]

Newfangled appliances run by electricity promised to lighten the housewife's load. A housewife shows off her new refrigerator in 1927. (Library and Archives Canada, Grayston, C.G.M.P.B. PA-122568)

The ad writers had homed in on exactly what the home cook wanted: certainty, cleanliness, economy. A housewife used to a wood or coal range would indeed be happy with a thermostat-controlled oven, and electric or gas kitchen ranges were by far the most popular of the new appliances produced after 1918. Manufacturers tried to build stoves for all situations, including a small, apartment-sized electric range with an attached side grill that, it was promised, would roast a large fowl at the same time as it cooked the vegetables.

Mechanical refrigerators with chemical coolants were introduced in the 1920s, but, expensive and prone to leaks, they didn't capture much of the domestic market. By the mid-1930s, some of the technical problems had been solved, but the average housewife was still left gasping by the price and could not be convinced even by persuasive editorial copy:

> In her own way, she is just as good a manager as any housekeeper of the nineties. Have you ever found her at a loss for something good to serve? Not with a mechanical refrigerator, for on its shelves, there are bottles and jars of fruit juice, cocoa, and other syrups for sweetening and flavoring, a roll of cookie dough, pastry ready for shaping, fresh fruit, crisp vegetables, milk, eggs and butter with their flavor unimpaired as well as other ingredients all ready to do their

During the Depression, housewives found ways to economize:

MONDAY SOUP

Add a shank bone to the bones from the Sunday roast. Cover with 6 cups of water, or more if required, and the liquor from the Sunday vegetables. Add any leftover portions of vegetables. Add 1 carrot, 2 onions, 2 or 3 outer stalks of celery and 2 tablespoons of dried peas or lentils. Simmer for 3 hours. When cooked, remove the bones and rub the soup through a coarse sieve. If too thick, thin with milk. Add more seasonings if required.

If there is any left-over porridge on hand, add it to the soup as well. The porridge will both thicken the soup and add to its flavor and nutriment.

Do not use strongly flavored vegetables (as turnip, cauliflower, Brussels sprouts, etc.), nor the waters in which they have been boiled.

—Jean Brodie, *A Guide to Good Cooking*, pp. 95–96.

Then, as now, women were eager to learn about new recipes, new ingredients, new ways of cooking. In 1933, hundreds of women flocked to an *Edmonton Journal* cooking and homemaking show. (Glenbow Archives ND-3-6274b)

share. There's probably the makings of a salad down to the last bit of crisp green, some savory mixtures in little jars for sandwich fillings or canapé toppings, a bottle of pudding sauce perhaps, or even some tomato or cream sauce which this ardent apostle of preparedness has made in quantity.[6]

New ingredients, a trend to lighter food, more types of canned food, and imaginative—though sometimes bewildering—recipes were presented as part of a modern era. Publications abounded in meal plans, laying out menus for three meals a day, every day of the month. A cooked breakfast was still recommended, with variations on eggs, waffles, pancakes, bacon, ham, pork chops, a steak, creamed haddock—and always cereal and coffee.

More and more produce came from large stores and supermarkets, but many housewives still depended on the open-air market supplied by area farmers; these women did their shopping at the Fredericton City Market. (Provincial Archives of New Brunswich P120/9/22)

As city transportation improved, men worked farther from their homes, and took their lunch pails with them; now, the big meal of the day could be at midday or at night. The recommended lunch at home included at least two courses—a main and a dessert— plus cocoa, coffee, or tea. Dinner included meat, fish, or poultry; potatoes and vegetables; a salad, such as cabbage, cheese, and pimento salad; dessert and coffee. If tonight's dinner was made of last night's leftovers, it must be disguised in some way and presented as something new.

Columnists and authors were also quick to declare how much and what kinds of food should be eaten, setting out, for example, a day's diet for 50 cents a person, 2,800 calories for an adult.

Ever more popular through the 1920s and 1930s were recipe books put together by housewives who were members of various charitable or social groups. The Kelowna Hospital Women's Auxiliary, for example, worked from the founding of the hospital in 1905 to provide much-needed linen and other resources for the hospital. Their 1936 recipe books, 50 cents a copy, contained advertisements from local and food-related businesses, family recipes, and lists and quantities of food needed to serve a family or a hundred people.

Housewives could buy more of their foods ready-made. At the same time, new inventions were making it easier to make their

Old skills survive in a modern era: Cape Dorset Inuit housewives clean walrus hide on Baffin Island in 1926. (Finnie, Richard S., Library and Archives Canada e002342623)

own. In the 1920s, for example, bottled fruit pectins such as Certo came onto the market. A booklet by the makers of Certo noted:

> It used to take a rather daring housewife to attempt jam and jelly making. You simply couldn't tell how it was going to turn out—your jelly might set and be beautifully clear, or, it might be a cloudy soupy mass—and not even the most skill-ful housewife could be sure. It was the one place in cookery where experience didn't seem to count. But now, things are different—use Certo to get successful results every time.[7]

As the Depression decade wore on, housewives on shrinking budgets sought ways to feed their families cheaply. Magazines and advertisers presented ideas for inexpensive meals, explaining what could be done with a can of soup, how canned meats fitted into a menu, and how new packaged foods could help the housewife.

RECIPES

This recipe won a readers' contest for recipes using Ingersoll cheese:

INGERSOLL CREAM CHEESE COMBINATION SALAD

   6 Tomatoes (medium size)

   1 small Cucumber (cut in cubes)

   $1/3$ cup Chopped Nuts

   $1/4$ cup Ham (minced fine)

   Salad Dressing to moisten

   Pepper and Salt to taste

   $2/3$ pkg. Ingersoll Cream Cheese

Select medium-sized firm tomatoes, wash, remove skin, cut in half crosswise. Arrange each slice on a bed of crisp lettuce or watercress and sprinkle with salt. Mix cucumber cubes, ham, nuts, cheese (half of quantity), and seasonings with enough salad dressing to moisten. Pile mixture on tomato half and top with a small ball of Ingersoll Cream cheese, rolled in chopped nuts.

— *Maclean's*, October 15, 1922, p. 39.

JEWEL CANDY FOR CHILDREN

   1 cup sugar

   $1/3$ cup white corn syrup

   $1/3$ cup water

   Watkins Certified Coloring

   1 teaspoon Watkins flavoring

Boil mixture until it crackles when dropped in cold water. Pour mixture into buttered plates. Add Watkins certified coloring and flavoring, let cool only long enough to handle. Cut strips of candy from plate into small pieces. Candy must be handled quickly as it hardens rapidly.

— *Watkins Cook Book*, 1936.

MOCK LEMON CURD

   1 pounds marrow (prepared)

   3 lemons

   2 pounds granulated sugar

   $1/2$ cup butter

Weigh the prepared marrow before cooking. Boil or steam it, then strain and mash it. Allow it to remain in colander for 2 or 3 hours, until all the water has drained away. When cold, add sugar and butter; simmer gently until the mixture is as thick as cream (about 30 minutes). Add the grated rind and juice of the lemons and simmer for 5 minutes longer. When cool, store in jars. Use for filling tarts.

— Jean Brodie, *A Guide to Good Cooking*, pp. 75–6, 175.

APPLE FILLING FOR 14 PIES

16 lbs. of tart apples, 2 tablespoons cinnamon, 7 lbs. sugar, 1 cup flour, $1/2$ cup butter. Pare and core the apples and cut into thin slices. Line pie pans with pastry and fill with apple mixture, dot with butter. Cover top with paste, trim and press edges together. Prick top well. Bake in a quick oven (425 deg.) for ten minutes, reduce heat to 350 deg., and continue baking for 20 to 30 minutes.

— *Kelowna Hospital Women's Auxiliary Cook Book*, p. 5.

POUDING CHOMEUR- "UNEMPLOYED" PUDDING

There are hundreds of recipes in Quebec for Pouding Chomeur— "Unemployed" Pudding, cake batter baked on top of a sugar syrup. One version, compiled from many:

Mix together:

   $1/2$ cup butter

   1 cup sugar

   2 eggs

   1 $1/2$ cups flour

   2 $1/2$ teaspoons baking powder

   a pinch of salt

   vanilla to taste

   $3/4$ cup milk

Syrup:

   1 $1/2$ cups water

   $1/2$ cup maple syrup

   2 cups brown sugar

   1 tablespoon flour

Mix the brown sugar and flour together. Heat the mixture until it melts. Add the maple syrup and water, and pour the mixture into a cake pan. Pour the cake batter on top. Cook at 375 degrees for 30 to 40 minutes.

"It's times like these which give us a chance to prove our housewifely virtues of thrift and good management, our skill in preparing wholesome, appetizing meals from simple, inexpensive ingredients," wrote *Chatelaine* editor Helen Campbell.[8] Cookbooks and columns in magazines and newspapers focused on using leftovers in imaginative ways and substituting inexpensive ingredients for more expensive ones.

But the poorest housewives—prairie farm women waiting out the drought, inner-city wives subsisting on relief or their husbands' paycheques for part-time work, widows or deserted wives—were beyond the reach of such suggestions. They were reduced to begging day-old bread from bakeries and bones from the butcher, sending their children to school with just a cold potato for lunch, and watering down and eking out the food they made for their families.

❧ THE HOUSEKEEPER ❧

"Can't you just picture the house when Grandmother went in for her housecleaning?" asked a newspaper columnist in 1935. "With her head swathed in a dust-cap, she went forth with her broom, and it was certainly up to one and all to 'clear the way.' What a different story now! Electric washers, ironers, polishers, vacuum cleaners, all have a part in helping the busy housewife to lighten her task."[9]

No housewife could mourn the days spent trying to keep carpets clean by the old methods of tea leaves spread and swept up, or beating rugs hung on the line outside. But she might be suspicious of the vacuums of the era, upright models that either used a fan to suck dust through a nozzle and into a bag hung from the handle or included a rotating head that was supposed to loosen dust so it could be sucked up. A vacuum and attachments cost about $65 in an era when the average monthly wage for a fully employed man was $80 to $120. "Although electric vacuums are now used in millions of homes," reassured a Hoover advertisement in 1922, "and are regarded as indispensable by their owners, occasionally the question arises whether this method of cleaning is injurious to

MY RE-MADE KITCHEN
My old kitchen was drab and dreary,
When night-time came I was so weary,
A thousand steps unnecessary
I made from dawn 'til dark.

My new kitchen is bright and cheery
With every unit gay and airy,
At dinner I am always merry,
My days are all a lark!

With space galore and cabinets many
Electric helpers all and any
And yet I didn't waste a penny
I need them all and how!

Now all my home seems recreated,
My old kitchen was so out-dated
My friends exclaim with breath abated
A perfect workshop now.

— "Remodelling Kitchen Contest Paves the Way for Profitable Sales of Kitchen Equipment," *Canadian Furniture World*, November 1932, p. 11, as quoted in Veronica Strong Boag, *The New Day Recalled*, p. 117.

A British Columbia farm woman in 1930 takes on one of the traditional chores of the housewife: keeping chickens. (Vancouver Public Library 11529)

rugs." Indeed not, said Hoover; "unfortunately many people have been influenced by these rumours."[10]

Housewives also had recourse to new cleansers; instead of making their own, they could buy Pine-Sol, a household cleaning liquid invented in 1929, or S.O.S. (for "save our saucepans") soap and steel-wool pads, invented in 1917. Old Dutch abrasive cleanser, around since the turn of the century, was popular in Canadian homes.

The new devices and cleansers lightened the housekeeper's load. But the devil finds work for idle hands, they say, and writers were certainly ready to suggest how the housewife might fill the time left empty by labour-saving machines. Put up new wallpaper; make or buy new curtains. "Get busy with the paper and the paint can. Get the menfolk interested, and maybe they'll give you some more money so you can do even more."[11]

In 1922, McClary's, a manufacturer of stoves and other appliances, produced a household manual aimed at helping the housewife plan her kitchen, clean the house, set the table, do the laundry, and choose and cook food. Among the cleaning hints:

> Wax is the preferred finish for a polished floor. Remember, however, that it will not cover soil and stain. The floor should be wiped over first with warm soft water—rainwater is best. Do not use any soap or oily cleaner. If the floor is too soiled to yield to this treatment, use a little turpentine. Especially stubborn stains will usually disappear after a vigorous rubbing with steel wool, moistened with turpentine.[12]

Dust storms plagued prairie housekeepers. In July of 1931, Jane Aberson fitted her spring cleaning in around caring for the chickens and garden, plus the usual routine of cooking and laundry—but saw her efforts go for naught:

> Even if it was a slow process this year, I eventually finished [house cleaning]. One evening I made the rounds of the whole house and thought, "Well this is all I can do about it this year. More important work is waiting."

Two days after that I had a bad disappointment, Although we sometimes have bad dust storms. . . we don't expect them this late in the year because the land is green and the soil is mostly covered. But one afternoon a strong wind set up like I have never seen! The roof of our machine shed was thrown high in the air and smacked down again, quite a distance away. . . . The sun disappeared behind kind of a yellow curtain. . . . It [the dust] penetrated through every nook and cranny. . . . When we came downstairs in the morning we found everything covered with a thick layer of dust. It had penetrated every cupboard and trunk in the house. . . . I walked disconsolately through the house and felt that I would not have the energy to start cleaning the mess up, after having just finished cleaning the whole house.[13]

CRACK FILLER

We have tried some of the most expensive ones on the market and found that, in time, it seems to dry out and all break out like powder. . . . the following recipe. . . . is still there, as solid as when filled in six years ago:

Take some flour and boiled oil to make a real stiff paste. Fill in the seams and leave for two or three days before painting over. If to be used on an already grained floor, then add light or dark oak stain to color the same shade as the floor, then, when dry, varnish over the whole surface. Be sure not to make the paste too thin.

— reader's suggestion, Toronto *Globe*, February 20, 1935.

❧ THE SEAMSTRESS ❧

Ready-made clothing, fashion fabric and patterns, mending and making do: the themes of the 1920s and 1930s built on those of the previous decade. Though the housewife could—if her budget allowed—buy most garments ready-made, many continued to make clothing for themselves and their children, spurred by saving money, getting exactly what they wanted, and a pride in their own handiwork.

The sewing machine had pride of place in most Canadian homes, but tailoring suits and making dress shirts suitable for the office was beyond the abilities of most home seamstresses. The

---

For an excellent and most economical floor wax buy:

2 ounces beeswax
½ pint turpentine

Dissolve the wax by putting it in a small tin and placing this in a larger one which contains several inches of boiling water. When the wax is melted, remove from the fire, add the turpentine and stir until well mixed....Simple as this preparation is, it cannot be improved upon, because it is made with the pure wax—no cheap gums or substitutes of any kind are in it.

Where the polish of your furniture was originally good, but has been very much dulled, here is a "reviver" which you can have your druggist make up for you, which will bring up the old finish and restore much of the beauty of your wood:

½ pint raw linseed oil
2 ounces vinegar
1 ounce spirits of camphor
½ ounce butter of antimony
¼ ounce spirits of hartshorn

Anyone who buys steel knives for table use now-a-days, should be careful to select those made of the new stainless steel. They require no cleaning, and are always spotless.

Wash any granite pan in hot soapy suds and a wooden toothpick or skewer should be used to clean the seams. A mild abrasive may be used to remove stains. To remove food that has been burned on, place a little fat of any kind in the vessel and warm it gently; this will soften the burned substance, so that it may be readily scraped off.

— McClary's Household Manual, 1922, pp. 13, 21, 24.

Another tool that is invaluable at housecleaning time is a dusting mop or "handle duster". Quite like a small floor mop, it covers a large area quickly and holds dust on its fluffy strings until shaken out of doors. What a contrast to a feather duster which flicked dirt from one thing to another! A handle duster is especially designed for cleaning the tops, backs and sides of book cases, chiffoniers, bureaux, pianos, sewing machines, gramophones, the legs and tops of tables and chairs, as well as banisters, wainscoting, paneling, bedsteads and springs. It does the work well and much more rapidly than is possible with an ordinary duster. For Windsor chairs and others with spokes or spindles, a split duster can be secured.

— Chatelaine, April 1928, p. 41.

Magazines and pattern makers offered patterns so that housewives could make fashionable clothes. (*Chatelaine*, 1933)

Sew where you will and as much as you like—always a pleasure with a Hydro Portable Electric Sewing Machine. You'll enjoy this sewing. No tiresome foot treadle that makes your body ache. You sew all day without fatigue—on any kind of fabric. Just press the foot control and the motor does the work. The whole outfit is no larger than a typewriter. Can be used anywhere—on the dining-room table, in the bedroom—anywhere you have a light socket....It's the last word in real sewing economy and comfort.

— The Toronto Hydro Shop, advertisement, Toronto *Globe*, April 9, 1920.

Today's my day for darning,
That's the time I think and plan,
And I solve the little problems
Which beset my smallest man.

I used to pounce upon these sox,
Rushing through with nervous speed,
To finish up the hated task
To rest or think or read.

Now I find the task of darning,
The time I like the best;
Time for retrospect or planning,
Time to sing and time to rest.

— from *Home and Country* magazine, as quoted in the Toronto *Globe*, February 13, 1935.

average housewife bought her husband's suits, shirts, and heavy work clothes at the store or through the catalogue. When it came to her own and the children's clothes, though, many housewives still snipped and sewed, using patterns from fabric stores or ordering from magazines that regularly featured fashion pages.

Eager to persuade housewives to spend more money on their sewing machines, companies such as Singer devised and sold attachments that would allow the seamstress to make looped carpets or try machine embroidery.

The difficult years of the 1930s re-emphasized the old arts of the seamstress: patching, darning, remaking, cutting down, handing down. Women knitted sweaters for themselves and their families and the arts of crochet, embroidery, and quilting were practised in both town and country. Flour and sugar sacks were never thrown away: they came in too handy for everything from household cloth to dresses (once the words were bleached out). Tapping into women's use of the sacks, manufacturers began making them in a variety of colours, and printing flowered patterns on them. Some even printed patterns for dolls or stuffed animals on the sacks, hoping this would convince housewives and their husbands to buy their product rather than a competitor's. An unpicked, unfolded sack provided about a metre of material.

⇜ THE LAUNDRESS ⇝

Electrical power companies were eager to sell appliances, especially during the Depression when their big industrial customers were using less power. Unsurprisingly, they thought their greatest success would be in selling washing machines. British Columbia Electric started its first major domestic sales campaign in 1925:

> All members of the sales staff who were connected in any way with the sale of washing machines were given their ammunition for the big drive on the housewives of Vancouver to be made during the month of March. The goal was set at 250 Thor washing machines. These 250 machines, if all operated at the same time, would require sixty-two horsepower and would wash thoroughly every 15 minutes 1,500 sheets. A clothes-line two miles in length would be required to dry the clean clothes from such a battery of washers.
>
> The foregoing gives a slight idea of the amount of work done by electric washing machines, but only the woman who has replaced the old type of scrub-board in a tub with a modern electric washer knows the amount of actual labour saved by the Thor electric washing machine.[14]

Though some housewives had mechanical washing machines by 1920, and many had electric ones with wringers or mangles by 1939, laundry was still the most physical and time-consuming task for the housewife. By the 1930s, many city housewives had running water and hot water heaters. But filling the tub with hot water,

Before the washing is started, the soap is shaved fairly thin with a knife, put into a saucepan, two quarts of cold water added for each bar of soap, and the soap slowly melted. A small granite cup is filled from the pan of hot soap, a little cold water added if necessary to cool reasonably, and this liquid soap is poured, a very little at a time, on the garment to be washed. Of course, there is soon a good lather in the tub and the melted soap need only be poured directly on spots or especially soiled parts. The dirt seems to fairly fall out by this method, and very little rubbing is required. The white clothes are usually boiled afterwards, with some of the soap solution. It is possible that a little more soap is used this way than in the ordinary process of rubbing the bar on the clothing, but undoubtedly clothes last much longer when washed this way and the labour is greatly lessened. It is particularly well worth while to wash woollens and fine things this way.

— *McClary's Household Manual*, p. 33.

New was better; new saved time and energy. Advertisers used comic strips to convince housewives that modern products could ease their days. (*Chatelaine*, May, 1933)

Recommended for various stains and spots:

Ammonia, washing soda, borax, lye, turpentine, benzene, kerosene, fuller's earth, paraffin.

TO MAKE STARCH
Thin Starch:

Mix ½ cup starch with ½ cup of cold water. Add to three quarts of boiling water with

> ½ level tablespoon borax
> ¼ level tablespoon lard,
>> kerosene or other fatty
>> substance

Cook fifteen to twenty minutes.

— *McClary's Household Manual*, 1922, p. 33.

shaving a bar of soap, and wringing out the clothes by hand or feeding them through a manual or electric wringer were still part of many housewives' lives.

To keep her linen sparkling white and her colours bright, the housewife was advised to have on hand an amazing number of potions and chemicals to remove stains and soften water. The 1922 McClary's manual advised:

> Javelle water (for white goods only), potassium perman-ganate in solution (for white and some coloured goods), oxalic acid (poison), ammonia water, hydrogen peroxide, French chalk, should be kept on hand, but safely out of reach in case of poisons, to prevent accident. They must be used quickly to prevent damage to fibres. Stretch the stained portion tightly over a bowl and apply chemicals from a medicine dropper or the point of a skewer or small stick.[15]

Wash was to be done weekly; on rainy washdays, clothes were

City dwellers might have electric power and appliances; farm dwellers rarely did. Housewives and their children do the wash outdoors in the 1930s on an Alberta farm. (Glenbow Archives, NA-3430-41)

dried indoors, in a cupboard behind the stove or wherever they could be hung—particularly unpleasant for those who lived in apartments or small houses, where damp clothes could take days to dry. And drying clothes outdoors on the dusty prairies could be particularly frustrating.

By 1928, manufacturers had devised a drying cupboard heated by electricity or gas. "What was once considered a three-day task now becomes a mere matter of routine, easily accomplished in the space of six to eight hours," enthused the first issue of *Chatelaine* in its "Domestic Workshop" column in 1928.[16] The magazine predicted the dryer would revolutionize washday, but consumers weren't so sure, and the heated closet didn't have a great deal of success. More successful was the umbrella outdoor dryer, a variation on the clothesline particularly useful for women with small yards.

Ironing, however, had become easier. Irons were made of lighter metals—or even glass. By the 1930s, electric and gas irons came with thermostats, so the housewife could control the temperature of the iron. Gone for the majority of households were the days when the iron was heated on the stove and was frequently too hot or too cold.

An advertisement for Hood's Sarsa-pilla—"makes rich red blood and promotes health"—got on the scientific bandwagon, then lapsed back into earlier jargon:

Don't be misled by sensational claims. There's nothing new about vitamins, except that scientists have just discovered and named them. They are in your food now, just as they have always been. Hood's Sarsapilla saves all the vitamins now, just as it has always done. It aids digestion, promotes assimilation, converts all the

good in your food into blood, bone and tissue, and is of great benefit for humors, eruptions, etc.

— advertisement, Toronto *Globe*, May 17, 1922.

The *Globe* told housewives they could keep their family well by buying food products that were advertised in the newspaper: they could trust the ads entirely, promised the ad, and "follow the high road to food economy":

Take this advice to protect the health of your loved ones. Every housewife

knows that sound health is the most priceless possession her family can have. Without it there is little real happiness in the home. So naturally she uses thought and energy to keep her husband, her children and herself fit and well.

The health and strength of the bodies in her care depend chiefly on the food she provides and prepares. Three meals a day—seven days a week. Truly she needs all her wits and ability to cope with them.

— Toronto *Globe*, April 5, 1935.

❦ THE NURSE ❦

The role of the housewife as family nurse came in for professional scrutiny after World War I. The campaign to prevent infant and maternal deaths gathered momentum, and mothers were encouraged to look to the health of their children with a proper regard for science. Books and articles by child-care experts could help them nurse their children properly through their illnesses and accidents. The doctor was the proper person to consult if a member of the family was ill, it was suggested, and also if a child was well. For the doctor had two roles: healing illness and preventing it.

Doctors talked about the need to prevent disease, especially the ever-present childhood diseases of diphtheria, measles, scarlet fever, and infantile paralysis or polio. Visiting nurses and well-baby clinics added their advice. In some cities, mothers could go to both pre- and post-natal clinics.

Yet the housewife still had a large role to play, looking after sick members of her family at home and tending to everyday tribulations. This task was subject to the same rules of organization and efficiency as other housewifely chores. In 1927, the *Canadian Home Journal* advised women on how and when to feed an invalid:

7 a.m.	One cup hot milk, flavoured with coffee or cocoa.
9 a.m.	One cup beef tea.
11 a.m.	Albuminized lemonade, orangeade or grape juice.
1 p.m.	Cream soup.
3 p.m.	One cup gruel made with milk.
5 p.m.	Egg-Nog.
7 p.m.	Albuminized fruit juice.
9 p.m.	Koumis.
11. p.m.	One cup malted milk.

The recipe for albuminized fruit juice was included: "Combine the juice of one-half orange, one-half lemon, one-half teaspoon sugar, white of one egg and one-half cup chopped ice. Shake in a covered jar until well combined. Serve when thoroughly chilled."[17]

The home nurse was further advised to make things as attractive as possible for the invalid, serving sustenance on the prettiest

Distant from doctors or nurses, housewives in the wilderness had to do the best they could. Elizabeth Goudie's child was badly burned when a stove exploded. Ill herself, she tried to look after her son until a doctor passing through the area arrived ten days later:

I said to Jim, "You better get me a juniper stick and I will boil it and use the liquid to bathe the burns." I had no dressing. I had a couple of sheets and I tore them up for dressings. There was a small wound of open flesh on his elbow and I was really afraid that would become infected. I hoped and prayed it would be all right. Jim got the juniper stick. I went to work and boiled it for four hours and started to bathe the wounds in the liquid.

On the second day, the spot on his elbow looked a bit red and infected, I took a piece of the stick and peeled the outside bark off and took the inside, the gummy bark of the stick, and beat it to a pulp. I sterilized my dressing by browning it on the stove and I placed a piece of the gummy pulp on his elbow. I greased the poultice with the castor oil and after six days, he seemed to be getting a lot better.

[The doctor tells Goudie she has done a marvellous job, the boy survives, and Jim goes back to his trapline.]

— Elizabeth Goudie, *Woman of Labrador*, p. 70.

Vaccinations were new for most mothers: they were encouraged to make sure their children were protected against a variety of diseases. (*Chatelaine*, 1938)

Time to protect me against **DIPHTHERIA**

Age 6 months

I nursed all my babies. I never gave them the bottle. I was a lucky mother because I was hefty and able to nurse them for ten months....I had an aunt who could not nurse her babies. She had to get a bottle for them. What she used for food was flour. She took the dry flour and packed it in a white cloth and boiled it for four hours. When she took it from the cloth it was like a piece of chalk that you use for the blackboard in school only it weighed about a pound. She would take a piece and grate it up and make a pap like a real thick gravy. She boiled it again and added sugar, a little butter and a little salt. She raised eight children like that....Some of them grew up to be old men and women. When put to the test we could always manage.

— Elizabeth Goudie, *Woman of Labrador*, p. 46.

china, with the best silver, and perhaps a single flower laid on the tray. And no noise, please, that might upset the invalid.

Though patent medicines were still available, many advertisers now suggested that prevention, in the form of the correct food, was the best medicine. This drink would build appetite and promote growth; that dessert was known by nurses to make mother and children healthy. Fleischmann's yeast was not, said its advertisements, a medicine or a cure-all, but a food: "the millions of tiny active yeast plants in every cake invigorate the whole system. They aid digestion—clear the skin—banish the poisons of constipation. Where cathartics give only temporary relief, yeast strengthens the intestinal muscles and makes them healthy and active, daily releasing new stores of energy."[18]

⊱ THE MOTHER ⊰

Though motherhood was still considered the ultimate achievement of a woman's life, and childless marriages were disparaged as a pale shadow of the real thing, the trend in mothering between the wars went from "mother knows best" to "mother must be helped." Reports, books, magazine articles, newspaper columns, doctors, visiting nurses, and public health programs heaped advice upon the mother and warned her against the practices of decades past.

Advice from medical professionals for childbirth and the infant years was part of the continuing campaign to reduce the deaths of mothers and infant children. Mothers should see their doctors for pre- and post-natal care, and were advised to have their babies in hospital. In rural areas, they should go to hospital, or at least to the town where a hospital was located, well before their due dates. The program seemed to be working: from 1921 to 1939, the rate of infant mortality slowly dropped.

In 1922, *Maclean's* magazine ran a six-part series that included advice on all aspects of a child's life. The material didn't just tell mothers what to do: it explained why at very great and scientifically detailed length. These articles were among many that dictated rules for every situation. The experts looked severely on rural women who might plead that they could not follow these rules because they couldn't reach a store to buy the recommended food. In that case, the mother of a baby should make a special arrangement with the farmer, "that the cow's belly, udders and teats should be wiped off with a damp cloth before milking; that the milker's hands should be washed before milking; that the few jets of the foremilk should be thrown away; and that as soon as the milk is drawn it shall be strained through absorbent cotton into a quart bottle suitably corked and placed in a pail of cracked ice."[19] You would have to pay the farmer extra, of course, but it would be worth it. The article didn't tackle the difficult topics of what you should do if you didn't have the money, or if the farmer told you to go to hell.

In Wayson Choy's novel, *All That Matters*, Siu-Dep, brought from China to marry a man she had never met, prepares for childbirth and motherhood:

Women friends brought Stepmother sachets of mixed leaves and bits of prune to brew pink-coloured teas, and jars of vinegared pigs' feet soup to reheat. A small pile of baby clothes sat unwrapped in her bedroom. The wooden crib was brought down from the attic and thoroughly washed. Bachelor Gee Sook from American Steam Company sent over eight baby-size cushions sewn from, and stuffed with, discarded fabrics. Eight was a lucky number....One month later, after considerable fussing by everyone, by Mrs. Lim with her potions and ointments, by Mr. Gu with his herbs, and by the mahjong ladies with their advice and with their share of special recipes...the baby boy had survived long enough to be given his official name. Third Uncle made sure that the herbalist approved. He even had the baby poked and prodded by a Western doctor.

— Extracted from *All That Matters*, pp. 152, 157, by Wayson Choy. Copyright © Wayson Choy 2004. Reprinted by permission of Doubleday Canada.

A senior member of a Nova Scotia medical school rails against women for not wanting to have babies:

They raise their children, in the average, by a rule of thumb that hasn't altered since Abraham was a lad.... If women took their work in life seriously, they could all be busy in the homes, and at the same time be preparing themselves for maternity.... But I hear the protest of angry women readers: "Are we nothing but baby machines?" "He ought to have a baby or two and see how he likes it!" "I wish a man could have a baby—it'd be the last."

O woman, woman! O blind, bemused woman!

Baby machines?

Is it given to man in all his lordliness to be a baby machine and produce a Christ, a Socrates, a Joan of Arc, an Einstein? Are all the automobile factories at work in this world of more value to the human race than one single womb that can bring forth a psalm-making Hebrew king or a playwriting bard out of Stratford?

O, blind bemused woman!

— "The Menace of Maternity," by Dr. Benge Atlee, *Canadian Home Journal*, May 1932, pp. 84–85.

In these decades, new foods were developed for babies. Gerber's baby foods appeared on the grocery shelves in the late 1920s, and in 1931 doctors at the Hospital for Sick Children in Toronto developed Pablum. A bland, precooked baby cereal described as tasting to adults like wet Kleenex, it provided most of an infant's nutritional needs. Pablum became a byword for baby food in Canadian households and was credited with giving children a good start in life. By the late 1930s, pasteurization of milk was declared mandatory in Ontario, with other provinces following suit despite opposition from dairy farmers, and child deaths from contaminated milk were all but eliminated.

The mothers' grapevine expanded to include Women's Institutes and other groups that often focused on a topic related to rearing a child. Women's magazines or pages in newspapers and other publications carried letters from mothers and columns with information gathered from a wide variety of sources.

"Any amount of sacrifice is worth while to protect the mother's health," an April 1925, editorial in the *Grain Growers' Guide*, declared, and listed the expenses a new mother might expect in providing for a first baby, from a crib and kiddy coop, to the doctor's bill (circumcision included), to clothing that included two barrow coats and two union vests. You could build some of the articles, such as the crib, at home, suggested the guide, and if you really couldn't afford everything, then you should skimp on the clothing rather than on the medical and nursing fees.

Especially as the Depression took its toll, some had nothing left to sacrifice. They needed help. By the end of the 1930s, seven provinces offered skimpy mothers' allowances to mothers whose husbands had decamped or died and who had no means of support. But to qualify, they had to prove to the eye of the visiting social worker that they were "deserving": clean, sober, and chaste.

Talk of contraception continued to be taboo, though many women found the information they needed from birth control advocates and women's rights campaigners. Especially in the Depression years, when adding another mouth to feed could be disastrous, it was increasingly important to prevent pregnancy.

For one Canadian woman, lack of effective contraception meant a virtual end to her marriage. "I lost twin boys in a 5 month miscarriage," she wrote to birth control advocate Margaret Sanger

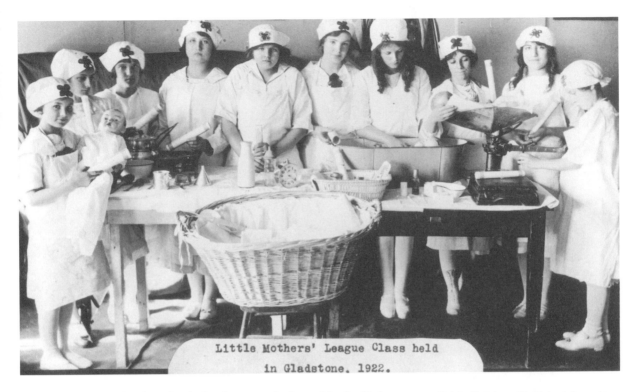

Little Mothers' League Class held
in Gladstone. 1922.

in May of 1927, pleading for help. "17 months later I had a little girl who died of pneumonia when 24 days old. In 15 months I had a 6 pound boy who came at 8 months. He got jaundice and died when 6 days old." She then had a boy who survived despite early jaundice. To her horror, she got pregnant again and delivered a handicapped child who died. She then suffered a series of health problems herself. Her only solution, unless Sanger could suggest an absolutely sure contraceptive: living apart from her husband. "I know I would never survive another pregnancy. Can you help me? Oh can You?"[20]

Girls in Gladstone, Manitoba, take part in the Little Mothers' League in 1922, learning the skills and information that motherhood will require of them. (Manitoba Archives N9342.)

❧ THE WIFE ❧

Young girls longed for it, older women gloried in it, those without it were pitied as spinsters and old maids. As ever, marriage was considered the norm in Canadian society between the wars. Through advertising and advice, girls and women were drawn a roadmap of the route to the wedding—and beyond.

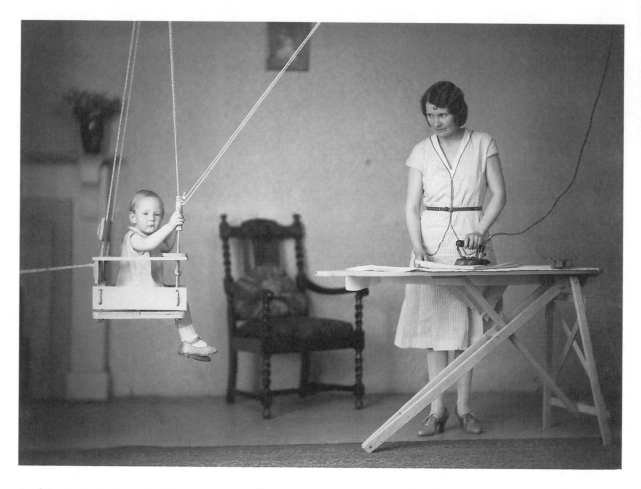

Carefully placed out of reach of a hot iron, an Edmonton child sits in an indoor swing while his mother tends to household chores. (Glenbow Archives ND-3-5802.)

For, once you were married, whatever went wrong with the marriage was the wife's fault. When runs in her stockings threatened to ruin her husband's budget, a wife could save her marriage by switching her laundry soap. If her husband looked askance at her sagging skin, she could rescue the relationship with a new toilet soap. Wives were reminded they were in a beauty contest every day of their lives. Forget to wear makeup, deal with body odour, cover the grey in their hair, dress stylishly, or cook the right meals, and who could blame a husband for having a wandering eye?

It was part of a double standard for men and women. Men's eyes—and other parts of their bodies—might wander, but single girls were under heavy pressure to stay virginal and divorce was rarely an option. A wife was expected to be forbearing, putting up with her husband's moods and bending to his will. If at all possible, women should even take physical abuse in their stride, since they would find it very difficult to support themselves and their children outside of marriage and, in any case, they had probably brought on the slaps or punches by their whining or demands or failure to behave as a wife should.

The stress and poverty of the 1930s Depression years was particularly hard on some marriages; farm wives and the wives of the chronically unemployed bore the brunt of their husbands' disappointments. Some women could stand it no longer: they sued for divorce on the only grounds allowed them, adultery. By the mid-1920s, women no longer had to prove desertion as well. Yet divorce was not easy; only six provinces had divorce courts, and women in other provinces had to petition the federal government.

For all the difficulties and disasters, most marriages went well and most wives were more or less content with their lot, working as partners with their husbands to raise their children and sustain their marriages. In this era of wage-earning husbands, there was much advice for, and discussion of, spending and budgeting. Some husbands simply turned their paycheques over to their wives, got back a little for their own spending money, and expected their wives to pay the bills and buy the food and other necessities. Others did the banking and issued their wives with a household allowance that they used for the weekly shopping. These husbands might trust their wives to do their best—or they might demand a penny-by-penny accounting of all that was spent. In every case, though, the housewife was urged to be frugal, efficient, and careful. She must make the right use of resources, planning ahead so that the family would not always be broke.

"It isn't nearly so easy to be carried away by the salesman's stress on the wonderful ease of the easy payments," wrote *Chatelaine*'s "Family Purse" columnist, "if one gets the habit of putting things down in black and white."[21] The wife must, suggested the column, adjust her Packard tastes to a Ford income. Planning, listing, budgeting, being businesslike over the household accounts: that was the way to change the scorn the man-of-the-house usually felt for his wife's accounting inefficiency.

In case of separation, the wife still had no legal right to the farm where she lived with her husband and family. During the Depression, though, she certainly had an official role to play. In

You will want your husband to fall in love with you every day, as he will surely want you to fall in love with him. Of course, you can't always be dressed up, but you can try to be always clean and neat, and you can welcome him always with a smile that comes so easy now. You will be tired, at times, with the labors and cares of the day; sickness may come upon you, and there may be days when the path will seem rough and hard; your purse may seem light; even the little comforts and luxuries of life which, perhaps, seem commonplace today, may be lacking; even the sting of poverty may be felt. If you have a true companionship with the man you love — a companionship grounded in mutual understanding and devotion and self-sacrifice — you will find yourself strong in the day of battle; and, what is of more importance, you will prove a source of strength and courage and inspiration to him in his conflict with the world. This is true marriage.

— Alfred Henry Tyrer, *Sex, Satisfaction and Happy Marriage*, as quoted on http://archive.salon.com/mwt/feature/1999/11/17/then/.

Though most housewives fought the Depression's woes with all the strength they possessed, some gave up:

She had just completed the hanging of Christmas decorations in her little home. Then with the home bravely adorned and spotlessly clean, she strangled one child, drowned the other in the bath, and killed herself by drinking a powerful germicide. There had not even been enough money in the house to buy the poison that killed her. She left a farewell note on the kitchen table bearing this out. "I owe the drug store 44 cents; farewell," it said.

— *Winnipeg Free Press*, December 18, 1933.

Many wives took on extra work in the Depression, trying to make a little cash to help out in the household. Else Seel, homesteading with her husband and children in northwestern British Columbia, helped out on their beaver farm, doing most of the work while her husband was out trapping or prospecting:

I toiled to feed the beavers, sank above my thighs in the snow, shoveled the door free and a path to the beaver-lodges, and dragged poplar trees over to the beaver-tank, sweat broke out all over me because of the effort, and tears ran down my cheeks, but they froze in the bitter cold. That made me realize how senseless it was to cry.

— Seel papers, *The Last Pioneer: My Canadian Diary*.

Ontario, for example, when a husband applied for a loan to keep the family farm going, inspectors were sent to check out the farm. A thrifty housewife, said the chairman of the Ontario Agricultural Development Board, was an excellent asset and often worth more than good stock or good equipment—or even a hard-working husband. "They make certain of ascertaining whether or not the housewife is thrifty," he noted of his inspectors.[22]

Sex was, as ever, an essential part of marriage. By the mid-1930s, attitudes to sex were slowly changing, as marriage manuals provided more complex advice. In 1936, the Marriage Welfare Bureau of Toronto published *Sex, Satisfaction and Birth-Control*, by the Rev. Alfred Henry Tyrer, revealing a degree of openness about sexual satisfaction in marriage. Who could doubt it when the T. Eaton catalogue the following year had an entire category for "Health and Sex Books"? Even masturbation and positions other than the missionary position were suggested as normal sexual activity.

Not that every married woman in Canada—for the books were very pointedly addressed to married folk—read and understood the manuals. Women wrote letters to advice columns, saying how little they knew of sex and pregnancy, and what they did know was probably garnered from friends and husbands, not from books. Advertisers were eager to help here as well. When she was too tired to go out because of inertia and premature aging caused by misunderstanding of the facts about feminine hygiene, a wife could solve her problems by douching with Lysol.

Zonite, a douche (though the ad never said so), claimed to be the very best for feminine hygiene. There was a need for scientific up-to-date facts on the subject, and "thousands who supposed they were using the best antiseptic for feminine hygiene have invariably been grateful for the knowledge that science has at last produced something better and absolutely safe as well."[23] No need, said the ad, to use powerful chemicals such as bichloride of mercury and carbolic acid, for if these products were not diluted, they could scar and poison, and if they were diluted, they were ineffective.

The discreet small print advised women to write for a booklet and talk to their doctors. What the ads didn't say was that products such as this were also meant to prevent pregnancy. Increasingly, mothers—and fathers—considered limiting their families to the children they could support without sliding into poverty. Though giving out information on contraceptives was still illegal, "rubber goods" were available at most pharmacies, wives traded information on pessaries or diaphragms—though these were too expensive for many women—and churches and court officers argued over whether allowing contraception would challenge the traditional authority of the husband as head of the household. Give a woman control over her own body, the argument went, and who knows where it will all end up?

Some voices suggested it would end up very well indeed. The Depression spurred organizations as different as branches of the United Farm Women, the National Council of Jewish Women, and the United Church to petition for legal birth control. Though these and other campaigns would not succeed officially until 1969, information and methods of birth control became more widely available in the 1930s.

◇◇◇

If your husband is spending the greater part of his evenings outside the home, you had better look for the cause, before it is too late. You will probably find that he is growing tired of your cold, indifferent, unsympathetic sexual nature and that you no longer stimulate the love side of his life as you did in days of yore. Or it may be that you are becoming careless as regards dress—especially morning apparel.

I would advise any woman faced with the problem to buy the most alluring house dresses and most charming negligee she can afford. Gay, dainty flimsy garments do not cost much if made at home.

— Georgina Sackville, typewritten manuscript, *Birth Control or Prevention of Conception*.

• 7 •

RATION BOOKS AND KNITTING SOCKS:

Housewives on the Home Front

They need warm clothes. They need woollen caps to fit under their steel helmets, warm sweaters to fight the damp and chill of long nights under bomb-fire. . . . They need clothing of all kinds. Will the women of Canada help? Can you sew? Can you knit? Do you want to help the gallant women of Britain? . . . Will you set aside a definite time each day during the long summer days and evenings to knit or sew for these men and women who need what you can send them so much? . . . The call has come direct to Canadian women! Let Canadian women send such a stream of warm clothing and comforts as has never been seen before in history!

—Byrne Hope Sanders, Chatelaine *editor, June 1941*

Knit for Canada, save food for Canada, work for Canada, save scrap for Canada. For most of the years 1939 through 1945, Canadian women were exhorted to be part of Canada's war effort. As thousands of men—and not a few women—poured onto battlefields and into army camps in Europe and the Far East, women discovered hidden talents and strengths and provided support and sustenance on the home front. They took jobs in war industries and replaced workers in offices and factories. They volunteered for the war effort in a thousand different ways. They watched husbands and sons leave home for war, and laboured at home under wartime regulations and housing shortages. They entered hasty marriages as men departed for the battlefield; they saw those marriages fall apart when the men returned—or before. For many, war brought the most serious change of all: the death of a husband or son.

For housewives on the home front, the war meant rationing, taking in boarders, learning to look after family chores that had previously been in their husbands' domain, and, if their husbands were overseas, developing a new social life. Though married women were never required to go out to work, many did and fought a constant battle to do their work and look after their children. The lessons they, and the hundreds of thousands of single women, learned in the war would have reverberations in the feminism of the 1960s.

As they had before the war, advertisers targeted housewives—but now their job was more difficult in the face of a shortage of goods and government injunctions to save, not spend. Manufacturing plants that were making guns or shells or ships couldn't produce refrigerators or stoves; food companies couldn't laud what wasn't

Help win the war with frilly apron and wooden spoon instead of a rifle: Canada's advertisers plugged their products with war-themed campaigns. This high-heeled housewife is encouraged to help the war effort by making nourishing meals. (Canada Starch Company advertisement, 1940s)

Home-front slogans on posters and in advertisements:

Roll out the rubber. Every ounce of scrap rubber is needed for our mobile forces. Get in the scrap.

Save waste bones; they make glue for aircraft, and are used for explosives. Get in touch with your local committee.

We're in the army now. Your aid is vital! Save metals, rags, paper, bones, rubber, glass; they are used in war supplies.

When troops move, keep tongues still! Don't gossip!

on the shelves. Just wait till the war is over, the advertisers told housewives: then you will have your new stove; then choice will return to grocery shelves. Take care of your old and chipped dishes; when the war is over, we'll have beautiful new china patterns ready for you. Many advertisers tied their ads to the war: "In wartime, eat one more slice of bread per meal," advised an ad for yeast. "¼ of Canada's wartime energy comes from bread."[1] Other ads lauded household cleaners or floor coverings that made housekeeping less time-consuming, leaving more time for work to support the war effort.

As families moved to cities with war-related industries, the housing shortage could be acute. In some cities, prefabricated houses were thrown up in a week or less. This Vancouver effort was built in a day; the housewife greets furniture movers at the door. (Harry Rowed, National Film Board of Canada, Library and Archives Canada PA-116137)

Governments saw housewives as volunteer home-front campaigners, recruiting them to monitor prices and report shopkeepers who overcharged. They weren't all angels: though government officials battled black marketeers, not a few housewives took advantage of the black market. There was always someone who knew where you could get a better cut of meat or a little extra butter—if you were willing to pay for it and able to deal with your own conscience. If not, magazines, newspapers, and the government itself helped out with pages of ideas for making do with what you had and recipes and hints for preparing nutritious and attractive meals despite food shortages.

~+ THE COOK ~+

Half a pint of milk a day—more than a pint for children. Some cheese as available. A serving of tomatoes or a citrus fruit, or their juices, and a serving of other fruits, fresh, canned, or dried, each day. A daily serving of potatoes and two of other vegetables. A daily serving of meat, fish, or substitutes; liver, heart, or kidney once a week. At least three or four eggs a week. For the first time, in 1942, Canadians had official directions on what to eat. This first edition of Canada's Food Rules was part of a national nutrition campaign that had housewives in its sights.

"Canada's housekeepers are in the forefront of this war against malnutrition," declared the campaign leaders. "We must put our kitchens into the fight and take up our action stations on this vital front to arm the nation with vim, vigor and vitality."[2]

To fight this war, housewives had to do more with less. Rationing began in 1941 as Canada sent food and other materials overseas and received less imported food. By 1943, each adult received coupons for half a pound of sugar per week; two pounds of meat,

THIS IS MRS. BAKER. OCCUPATION: HOUSEWIFE. She has two children and the best husband in the world. He pays the taxes and the rent and gives her the housekeeping money every week.

She buys food and clothes and things like that. So there's not much left by Friday.

Just pin money, really!

She told the Victory Bond salesman, "I could never save enough out of my money to make any difference. Mr. Baker takes care of that downtown."

BUT MRS. BAKER…Did you know that you, and all the Canadian housewives like you, every week spend…

More than Ten Million dollars for food?

Four million dollars for clothes?

A million and a half dollars in drug stores?

If every housewife in Canada saves just one cent out of every dollar she spends…Then the housewife alone would buy enough Victory Bonds every month to pay for two corvettes to sweep the seas and guard the

lifeline that carries supplies to their husbands and sons and brothers in the battle line!

So, Mrs. Baker, won't you help this time by saving your pin money and putting it into instalments on a Victory Bond of your own?

You'll be surprised how good it will make you feel.

— Victory Bond advertisement sponsored by the Kellogg Company of Canada Limited, Toronto *Globe and Mail*, May 4, 1943.

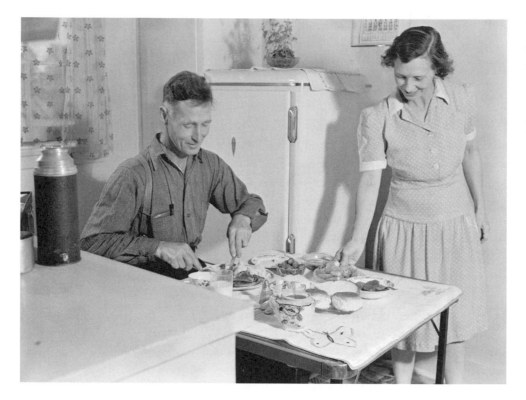

The housewife should keep her man happy so he can work hard to help win the war. This Vancouver woman has prepared a good dinner and has the thermos ready for her husband, who is headed for the night shift at the shipyard. Whether or not she normally ate with her husband, the photographer has posed her as serving him. (National Film Board of Canada, Library and Archives Canada PA-145667)

carcass weight—with a good proportion of that cheaper cuts; half a pound of butter; an ounce of tea; and four ounces of coffee. There were also shortages of cheese and certain types of canned food. Especially if she worked outside the home, the housewife had more money now than in the Depression, but less to spend it on.

Magazines and newspapers and government publications gave budgeting advice and printed economical recipes. "Use your cook stove to cook Hitler's Goose," suggested the headline on an article that based four days of menus on the new Canada Food Rules.[3] Some injunctions had a decidedly modern flavour. "Some of our old ways have been proven wrong by scientific discoveries about how to buy and cook," a *Maclean's* writer opined in 1942, outlining the "new cooking." The article suggested that, since freshness was good, housewives should not buy a lot of vegetables and keep them in the fridge; that they should cook vegetables in as little water as possible, and save that liquid for gravies and stews; that vegetables shouldn't stand peeled in water and that they should be cooked quickly, since slow cooking took its toll in colour, flavour, and food value.[4]

One way of dealing with shortages of produce was to grow your own. Copying a British program, Canadians planted Victory Gardens, growing vegetables for themselves and for others on any spare piece of ground—a job that sometimes fell to older men and sometimes to housewives. Women's Institutes supplied economical recipes to be distributed to the general public and women's groups across the country stopped serving food at their meetings, to set an example in food conservation.

Housewives helped fill shortages overseas. An amazing campaign saw volunteers fill thousands of jars and tins with jam in city and country kitchens. The Women's Institutes of British Columbia, for example, made and sent overseas some 325,000 pounds of jam, 1,300 parcels and boxes of food, and half a ton of canned fruits and vegetables. The Point Grey Women's Institute opened and tested every four-pound tin and dispatched the jam to Britain.[5]

RECIPES

TOASTAROONS

6 cups cornflakes

1 can (14–15 ounces) condensed milk

Preheat oven to 325°F and grease a baking sheet. Combine the cornflakes and condensed milk, mixing lightly. Drop by teaspoons onto the greased baking sheet, and flatten slightly, shaping the edges with a spoon. Bake for 12-15 minutes. Remove from the baking sheet immediately, using a knife or spatula. If the cookies stick, place the baking sheet over very low heat for a few seconds.

— Devonna Edwards, *Wartime Recipes from the Maritimes, 1939–1945*, p. 75.

The same page that carried the recipe below also included a recipe for fish and chips as an out-of-the-ordinary party dish, the "poor man's feast."

How to s-t-r-e-t-c-h your salmon ration. The supply of Clover Leaf is limited…it is rationed so that everyone may have an equal opportunity to purchase their share.

SALMON SOUFFLÉ

2 eggs, separated

½ cup milk

½ pound can Clover Leaf Salmon

½ teaspoon salt

½ tbs. finely-chopped parsley

¼ teaspoon pepper

2 stalks finely-chopped celery

Flake salmon, add seasoning, parsley and celery. Beat egg yolks until light and fluffy, add milk. Beat egg whites stiffly then fold into egg yolk mixture. Carefully fold in salmon mixture. Turn into well-greased baking dish, cover and place in pan hot water. Bake in moderately slow oven, 325 F. 40 to 50 minutes. Serves 5.

— *Halifax Herald*, February 28, 1944.

No husband here to do his chores? Don't sit down and cry; do them yourself. With their husbands fighting overseas, women learned to do tasks formerly in the male realm. This housewife fills the humidifying pan on her coal furnace. (National Film Board of Canada, Library and Archives Canada PA-108029)

During the war, Kate Aitken, the best-known voice of the Canadian homemaker from the 1930s through the 1950s, wrote a pamphlet on feeding a family of five in wartime on $12.50 a week, with menus and recipes for every meal of the week. The following is the grocery order for the meals, including everything except condiments, jams, and preserves, which the housewife already had in her fruit cupboard:

16 quarts milk	$2.08	1 bottle of apple cider	.17	2 doz. eggs	.78
1 lb. Canadian cheese	45	5 grapefruit	.25	6 oranges	.20
3 ¼ lbs. butter	1.27	6 lemons	.11	3 ¾ lb. sugar	.30
15 lbs. potatoes	.40	6 quart basket baking apples	.59	4 lbs. chuck roast	1.00
22 lbs. fresh vegetables	.63	1 lb. prunes	.14	2 lbs. flank steak	.50
1 lb. lima beans	.14	½ lb. dates	.05	2 lbs. chuck steak	.50
1 lb. split peas	.15	½ lb. raisins	.04	1 shoulder pork	.32
2 cans tomatoes	.23	1 lb. shortening	.19	1 lb. tin pink salmon	.18
1 can peas	.11	7 lbs. cereal and flour	.29	1 lb sausages	.30
1 can tomato soup	.09	⅓ lb. tea	.25	1 ½ lbs. liver	.23
1 large can tomato juice	.10	⅓ lb. coffee	.15		
1 large can apple juice	.19	¼ lb cocoa	.11		$12.49

— *Feeding Your Family in Wartime*, p. 16.

The Housekeeper
and the
Laundress

With outside work and volunteer efforts occupying her days, the wartime housewife needed to use her time wisely when it came to cleaning house and doing laundry. She also needed to pay attention to recycling: she was expected to save everything she couldn't use, be it fat, bones, or metal, and turn it in at scrap drives or to garbage collectors.

Before the war, much of Canada's supply of vegetable oil had come from the Far East. The war put an end to that, and substitutes were sought. "Out of the Frying Pan, into the Firing Line," read one appeal for fat that could be used for making soap or for commercial baking. Bones could be used for airplane glue and fertilizer. Rubber was in short supply, so even bathing caps were recycled. Waste paper could be used for many wartime purposes, even paper parachutes to carry food to isolated members of the armed forces.

An advantage of the war for those who hated housekeeping was a somewhat relaxed standard, especially if a woman was working outside the home: immaculate floors and carefully dusted knick-knacks were less important when bombs were raining down overseas. Save time and energy with appliances, suggested ads early in the war: an electric iron, an electric refrigerator, an electric washer, all made life so much easier for the housewife. But, as the war continued, there were no new appliances to be had, and it was harder and harder to repair old ones. With a shortage of aluminum—most was used for building airplanes—pots and pans were also in short supply, so the housekeeper had to look after the ones she had.

With accommodation increasingly scarce anywhere that men worked in war industries, the government encouraged women to take in boarders, to fill that spare room, and give a man—or even

Simplified housekeeping is a "must" with women on the home front. A full-time war job or voluntary services in hospital, Red Cross or other vital work takes precedence over housework. With Linoleum floors to slash hours from her housecleaning schedule, today's busy housewife can still find time to handle both home and war work capably.

— 1943 advertisement for linoleum, as quoted in Jean Bruce, *Back the Attack*, p. 121.

Space was at a premium in any town or city where war production occurred. A Kingston, Ontario, woman deals with cramped conditions in a rented apartment. (National Film Board of Canada, Library and Archives Canada PA-142398)

a man and his family—a chance. Many housewives cooked, cleaned, and laundered for their boarders as well as for their own families. At least the extra work brought extra food and income, as boarders contributed a ration book and money to the household.

ᚷ THE SEAMSTRESS ᚷ

Want cuffs on your pants? No, sir. A long dress? Not a chance. And heaven forbid that you might want decorative pockets or frills. Canada needed huge amounts of fabric for military uniforms, so fabric mills and garment factories turned to the task of making suitable cloth and turning it into uniforms. Ready-made clothing for civilians was restricted to a narrower range of sizes and colours, and, as in other parts of their lives, women were asked to make do.

Though she no longer had her house, life still had to go on for the housewife in the internment camps of British Columbia, where Japanese Canadians were imprisoned from 1942 to 1945. An unnamed woman does the family washing at one such camp. The official caption reads, "Space-saving community washroom with staggered washing hours are a feature of each camp," an official attempt to make the camps seem bright and modern. (Jack Long, National Film Board of Canada, Library and Archives Canada C-067496)

Early in 1943, the wartime prices board that regulated supply and prices of consumer goods announced a new campaign against waste. "We will have people demonstrating how easy it is to make over an old garment taken out of an attic or trunk, into something smart and useful for the children," a board spokesman declared. "It really is surprising how good your wife can look in a suit made over in 1943 from a 1914 tuxedo."[6] At the same time, the various companies that made sewing patterns pooled their resources to produce simpler wartime patterns, and new garments made from old were taken on a multi-city exhibition tour.

Housewives did what housewives had always done: improvised. They made over children's clothes or passed them on to younger children. They darned holes, turned sheets side to middle, and

The village women came to make things to send to England. There was the blacksmith's wife, and the village handyman's wife. Poor people are so much more inventive; they know how to make things over.

We had a big roll of cotton to make diapers for English children, and the roll was too wide. There was eight inches or more to spare on the side. And do you know, we made children's pyjamas out of those eight-inch strips, piecing them together.

— woman from Thornhill, Ontario, in an interview with Jean Bruce in *Back the Attack*, p. 3.

Don't buy new; re-use, recycle. Children model clothes that have been made over to save on fabric in the Re-Make Review, staged by the Wartime Prices and Trade Board in Toronto in 1945. (Ontario Archives 10002721, C 5-1-0-101-10)

rejuvenated old and tired dresses with new trim from some other piece of clothing. It's doubtful, though, whether many women heeded the prices board suggestion to make dresses from old table linen or aprons from worn-out men's shirts.

Housewifely skills were called upon in making things for Canada's troops overseas and people in Britain. Across the country, church guilds, Red Cross groups, Women's Institutes, women's auxiliaries, and neighbourhood groups met to knit and sew. The United Church alone saw 60,000 volunteers produce 267,372 pairs of socks, 50,223 sweaters, 18,522 pairs of wristlets, 33,275 scarves, and 22,024 pairs of gloves and mittens in the one year of 1940.

Some companies provided wartime daycare for the mothers who did war work. These girls are learning early how to be housewives and mothers at the General Engineering Company munitions factory in Scarborough, Ontario. (Ontario Archives, 100004936, F 2082-1-2-12)

꿍

THE MOTHER
AND THE NURSE

꿍

Being a mother didn't get any easier during the war. If you were working outside the home, it actually became more difficult, because you had to deal with the question of what to do with the children. Especially in Quebec, the church and politicians railed against working mothers. Serious articles bemoaned the latchkey kids—a term first used during the war to describe children whose mothers were not there when the kids came home from school.

Knowing the importance of daycare for working women, the federal government offered to pay for day nurseries for women in war work. Only Ontario and Quebec took them up on the offer, but neither province came anywhere near to filling the need. Some factories started daycare centres for their employees. Newspapers reported that a few mothers left their very young children alone in the car or at home while they worked or played. But most working women whose husbands were overseas moved back home with parents, left children with relatives, or paid someone to look after the children. Women who stayed home were still exhorted to see their doctor as soon as they became pregnant and to plan with him—almost all doctors were male—their care and nutrition throughout pregnancy and when the baby came. "A nation's babies are its strongest link with the future," a magazine article declared, citing the fact that one baby in 17 died. "To provide the best of care for expectant mothers is no extravagance. It can't be put off until after the war."[7] If some women couldn't afford to do this, the article suggested other women should try to help, individually or through their organizations.

A major problem for families was the lack of decent accommodation at a reasonable price. As families moved to cities for work in war industries, existing accommodation was soon exhausted. Story after story told of families living in inadequate housing: a family of three in a hotel room they couldn't afford, a family of 12 in four small rooms with the children sleeping five to a bed, families

The war changed women's roles—though not forever. Two married women cement 25-pounder shells at a factory in Montreal. (Harry Rowed, National Film Board of Canada, Library and Archives Canada PA-116925)

turned out by landlords or made to pay extra or unable to afford coal for heating. Though the government instituted rent controls and began to build wartime housing, the problem remained acute.

❧ THE WIFE ❧

The wife whose husband was serving overseas—or absent doing other war work—entered new territory, for she felt neither married nor single. Things that her husband had done, from tending the furnace to going to the bank, were now her jobs. Used to depending on her husband for companionship, she now had a choice of being lonely or of finding new companions. She had to be a single parent, but one who still tried to do things as her husband would wish. Those whose husbands were killed in the war needed to take on a variety of roles for the foreseeable future.

This was my first experience of being alone, and I saw the house in a completely different way. Areas which had been completely male, like the furnace room, like the hot-water tank, like the garage, became my domain, my responsibility....I had never carried on the day-to-day financing, paying the coal bills, the electricity bills, the taxes....I found you could still go to symphony concerts, that a woman didn't need an escort to go out....It was the first sharing of my life with women, finding the depth of companionship that there is in a woman-to-woman relationship, and how supportive that relationship can be.

—Jean Bruce, *Back the Attack*, interview with a Winnipeg woman, p. 17.

As the end of the war approached, commentators debated the future role of married women:

If a married woman with means of support is crazy enough to want to earn a living—let her go to it!

But I do not believe many woman will want to keep on with the daily grind of earning a living after the war, when their men are home to do it for them. I do not believe that any woman really likes to dig out of her home, be it ever so humble, morning after morning, and spend the rest of the day in the business world, being bossed around by someone else. She'd much rather be home where she can do some first-class bossing herself.

— Radio commentator Claire Wallace in the Canadian Women's Press Club *Newspacket*, November 1944, as quoted in Jean Bruce, *Back the Attack*, p. 169.

Many married women relied on the companionship of other women in similar circumstances, going to movies or other entertainment together. Some, though, emboldened or embittered by the absence of their husbands or the thought that those husbands were enjoying themselves with women overseas, had their own flings with single men or Allied troops in Canada for training. Still lacking reliable birth control, some who played also paid: men who came home after months overseas walked away from wives who had had affairs or other men's children.

For wives in unhappy marriages, working outside the home provided an escape and a chance to make money of their own. Though commentators repeatedly stressed that the situation was only temporary, that after the war women could return to their appointed role as housewives and mothers, many relished the chance to prove themselves in factories and offices. "I didn't mind how dirty, how filthy it was, it was just great. It was a release from a marriage that was no good," commented one.[8]

Farm wives whose husbands were away had to work even harder to accomplish the farm routine, taking on the jobs that their husbands had done. Driving the tractor, hauling water, getting crops to market, and being alone in winter storms taxed farm wives. Some were able to hire help, but the help rarely seemed to be as reliable or as efficient as their husbands had been.

Housewives were urged not to take their men, absent or present, for granted. If he is home, remember that marriage comes first: work for victory, but keep your hands soft and attractive with hand lotion—and make sure those remade clothes are pretty and alluring. If he is away, write letters that remind him of you and the children in a positive, not a nagging, way. Make sure you can compete with those attractive women he is meeting "over there." "Do you study to hold that man 5,000 miles away?"[9] they were asked—and they knew that the answer had better be "yes."

Being alone with a husband overseas was difficult; having him come home might be even more so. Children who were babies when he left were toddlers who didn't know their daddy when he returned. Women who were used to making the family decisions themselves often found it difficult to return to a subordinate role. And men who had seen horrendous sights in battle, or who had got used to constant action and heroics, found it difficult to return to civilian life. For wife and husband both, postwar would be a difficult time.

———————————————————————————————————————

The only answer men can give as a solution to industrial problems is: let the women go back home and then the men will have plenty of work to do. "We need more children; let the women fulfill their role by bearing more children. That's all they have to do."....It's not right that one half the human race should live under the dictatorship of the other half....Let women work. Let there be no barriers against them because of their sex. First and foremost, they are citizens, neither superior nor inferior to men....The old grey-beards won't have to worry about the declining birth rate if they will do a little progressive thinking and take some progressive action.

— Saskatchewan journalist Dora Dibney, in the *Newspacket*, August 1944, as quoted in Jean Bruce, *Back the Attack*, p. 173.

· 8 ·

MIRACLE FABRICS AND MARSHMALLOW SALADS:

Housewives in the '50s

Which profession would you say requires the most personality or versatility? I would nominate the humble housewife. To be successful, she must be a dietitian as well as a cook, to preserve the health of her family. Speaking of health, she is one nurse who doesn't stop at an eight-hour day! She must keep her home neat and clean, be a social secretary, bookkeeper and economist, for women do most of the saving as well as the spending. She must be an expert seamstress as well as an interior decorator. She is still the reliable laundry where Dad can send his shirts and get them back in less than a month. Sometimes, too, she's the family painter, gardener and chauffeur. If there are children, her responsibilities are multiplied. She must then be teacher and psychologist, and sometimes judge and jury. . . . The amazing thing is that so many women do all this and even find time to develop special talents and interests. And so, hats off to "the Humble Housewife."

—Toronto Globe and Mail, *May 20, 1946*

After the war was over, Canadians yearned for prosperity, normalcy, home life. The 1950s fulfilled those yearnings. Incomes rose steadily, women left the work world to stay home with their families, the birth rate increased in a postwar baby boom, vast numbers of immigrants—most from Europe—boosted the population, and householders filled suburbs of new houses with labour-saving appliances. Yet just behind the technological changes, the renewed emphasis on home, and the baby boom came a vigorous social rebellion that changed women's lives. The 1950s were the last decade when the full-time, lifetime housewife was the norm. They also marked a transition from traditional Canada: the 1951 and 1961 censuses showed Canadians of British origin steadily losing ground to Canadians whose origins lay elsewhere.

One million women worked outside the home during the war. When the war ended, war industries shut down, and 750,000 demobilized servicemen went looking for jobs. Polls suggested that men and women alike thought men should have preference for employment. Government, manufacturers, advertisers, and many commentators, male and female, encouraged women to return to their roles as housewives and mothers. The excitement of wartime employment was over: "help wanted, female" columns no longer called for welders or mechanics, but for clerks and secretaries. Most women went home willingly, trading the tumult of the war for the normalcy of home and family.

Some who stayed in the workforce looked down on those who returned home. In 1950, a working woman poured scorn on housewives. "You can't say: 'She is a housewife, so she is blond.' You can't say: 'She is a housewife, so she is fat.' You can't even say:

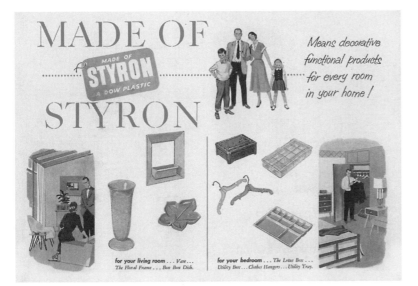

Plastics were everywhere, making families happy, in postwar Canada. (*Chatelaine*, September 1952)

'She is a housewife, so she is a good cook.' But nine times out of 10 you can say: 'She is a housewife, so she is unhappy,'" wrote Beverly Gray in a sweeping condemnation of housewives in the March 1950, issue of *Chatelaine* magazine.

The modern housewife, wrote Gray, was miserable, frustrated, underprivileged, abused, and oppressed—at least in her own mind. "Chat with any housewife for five minutes, and she will tell you how she suffers." Her complaints of poverty, loneliness, and drudgery were not valid. Her mental development stopped the day she married and her life was confined to a narrow domestic tunnel.[1]

Not surprisingly, Gray's diatribe—simplistic, one-sided, and surely intended to create a backlash—brought forth much angry and thoughtful commentary from housewives across Canada. *Chatelaine* received more than 500 letters of dissent.

"Miss Gray is guilty of the most sweeping generalizations," wrote one observer. "She takes a few of the most unattractive human emotions—frustration, envy, suspicion, discontent and laziness, and she has landed them squarely in the housewife's lap. She has allowed for no individual talents or virtues, condemning in one sweep every woman who dares possess husband, hearth and home."

Who volunteers for every charitable organization, asked the letter writers? And what husband prefers theories on Russia and future war to a fresh-baked lemon meringue pie? "In my opinion,"

Chatelaine, July 1946, defines the essential housewife—and, despite the fact that the native woman is and does all these things, quickly eliminates her from consideration:

A housewife in Yellowknife is just like you or me or your Aunt Susie. She has to get three meals a day, make beds, wash dishes, keep her husband well fed and in good humor, and have babies.

To be honest about it, there are no original housewives in this far land, unless you would like to call a native Indian woman at the door of her shack, a housewife.

— Edna Jacques, "Housewives of Yellowknife," p. 81.

The magazine advertisers' council told housewives they could depend on companies that advertised to make their lives happier and more efficient. (*Chatelaine*, September 1952)

Victoria—Women should take more interest in world affairs, says Vera Britain, the distinguished British writer. "Most women these days are as intelligent as the men and should not be content to stay buried at home," she said in an address here. 'They seem to be anaesthetized—you might say stupefied—by little domestic details. They should run for political office and things like that. Children and a husband all have their place, but housewives should follow what's going on around them locally and on an international basis."

— Toronto *Globe and Mail*, April 13, 1959.

"I wish I could press a button and the housework would be done!"

wrote another, "the term housewife is outmoded. The next time the census man comes to the house and asks, 'Occupation?' I'm going to reply 'Homemaker,' or 'Nation Builder,' or 'The most important job in the world,' instead of answering meekly 'Housewife.'"[2]

After the Depression years of not being able to afford new appliances and improvements, after the war years when supply was very limited, housewives had more tools with which to do that "most important job." The postwar years promised vast numbers of refrigerators, stoves, vacuum cleaners, washing machines: all the technology that would make the housewife's lot easier. Every newspaper and magazine was stuffed with advertisements for labour-saving devices that would be available as soon as factories converted their assembly lines to peacetime production. Once the appliances began to arrive in stores, the emphasis was on saving time and energy. Hotpoint appliances were headlined "Breakfast Speeder" for the toaster, "Minute-Saver" for the electric kettle, "Comfort-Maker" for the heating pad, "Hour-Saver" for the featherweight electric iron, and "Leisure-Maker" for the vacuum cleaner.

In 1946, the *Canadian Home Journal* trumpeted a series of innovations that the author said would bring amazing war time developments in materials and technology to home use. A spin-dry washer still in the blueprint stage, for example, would do a family wash in less than an hour and an electric blanket with a brain was "built along the lines of the special suits so essential to high-altitude flying." A pressure cooker would cook a stew in 15 minutes, peas in 15 seconds.[3]

Throughout the 1950s, every new appliance, every new device was advertised as a way to make the housewife happier, more frugal, a better wife and mother. Speedy carefree cooking and penny-wise meal-making were the result if the family bought a Frigidaire, a Hotpoint, or a Westinghouse.

Postwar was also the age of plastics. Transparent, opaque, flexible, rigid, colourful, colourless, big, and small, things made of plastic were ubiquitous in the Canadian household by the end of the 1950s. Garbage bins, food storage containers, laundry hampers, blanket bags, even coleslaw shredders were made of plastic.

For many housewives, Tupperware was the pinnacle of plastic, affording them both versatile containers and an opportunity to get together with other women. Invented in 1945 by an American entrepreneur, the vacuum-sealing plastic containers came in a huge range of sizes and shapes and were sold at Tupperware parties, each organized by one neighbourhood woman—a hostess—who sold the containers to her friends and her friends' friends. These early home sales parties that began in the early 1950s signalled a wave of home-based sales businesses reliant on the housewife network.

This was the other face of the postwar Canadian housewife: above, signs at the Ontario legislature in 1946 to protest against high milk prices. (City of Toronto Archives, John H. Boyd, Fonds 1266, 108431)

Above right, working-class housewives crowd onto a train headed for Ottawa to protest rising prices. (*Canadian Tribune*, Library and Archives Canada PA-093685)

The parties gave women who stayed at home a chance to get together, something that was becoming more difficult as postwar housing went up in the new suburbs on the outskirts of growing cities, with rows of modern cookie-cutter houses and big backyards for the children to play in. Suburbia was very much a new concept for Canada; now that most families had cars, it was possible to design and build a residential area distant from public transportation and the workplace. The idea of separating homes from businesses even spilled over into small-town Canada, in places such as Kitimat, a 1950s-built model town in northwestern British Columbia. Such models were sometimes impractical: in Kitimat, for example, planners decided that housefronts should face green space rather than the street, an intriguing concept but one somewhat divorced from domestic reality. Where, asked the housewives, were they to put their clotheslines, in the "front" yard or in the backyard facing the street?

By the late 1950s, some were seriously questioning whether suburbia was a good thing, suggesting that it did not provide the variety of ethnic backgrounds, ages, and income levels that made a good community. An October 1958 *Chatelaine* article suggested that suburbia fostered a pointless race for more possessions of the latest kind and that it resulted in confused gender roles as women did the household chores more properly done by their husbands. The article provoked an avalanche of mail, almost evenly split for and against suburbia.

The suburbs certainly created a different milieu for the housewife. With the two-car family rare in the 1950s, the suburban housewife was usually at home for the day once her husband went off to work, with no easy access to shops or city amenities. Kaffe klatsches, telephones, and television replaced big-city bustle or small-town Main Street. By the mid-1950s, almost every household in the city, and many in rural areas, had a telephone, and women who in a previous era talked to their mothers or sisters or friends by walking next door or down the street—or just by turning around in the kitchen—connected by wire. The first television programs hit the airwaves in 1952; by 1954, almost a million Canadians owned television sets, and television broadcasting was available to about 60 percent of the population. The television set became the focus of many living rooms and the first TV dinners—roast turkey or pot pies—signalled an era of convenience food.

Not only the cities were changing. Almost all provinces conducted rural electrification drives that saw the number of households connected to electricity rise from less than half in 1946 to almost all except in very remote areas by 1960. Family income, not location, would now even more be the determining factor for the lifestyle of the housewife.

Though advertisers flooded the marketplace with paeans to consumer products, not all housewives were willing and obedient consumers. Fresh from serving with the Consumer Branch of the federal government during the war, some savvy housewives wanted to continue the fight. But, as with any other large group of people, there were different opinions on how to proceed. In the dark Depression days, left-wing housewives had formed the Housewives' Consumers Association (HCA), to fight against a capitalist system that they believed worked for the rich and hurt the poor. Now the HCA continued the battle for consumer rights.

In early 1947, the association organized housewives across Canada to protest prices that rose as wartime price ceilings were lifted. In April, western women sent a delegation to Parliament Hill to plead their cause. In May, in Montreal and Toronto, Saskatoon and Victoria, they talked of organizing a buyers' strike. Vancouver housewives declared a seven-day boycott of jam, marmalade, peanut butter, and canned fruit. Regina housewives paraded against high prices. In Winnipeg, women protested the prices of veal chops, round steaks, sirloin, side bacon, butter, shortening, bananas, and tomatoes. Edmonton housewives took the ultimate step of boycotting Mothers' Day, opposing gifts that would cost any more than in 1939. In June, some 100 housewives, representing groups across Canada, stormed into Ottawa with decorated rolling pins, demanding an audience with their members of Parliament.

My DREAMS are coming CLOSER all the time.... Naturally, buyers are not able to get everything they want the minute peacetime production starts. It takes some time to secure materials, set up machinery and produce a sufficient quantity of new Westinghouse appliances to permit nation-wide distribution. But your new Westinghouse Radio, Range, Refrigerator, Washing Machine and Table Appliances are "on the way". Your dreams of a modern Westinghouse electrical home are coming true.

— Westinghouse advertisement, *Canadian Home Journal*, December, 1945, p. 63.

But postwar was Cold War, the battle of capitalism against communism. The activities and left-wing connections of the HCA led some media and politicians to dub them Reds, and the RCMP investigated them. When Montreal police raided a party held by the far-left Labour Progressive group, supposedly for liquor sales violations, the newspapers noted that among the papers found in the briefcase belonging to the editor of a banned newspaper were "several press releases about to be distributed by the Toronto Housewives' Consumers Association."[4]

The Canadian Association of Consumers (CAC), an all-women organization formed in 1947 to speak for the Canadian housewife, led a more centrist campaign with advice to housewives not to be sucked into paying more than an item was worth.

Red or not, relevant or not, the housewives' price campaign was doomed. By the end of 1947, price controls had been torpedoed and the prices of such essentials as bread and milk were allowed to rise as the market dictated. The CAC grew, but the HCA slowly faded into oblivion.

"Mrs. Canadian Housewife" reads the caption on this picture taken in Ottawa in the early 1950s. With her child in her grocery cart, this woman marvels at the supply of cookies, canned peaches, salmon, and luncheon meat—even canned hamburgers. (Malak, Library and Archives Canada, PA-145867)

The CAC also led the campaign to make margarine a legal product. Since 1886, the manufacture and sale of margarine had been prohibited in Canada. Postwar, housewives and the CAC, plus would-be margarine manufacturers, battled to break the ban, citing the rising price of butter and the housewife's need for a cheaper substitute. They were successful—though the battle went all the way to the Supreme Court of Canada, and Quebec temporarily bowed to the dairy-farmers' lobby and prohibited the sale once more.

In many parts of Canada, though, margarine could not be coloured. Every housewife of that era recalls the squishing and squeezing, the thumping and rolling, to spread the little envelope of yellow colouring through white margarine. Housewives and the Institute of Edible Oil Foods were victorious here, too: coloured margarine was available in most of Canada by 1959. In 1961, the last ban, in Quebec, was lifted.

It was a small victory, one aided by powerful marketing from the margarine-makers. When housewives railed against trading stamps, they were less successful. These small stamps given for every purchase at specific stores, then pasted into a book to be redeemed—one day—for other products, brought forth a howl of condemnation. Trading stamps were an insult to housewives, said those opposed; they increased the cost of foods and added to the chores of housewives who must lick and paste. Letters to the editor and CAC campaigns notwithstanding, trading stamps were ruled to be legal, and a generation of housewives filled drawers with little books of green stamps.

In the late 1940s, writer Kate Aitken provided word pictures of housewives across the country in a series of articles about Mr. and Mrs. Canada published in the *Montreal Standard*. A woman in Saint John canned salmon and other food for her family in her kitchen; owned an electric refrigerator, washing machine, and iron; burned coal in the furnace year round as mornings were always cool; handled the household accounts; and paid her bills from the cash she put in her glass-fronted cabinet. A Prince Edward Island fox-farming family grew all their own vegetables in their garden and canned fruit and vegetables. In British Columbia, the family described had tea in the afternoon under the apple trees and ate homemade bread

I saw their houses, admired their taste, and heard that they spend hours doing leatherwork and bookbinding. I inquired if they read enormously and played the piano, but I rather gathered that when it is as dark as that all day they prefer to gather together and do handwork of various kinds....In my daily life, and that of most women, "choosing" plays an enormous part in one's leisure hours....These women have no choice at all of any kind. They have one small shop—the Hudson's Bay Store....For their food they have little choice: there are no eggs, no milk, except in tins—no fruit or vegetables, except, of course, in summer....They can write for things from Edmonton—but it takes a long while to come by water and it is expensive by air. They cannot choose their company either, and there is nowhere to go.

— "A Flying Visit to Far Northern Housewives in Canada, Where Women Have No Choice in Winter," *The Times*, September 8, 1955.

and fresh cake made with cream because of the shortage of short-ening. The wife made all her daughter's dresses. The family used sawdust for fuel in a stove that stayed lit day and night. An Alberta war bride was disappointed in the lack of children's clothing in Canada—her baby had to wear diapers made from one of her old silk vests. She cooked with soft coal and bathed her baby in a tin tub filled with rain water heated in the stove reservoir.

The Manitoba family kept adding onto or rebuilding their house: from two rooms in 1924, they had advanced to a six-room house with electric lights, stove, and fridge; hot and cold running water; a telephone; and central heating. The wife of a university professor in Saskatchewan employed a full-time maid while she was teaching, a cleaning woman once a week while she was not. She had an electric stove, washing machine, floor polisher, iron, toaster, and radio. She sewed overcoats, trousers, and suits for herself and her daughters, and everything was worn to the last thread before it was discarded. She had a garden, liked to serve lettuce or celery with meals, used more eggs than meat, lectured on childcare to home-makers, and, worthy of special note, did her housework in slacks.

A family in Sherbrooke, Quebec, lived in a 12-room house and rented out the top floor apartment; bought their furniture at auction and refinished it themselves; had a vegetable garden; and enjoyed electric lighting, an electric fridge and stove, a MixMaster, washing machine, and iron.

Aitken wrote about the Ontario family:

> Mrs. Strauss is a wonderful manager. Their garden puts in two hundred quarts of canned fruits and vegetables in the fruit cellar each year. She lays out her weekly menus and shopping list to the last penny; if, as last week, she has the odd fifty cents left over, it goes toward treats for the chil-dren. Kathe makes all their clothes, is teaching the twins and Rose Marie to sew and knit. The children, small as they are, hang and pick up their own clothes, wash the dishes, help with the shopping. Monday is a busy wash day with an average of 28 dresses on the line; they must all be ironed on Tuesday. Friday is another busy day, baking day; Kathe's average baking is five pies, a cake for Sunday, a batch of cookies and a fruit loaf.

From the moment the modern house-wife wakes up to the moment she goes to bed, electricity plays a big part in her life. It starts with morning coffee and throughout the day helps to light-en the burden of housework.... For the housewife electricity is a lifeline. With-out it she would be back to the days of the inefficient hand-scrubbing and polishing, the wood-burning stoves and the oil-lamps. Electric appliances today number over 60 different kinds and they can help make life as easy as we want it.

— Toronto *Globe and Mail*, February 6, 1958.

Immigrant traditions survived through food. These Calgarians work their way through the eight meatless dishes of a Ukrainian Christmas in 1954. (Glenbow Archives NA-5600-7498a)

The Strauss' enjoy a game of cards, play often with the upstairs tenants and other friends. They enjoy bingo but see few picture shows; Cyril bowls, summertime he gardens.

The Strauss' are good church people, good neighbors, good managers and good Canadians.[5]

❧ THE COOK ❧

Cooking still lay at the centre of the housewife's life. In 1953, writer and media personality Kate Aitken advised the new bride:

If anyone tells you that the old adage, "the way to a man's heart is through his stomach" is not true, don't believe them. No matter how charming you may be, no matter how fascinating your little housedresses and aprons are, no matter how much sterling silver flatware you got from your grandparents, the thing that really counts is that you should be immaculately clean, pleasant any hour of the day when your husband's around and produce good meals right on the dot when your husband is ready for them.[6]

These Manitoba Mennonites who gathered at the family table in 1955 were much more sombre. (Manitoba Archives N12963)

Aitken further told the new bride that there were only seven basic recipes in the world—a white sauce, homemade rolls, tea biscuits, light cake, plain pastry, cornstarch desserts, and salad dressing—and if she could master these seven, she was well on her way to a long and happy married life.

Slightly revised for the 1950s, Canada's Food Rules and meal recommendations still stuck with the old standbys. Breakfast was citrus fruit, whole grain cereal, bread, and perhaps an egg. Dinner, at noon or at night, was meat, fish, or poultry with potatoes, one other vegetable, and a fruit dessert. Supper or lunch included cheese, egg, or other protein, plus a vegetable and more bread. Children should drink milk at all meals.

Magazines and newspapers offered up reams of recipes and hints guaranteed to make the family smile even when rationing still ruled in the immediate postwar years. Add a few cloves to the fat when you're frying doughnuts; scatter some chopped onion, parsley, and lemon juice in diced ham fat over half a slice of ham when you can't afford a whole slice. Serve boiled cucumber topped with cheese sauce and bread crumbs or scalloped tomatoes made with crumbled shredded wheat cereal. As the 1950s wore on, housewives were introduced to a raft of innovations in the kitchen. "Just add water and stir" was becoming a household phrase; by 1959, half the

Does your husband yawn at the table? The things women have to put up with. Most husbands, nowadays, have stopped beating their wives, but what can be more agonizing to a sensitive soul than a man's boredom at meals? Yet, lady, there must be a reason. If your cooking and not your conversation is monotonous, that's easily fixed. Start using soups more often, with lighter, more varied dishes to follow. Heinz makes 18 varieties. You can serve a different one every day for three weeks. Use them in your cooking too, and strike some new flavours that will lift ordinary dishes out of the commonplace.

— from a Heinz Soup ad, *Canadian Home Journal*, June 1950, p. 35.

RECIPES

Pineapple and marshmallows were favourite ingredients for company dishes. This recipe comes from the *Labtec Cookbook*, compiled by members of the Saskatoon Academy of the Canadian Society of Laboratory Technologists in 1955, p. 45.

FRUIT MARSHMALLOW SALAD

1 ½ teaspoons gelatin
¼ cup water
¾ cup pineapple juice, heated
30 marshmallows
½ cup chopped almonds
½ cup grapes, pineapple
  or bananas cut up
15 cherries, cut in fours
½ pint whipped cream
2 egg whites

Soften gelatin in water for 5 minutes, dissolve in heated pineapple juice, cool. Whip, when well whipped add marshmallows, fruit and nuts. Fold in stiffly beaten egg whites and whipped cream. Mould. Keep in fridge. Serves 15.

— Joan Dave, Lethbridge, Alberta

Make your salad with Spork and you serve pure nourishment with not a smidgin of waste. Start with salad greens and tomato tossed in French dressing. That takes care of vitamins.

Now for the all-important proteins, Pile Spork, the delicious blend of luscious pork shoulder and tender lean beef, in the centre of your salad. It looks so attractive and it's easy to serve. Garnish with cheese and hard-boiled eggs for extra protein-green onion for extra vitamins."

— from an advertisement for Burns Spork, the *Halifax Chronicle-Herald*, Sept. 2, 1959.

Almost every 1950s housewife had a tuna fish casserole, usually made with cream of mushroom soup. Some were topped with potato chips; some, like this one from *Personality Cook Book*, published by Victoria's Emmanuel Baptist Church in 1955, used bread crumbs:

COMPANY CASSEROLE

1 6 oz. pkg egg noodles
dash of pepper
1 can cream mushroom soup
2 chopped hard-boiled eggs
1 c. milk
1 7 oz. can tuna fish
1 c. grated cheese
½ c. buttered crumbs

Heat oven to 350. Cook noodles in boiling salted water until tender. Empty soup in pan, add milk, stir and heat. Add cheese and stir until melted.

Combine noodles, pepper, eggs and tuna fish with sauce. Place in greased casserole. Sprinkle crumbs on top and bake 30 minutes.

CREAMED PEAS AND CELERY

1 No. 2 can peas
2 tablespoons flour
1 cup sliced celery
1 ½ cups milk
2 tablespoons butter
¾ teaspoon salt
Paprika

Cook celery in small amount of boiling salted water about 10 to 12 minutes until tender. Melt butter in saucepan; add flour; stir until well blended. Add milk slowly. Cook, stirring constantly, until mixture thickens. Drain peas and celery, reserving liquor for soup or vegetable juice cocktails; add to sauce; add salt; heat thoroughly. Serve in warmed vegetable dish or individual dishes. Sprinkle top lightly with paprika. Serves 6.

— from an advertisement for the American Can Company: "Wise Wife! Good Mother!…Smart Woman!… YOU CAN'T BEAT CANNED FOODS," *Canadian Home Journal*, March 1946, p. 69.

New vacuum cleaners were among the most appreciated appliances. (National Film Board of Canada, Library and Archives Canada PA 150867)

Women were learning to worry about their weight. Here are Wednesday's menus for the Trick or Treat Diet in the Toronto *Globe and Mail* "Why Grow Old?" column, October 13, 1959.

BREAKFAST

½ grapefruit

½ cup whole wheat flakes

2 teaspoons sugar

1 glass skim milk

Black coffee

LUNCHEON

1 cup consommé

2 scrambled eggs with one teaspoon of butter, and a dash of skim milk (cook in double boiler.)

1 piece toast

Tea with lemon or coffee black.

DINNER

4 ounces calves' liver, broiled with onions

½ cup of string beans with a few pieces of canned mushrooms, and two tablespoons skim milk, salt, and sprinkle with parmesan cheese.

½ cup brown rice

A medium fruit cup (fresh fruit or water packed canned). Just a teaspoonful of wine or liquor will give it zest.

cups of coffee served in Canadian homes were the instant variety. Instant potatoes, frozen orange juice, cake mixes, Minute Rice, Saran Wrap, Cheez Whiz, whipped cream substitutes in a can were all products of the 1940s and the 1950s. There were predictions of boneless turkey rolls, pre-fried bacon, and vacuum-packed fruit juices, and talk of a hot-air dryer to be installed on the shore of Hudson Bay to dehydrate seal meat for winter use by the Inuit.

Though the first McDonald's and Burger King outlets wouldn't open in Canada until the 1960s, Dairy Queen and Kentucky Fried Chicken opened in the 1950s, and chains like Vancouver's White Spot restaurants expanded, pointing the way to family dining out that was simpler, cheaper, and easier.

The modern home kitchen was soon available even in rural areas. The newspaper in Claresholm, Alberta, a small town in the ranchlands between Lethbridge and Alberta, was ecstatic in July of 1948 about a Massey-Harris model kitchen display travelling throughout southern Alberta. "It contains all the latest domestic conveniences to enable the farm wife to enjoy more leisure time and to lighten her household duties," said the newspaper writer, citing a coal-burning stove, deep-cooling unit, washing machine, powerful water pressure system, and electric cream separator. "All

Science was touted as the answer to a housewife's woes. A postwar housewife happily settles in to cleaning her sink with a wonder cleanser. (William B. Edwards, Library and Archives Canada PA-080774)

The man who first thought of a perpetual motion machine must have spent a lot of time observing a woman in her endless war on dirt. From washing dishes three times a day to the annual spring housecleaning, the everlasting fight goes on.

No one has yet found a way to turn housecleaning into play, but it needn't be a nerve-wracking chore that upsets the whole family and reduces mother to a mere shadow of her former self. Time spent in planning, on paper if that's a help, is time well spent in the resulting order and efficiency when you finally get down to business.

— "Housekeeping Ahead," *Chatelaine*, April 1946, p. 94.

the kitchen utilities were made by Massey Harris for the purpose of raising the standard of living on the farm to a level comparable to that of urban dwellers. . . . These appliances can be run on a rural electric line or on a farm lighting plant and are therefore within reach of all."[7]

Adding to the comfort were other innovations, such as radio and television. "Peeling potatoes to sweet music by Frankie or Bing is much more fun than just peeling potatoes," noted a *Chatelaine* columnist.[8]

❧ THE HOUSEKEEPER ❧

All the advances in household technology should have made it easier to keep the house clean and tidy—and, to some extent, they did. The 1950s housewife could use appliances and products that didn't

This unidentified woman and child were photographed for *Weekend Magazine* in Montreal in 1949. "I'm a housewife again," reads the caption—though the child doesn't seem too happy about the idea. (Andy Graetz, *Weekend Magazine*, Library and Archives Canada PA-115226)

Newspaper columnist Margaret Munnoch beseeches women to just say no to the whims of interior designers:

I am quite convinced that if all the accent cushions in Canada were put end to end, they would stretch, to put it patriotically, from sea to sea. I am equally convinced that it wouldn't really matter if they didn't. My point is that the accent cushion, the stock-in-trade of the interior decorator, has become symbolic of a deplorable state of affairs.

In an era that prides itself on simple, functional interior design, what possible purpose does the accent cushion serve? None. It is too small to fit behind your back, too large to stop the mouths of howling children, too hard to rest your head on and too bizarre to ignore. They say it adds sparkle to your room, but so would a piece of rock crystal—with the same degree of comfort.

— Toronto *Globe and Mail*, August 18, 1959.

exist a few decades earlier to lighten her housework load. But technology came with a price: the expectation that now the housewife would keep her place even cleaner, and that she would follow all the trends in home decorating.

Increasingly, housewives added floor polishers and vacuums to their roster of house-cleaning equipment. They could choose from three kinds of floor wax—paste wax, a water emulsion wax, and a liquid wax. Washing dishes was more complicated: the new acrylics, for example, should be washed in lukewarm soapy water, not in scalding hot water. And details were important: one

Not everyone benefitted from innovations and inventions. On the eve of Confederation in 1949, a housewife carries water from the community well in Portugal Cove, Newfoundland. (National Film Board of Canada, Library and Archives Canada PA-128013)

〰〰〰〰〰〰〰〰〰〰〰〰〰〰〰

Manufacturers fancied up their products with scientific-sounding names:

To give you faster, easier cleaning than any other cleanser.... We've activated Seismotite in Old Dutch Cleanser.

— from an Old Dutch advertisement, *Chatelaine*, February 1950, back cover.

〰〰〰〰〰〰〰〰〰〰〰〰〰〰〰

Though few followed up, housewives and their husbands were encouraged to protect their families in the Cold War days of Red-under-the-bed scares and nuclear threats:

An atomic fall-out shelter has been incorporated in plans for a subdivision in Aurora.... For about $1,500 extra, a family can have this basement protection against nuclear fall-out.... Its dimensions are almost 11 feet by eight feet. Folding sleeping cots, emergency escape tools, a chemical toilet, water containers, food supplies and utensils, a telephone extension and radio equipment should allow a family to remain relatively comfortable for the seven to 14-day danger period, the builders claim.

— Toronto *Globe and Mail*, January 17, 1959.

newspaper household hint advised the housewife to paint the inside of her salt shaker's metal top to prevent rust or tarnish.

As homes went up rapidly in the suburbs, housewives—and their husbands—were prompted to buy wall-to-wall carpet, fine furniture, new appliances. A housewife looking for ideas on how to keep her house up-to-date need look no further than the advice columns of the daily newspaper and the monthly magazine. Decorating hints or suggestions on furnishing new houses were now as numerous as the simple instructions from earlier decades about how to clean this or polish that. Housewives were prompted to lay coral-coloured linoleum in the dining room and orange carpet in the bedroom and treat their new acrylic containers with care.

A housewife uses her new sewing machine under an electric light. (National Film Board of Canada, Library and Archives Canada PA 150868)

Mending for your mites and men—and yourself—can save many dollars. And machine-mending can be quicker by many a wink than hand-sewing—and hold better!

...examine clothes regularly. Always mend before laundering. When a seam gives or frays, stitch it a little deeper than the original.... If a dress has become short-waisted, rip out waistline stitching and sew in a set-in belt.... When you put up cuffs of a boy's pants, leave enough turn-in allowance in addition to cuffs so they can be let down again and perhaps again.... So many features of a man's suit show wear that YOU can repair: front coat edges, buttonholes, cuffs, pocket edges, inside pockets, crotch. And men's lapels are so much narrower! Even this remodelling you can do.

— *Halifax Chronicle-Herald*, September 8, 1959.

There were some hints that Canadians were entering into the age of disposable commodities. At a conference about house-building, a vice-president of the National Home Builders Association expressed the fear that houses built in the 1950s would last too long—50 years!—and be out of style before they wore out. "I am not saying that we should cut quality, but we should temper it with realism." Several observers said that the speaker was only joking.[9]

❧ THE SEAMSTRESS ❧

Gone were the Depression and war-era admonitions to make over this and mend that. The seamstress of the 1950s was busy at her sewing machine making new clothes from new fabrics for herself and her daughters.

She could choose from synthetic fabrics and postwar patterns aimed at making her fashionable at an economical price. The strange-sounding names of terylene, polyester, dacron, and acrylic joined the fabric lexicon; nylon, invented at the beginning of the war, again became available. Housewives rejoiced in the concept of "wash and wear," dreaming of leaving behind their irons. Most, though, still relied on cotton, wool, and earlier synthetics such as rayon for most of their sewing. The thrifty housewife found remnants on sale that would easily make up into a skirt or blouse.

Sewing machines were getting fancier: completely automatic, free arm, attachments to do special stitches. Some manufacturers boasted that their machines could sew on buttons and do blind-hemming without any attachments at all.

Many housewives bought clothes instead of making them. An ad for Eaton's, for example, suggested its wash frocks would help the housewife "look cheery and trim as a tulip when you toss up an omelet, swish the mop around or set forth with pram and shopping bag on a Summer morning. Easy to do the comely-housewife act in these fresh, new attractive dresses."[10]

Women were also busy knitting sweaters for their husbands, children, family, and friends. The late 1950s were the age of the Mary Maxim, a heavy wool sweater with a uniquely Canadian image knitted into the pattern: totem poles, beavers, reindeer, ducks. Even prime ministers were known to wear Mary Maxim sweaters.

The frugal housewife was still with us despite postwar prosperity; many families struggled to keep up on incomes much lower than average. A Winnipeg writer gave advice on saving money:

Even if your Christmas list is long, you can add this personal touch to your yuletide giving with presents made from cotton bags. These containers come as a bonus when you buy feed, flour, and other commodities, so they're a handy source of low-cost, high-quality sewing fabric.

If you live on a farm or in the suburbs, you probably already have a supply of sacks on hand.... Cotton bags come in colorful prints, soft cambrics, and durable osnaburgs, and in five to 100-lb sizes. You can use the larger containers to make gay holiday aprons or luncheon cloths for your favorite homemakers, brunch coats for teenage daughters or nieces, shirts for the man in your life and yule accessories for your home. Smaller bags are handy for toys, potholders, novelties, and doll clothes.

— *Winnipeg Free Press*, December 5, 1959.

Laundry the new way—a happy Calgary contest winner turns in her old washing machine for a fancy new one. (Glenbow Archives, NA-5093-48)

Skillful knitters made up their own patterns that reflected the interests of their husbands or children—though a cartoon suggested the only image fitted for one woman's husband was a TV set.

⤳ THE LAUNDRESS ⤳

By the 1950s, most Canadian housewives had seen an end to the worst of laundry drudgery, as electric or gas-powered washing machines and new detergents made this task a little easier. Not perfectly easy, of course. In most washing machines, the laundress had to feed the clothing through a wringer into a laundry tub for rinsing, then back through the wringer and into the clothes basket.

"To help relieve the soap shortage," noted a 1947 news story, "a new industry has been developed, that is, the manufacturing of

"Tide," the new package laundry soap made by Procter & Gamble of Hamilton, Ont., moved into the grocery stores this week and is now on sale in Red Deer and throughout the district. The product is the newest development in the package laundry soap field, and is quicker, cleaner and more efficient, it is exceptionally good in hard water and rinses out easily. The new product is being introduced with a powerful newspaper advertising campaign and a full page ad. appears in this issue of the *Advocate* on page 17.

— *Red Deer Advocate*, June 2, 1948.

Not only did modern appliances lessen the workload they also—or so the advertisers said—kept women lovely. (*Chatelaine*, January 1951)

Lovely Hands

BELONG TO WOMEN WHO OWN A...

Thor
AUTOMAGIC WASHER

*T.M. Reg.

YOUR HANDS NEVER TOUCH WATER

When You Wash Clothes

or Dishes

After the war, we had the old flat-irons—the sadirons. And then we had a gas iron. We children weren't allowed to touch that. It would burst into flame. I think it was the main reason we got propane on the farm.

— Selma Adams, author interview

This is the day of lavish cleanliness. You too can scoff at the drudgery of "blue Monday," enjoy the luxurious daily changes of personal linen, towels and sheets, thanks to modern laundry facilities.

— "Washing and Ironing the Right Way," *Canadian Homes and Gardens*, February, 1946, p. 65.

a detergent product which does almost the same work as soaps. These detergents have been improved to the point where they are now preferred to soap by some housewives for certain work, and they are expected to remain as a standard household require-ment after soap returns to full supply."[11] Though detergents had been developed in the 1930s, only in the 1950s did they become household essentials. Simpler to use, easier to rinse out of clothes, detergents also meant that the housewife now must pre-soak only the dirtiest of clothes.

Spin-dryers were still in the future; the clothes line ruled the drying of laundry. In city apartment buildings, laundry lines stretched across the fire escape or along the balcony.

The development of the thermostat-controlled iron in the 1920s had made the task of ironing much easier—no more scorching when the iron was too hot, or ironing clothing twice if it was too cold. Housewives continued to iron handkerchiefs, underwear, and sheets.

⊁⊹ THE NURSE ⊹⊰

In the 1950s, the housewife's role as nurse revolved around preventive medicine, with a focus on proper nutrition and exercise for her family and early diagnosis of any ills. Give them their vitamins and minerals, mothers were advised, and a daily dose of cod liver oil to keep them healthy and strong.

Mother nursed the minor bumps, bruises, and scrapes her children incurred, and was expected to look after both children and husband if they were home with colds, flus, or other ailments. Parents were encouraged to make sure their children were immunized against diphtheria with a vaccine that was developed in 1923 and against whooping cough with a vaccine developed in 1926. Most children still caught several of what were regarded as the usual childhood diseases: vaccines against measles, mumps, and chickenpox emerged only in the 1960s.

Mothers cared for children who caught these infectious diseases at home, instructed to keep them away from other children. "For measles, we kept children in a dark room and tried to keep the fever down with damp cool cloths or a bath in tepid water, and put calamine lotion on the spots," recalled one 1950s mother. "For chickenpox, we put a handful of oatmeal in a cool bath—that was to dry up the scabs. And we used calamine lotion for the spots, too."[12] Mothers of the era were told to keep a boy who had mumps lying down, lest the disease spread to his testicles and render him sterile.

Mothers—especially from low-income families—still hesitated to call the doctor for minor ailments but most would hurry their children to the doctor's office for anything that looked serious—or ask him to make a house call if the child was very sick. In these days

The Metropolitan Life Insurance Company advised people on how to avoid colds in one of a series of health advertisements in 1951:

DON'T GIVE A COLD A CHANCE!
Keep physically fit, particularly during the winter months.

Get sufficient rest and sleep and eat a balanced daily diet.

Dress warmly when going out-of-doors and avoid damp, inclement weather where possible.

Stay away from people who cough or sneeze carelessly.

— *Chatelaine*, January 1951, p. 3.

Mrs. Kay Crowe, director of the department of family life and parent education at Montreal's Mental Hygiene Institute, was quoted in an article on women and depression:

It's becoming a matter of prestige to have a large family these days. When a woman says, "I'm having our fifth baby," everyone tells her how wonderful it is. But it isn't so wonderful if she can't get help. She becomes too tired to cope.

— June Callwood, "Could You Have a Nervous Breakdown?" *Chatelaine*, December 1959, p. 62.

Nursing and baby clinics were held in all parts of Canada. Here, Soudlo, a resident of Pangnirtung, NWT, prepares powdered milk formula for her baby, Quaga, held in a nurse's arms. (George Hunter, National Film Board of Canada, Library and Archives Canada PA-166452)

〰〰〰〰〰〰〰〰〰〰〰〰〰〰

Gloomy, tired, bored mothers. What can be done for them? Here is a suggestion:

A mother who has one or more preschool children can find a perfect outlet in a cooperative nursery. She does committee work with other young mothers and goes to the nursery once a week to help teacher. Four other mornings a week her child is in nursery school for two hours, affording her a little breather in which to rest, read or recreate.

…When we campaigned for tax support of a nursery school program, the opposition piously hymned one theme… : "the mother should stay home and take care of her children."

This hidebound view fails to take account of the fact that today's suburban population is probably further removed from near relatives than any group in human history. Very few of us have an aunt or granny to help, even in times of dire illness.

— *Montreal Gazette,*
September 21, 1959.

before Medicare, though, a serious illness could bankrupt a family, or lack of money could make it impossible for the illness to be properly treated.

Perhaps the housewife's greatest fear in the early 1950s was that one of her children might get polio, which attacked the nerves along the spinal cord, often resulting in paralysis. Some children stricken with polio were condemned to months in an iron lung, a cumbersome machine that kept them breathing by mechanical means. An epidemic in 1952 and 1953 saw some 14,000 Canadians stricken with polio, and advertisements for polio insurance ran alongside ads for crop insurance in prairie papers. By 1954-55, a vaccine had been developed against the disease, and thousands of Canadian children were vaccinated.

❧ THE MOTHER ❧

The postwar days turned advice for mothers upside down once more. One mother commented that, without thinking about it, she had treated her three children differently, depending on the prevailing wisdom when they were infants: one was expected to eat what was in front of him regardless, the next was given some latitude, and the third was allowed to do as he wished.

Perhaps the greatest influence on the mothers of the postwar period was Dr. Benjamin Spock's *The Common Sense Book of Baby and Child Care*, first published in 1946. For more than two decades, doctors, nurses, and social workers had set out rules on discipline, toilet-training, eating, and almost every other aspect of caring for infants and children. Dr. Spock told them to throw all this away: mothers—and fathers—knew best. They should be flexible, see their children as individuals, and—above all—enjoy the parenting process. He also underlined the need for a steady loving person—presumably the mother—to be at home to give the child the security he or she needed.

Dr. Spock's books on matters medical and maternal became the child-care bibles for millions of mothers across North America. Since so many mothers now lived far from their own mothers and other family members who could give them advice, they were more than willing to turn to this generation's expert. Yet many immigrants who came to Canada after the war still relied on the old ways and were deeply suspicious of the new.

Family income level continued to limit what a mother could do for her children, though families got some government help from 1945 on, when a system of family allowances was established. The cheques, monthly, with a set amount for each child dependent on age, were made out to the mothers—in every province but Quebec. Women had to stage a rebellion of sorts in that province before the provincial government relented and allowed mothers, not fathers, to get the allowance.

The cheques went out to millions. Prosperity and hope combined to convince couples to have two, three, or four children. Almost all mothers except those most distant from town had their children in hospital. Public health improved and each year, fewer

Sam saves Roger and Gloria's marriage, in fiction in *Chatelaine*, January 1951:

"You've got to be firm. You've got to be the boss and lay down the law. Gloria's that sort of girl. She can't respect you if you're putty in her hands.... Be firm. Gong her if you have to."

"You mean—hit her?"

"Like Noel Coward said.... Gong her."

Later: "I was so darn angry I turned her over my knee and let her have it. She apologized.... Boy, were you right!"

— from "The Reporter and the Redhead" by Alec Rackowe, p. 46.

and fewer children were stillborn. By 1961, the infant mortality rate had dropped to a quarter of what it had been in 1921.

Though most women stayed home in the 1950s, a small but growing number went out to work, leaving their children with babysitters or making arrangements for someone to look after them after school. Whether they worked out of necessity or simply because they wanted to, they were still condemned by many. "Working mothers are sewing seeds of teenage drinking, carousal, gambling and sexual promiscuity," thundered Rev. Dr. James Mutchmor, United Church moderator, in 1958.[13] His attitude was echoed by many, despite the fact that many women who worked did so because their families needed the money. But the naysayers wouldn't stem the growing tide to working mothers that would mark the next decade.

Our role was clear. We were to be utterly supportive. We were to make the adjustments because we were the fortunate ones. We had been on the cozy home front, and we knew if anything went wrong with this reunion it was the wife's responsibility.... Someone would say to you, "I hear John will be home tomorrow, isn't that marvellous?" and the only possible response was, "yes, it's going to be the most glorious day of my life." Well, it wasn't the most glorious day, usually. It was the scariest day. It meant beginning again...he's not the same boy who went away.... When a woman who is alone with two or three children for six years and has learned how to handle money, and how to make the furnace work better than it used to work, it wasn't easy to give up those skills.

— Winnipeg woman, interview with Jean Bruce, *Back the Attack*, p. 161.

The Wife

Despite the growing number of married women working for wages outside the home, being a full-time housewife was still the choice of the great majority of women. Nonetheless, towards the end of the decade, some commentators suggested that women were getting a little out of hand and usurping the proper role of men.

A Montreal psychiatrist who wrote about suburbia for *Chatelaine* quoted a sociologist colleague as saying, "Men must put a higher value on themselves and re-evaluate their women. It is a woman's role to cook, clean, and raise children and men must insist that she concentrate on these functions. It takes a lot of man to believe that he is important enough to be served by a woman. If he feels this strongly, she can regain the sense of accomplishment women used to derive from baking pies and waxing floors."[14]

Though some female readers agreed, most were aghast or amused. "The idea of a male ruler and a female servant degrades the best in human relationships," expostulated one reader.[15]

Yet the view the psychiatrist expressed, while extreme, was not out of line with the image of the wife in the 1950s. There was a new emphasis on looking good while keeping house. The comely housewife was in style, wearing an attractive housedress and—if the

**"ME, JOHN? ME—
UNRESPONSIVE—COLD?"**

...DOUBTS...INHIBITIONS

*Frozen by unsureness, wives may lose love . . .
through one intimate physical neglect*

The wife's at fault again: an advertisement for Lysol as a douche shows how the devil of doubts and inhibitions can freeze a wife into losing her husband's love. Accompanying copy hints at, but cannot legally promote, Lysol's use as a contraceptive. (*Canadian Home Journal*, May 1950)

Dear Mrs. Thompson:

...Just this last while my husband doesn't pay any attention to me or the children. He used to come home early in the evening and take us visiting or car-riding. Now he doesn't seem to want to do anything for me at all. I have asked him if there is something bothering him but he won't give me an answer at all.

Before this, he used to drink a little. Now there is never a day goes by that he doesn't drink....When he comes home from work I don't say much to him. I mean I think I was more or less nagging him. All I do is ask about his work.

....Perhaps your husband is just getting tired of responsibility, after six years of marriage....Part of your job is to make him think it is wonderful to be a husband and father....Don't complain about anything.

— "Mrs. Thompson Gives Advice,"
Globe and Mail, March 27, 1959.

advertisements were to be believed—high heels, as she swept the floor or put the roast in the oven.

A woman was urged to feed her man properly, keep a clean house for him, ask about his day but never complain about hers, keep the children from bothering him when he was tired, make the very best of his paycheque, and always be cheerful and ready for whatever he suggested. Though she must be a skillful housewife, she mustn't overdo it. In a magazine short story, a wife was losing her husband because she was so good at her household job, putting up hundreds of jars of beans and tomatoes, caring ceaselessly for the children, too busy or too tired when he asked her to go for a walk in the moonlight. Little wonder, then, that he took up with the female boarder. This woman took a good look at herself and reformed, and everyone—except, presumably, the female boarder—lived happily ever after.

The magazines were ever ready to help out with various crises, real and imagined. Feature writers tackled many a topic to keep marriages from foundering, including how to know if you were normal, whether you were headed for a nervous breakdown, whether your husband might commit suicide, and how you should cope with being the wife of a travelling salesman.

Some marriages did founder. Although adultery was the only official grounds for divorce, the divorce rate spiked during and just after World War II, as war pressures, absent husbands, and female freedoms resulted in more marriage breakdowns. Ontario led the parade: there, one marriage in 13 ended in divorce. The other 12, though, thrived or survived. "I was determined to make it work," was the standard response from women who thought about splitting but decided to stay, "because of the children."

Echoing a theme—and a solution—from the 1930s and the war years, advertisers suggested it was the woman's responsibility to make sure the marriage endured. "Ooh? Domestic Crisis!" read one magazine ad—for Tom was treating Sue badly and Sue was furious. But—wouldn't you know it?—it was all Sue's fault. She had become neglectful about her personal hygiene. Off to the doctor she went; he told her she must use Lysol disinfectant for douching every time. So Sue and Tom now had a heavenly home-life, thanks to Lysol, far more dependable than salt, soda, or other home-made solutions.[16] As in earlier decades, douching with Lysol was regarded as a method of birth control.

Not all women bought into the standard expectations of a wife. Long before such topics were openly discussed in most forums, editorials and articles in Chatelaine, the leading Canadian women's magazine, argued for women's rights. "Our abortion law," wrote Joan Finnigan in 1959, "multiplies tragedy and human anguish, causes needless deaths and leaves orphans. It also fails to recognize an important new social principle—the welfare, and not merely survival, of the child. It should be changed—and soon."[17] Denounced and harassed for running the article, editor Doris Anderson refused to back down. She kept her job.

Another article in *Chatelaine* in 1959 touched off more controversy—this time among readers who deplored the double standard and denounced a male author who wrote that a woman should just put up with her husband's philandering. "Let us picture [the writer]," responded one irate letter writer, "coming home three or four evenings a week to find his dearly beloved Esther has chosen to spend the night with an eligible bachelor of the neighbourhood. I doubt if he would even consider a marriage counselor. He would dash off to a reputable lawyer and start divorce proceedings, declaring his wife to be unfit as the mother of his three children. What is sauce for the goose should be sauce for the gander."[18]

In such responses were the seeds of the decade fast approaching. The 1960s would bring the feminist rebellion, the birth-control pill, and a virtual end to the stay-at-home housewife as the Canadian norm.

◇◇◇

"I'm never getting married," I announced peevishly that spring over a supper of meatloaf and mashed potatoes. "I'm never going to be trapped in a house with puking babies and have to wash clothes and scrub floors and make supper for everyone like a slave. It's disgusting."

Elsie paused, a homemade pickled beet on her fork, and looked at me levelly. "That's what they all say," she smirked.

—M.A.C. Farrant, *My Turquoise Years*, a memoir of growing up in the 50s and 60s in coastal British Columbia, p. 46.

LIFE AND TIMES
OF THE HOUSEWIFE IN CANADA

꙳

1600–1763

CANADA EVENTS		꙳		HOUSEWIFE EVENTS
French establish Port Royal on the Bay of Fundy); no women in colony	1605		1605	First European garden in Canada
Colony abandoned	1607			
Champlain founds Quebec	1608			
New French colony on Bay of Fundy	1608 on			
			1617	Canada's first housewife, Marie Rollet, wife of apothecary Louis Hébert, arrives at Quebec
			1620 on	French colonist women put their household skills to work in their New France houses
			1630	First French housewives establish themselves in Acadia
Montreal founded	1642			
			1663–	*Filles du roi*, hundreds of women
British take over Acadia Louisbourg founded	1713		1673	who will marry settlers in New France and start families, arrive in Quebec. Population growth accelerates
Acadians expelled: 11,000 of about 15,000 leave for France, Louisiana, West Indies	1755– 1763			
British conquer Quebec	1759			
New France ceded to British	1763			

1764–1850

CANADA EVENTS		HOUSEWIFE EVENTS
American Revolution	1775– 1783	
James Watt invents steam engine	1776	
United States becomes an independent country	1783	
Loyalists arrive in Canada: 20,000 to Nova Scotia 14,000 to New Brunswick 1,000 to Lower Canada (Quebec) 6,000 to Upper Canada	1783– 1800	
Colony of Quebec divided: Lower Canada (Quebec) Upper Canada (west of Quebec)	1791	
York (Toronto) founded	1793	
	1798	Smallpox vaccine developed, the first in a series of vaccines that will make life easier for the housewife-as-nurse
European immigrants pour into Upper Canada	1800– 1850	
	1810	Metal cans invented; opened with knives or other sharp implements
U.S. invades Canada, but is driven back	1812	
Red River Colony founded in what will become Manitoba	1812	
	1820 on	First sewing machines developed: tailors in France smash them as unfair competition
	1820 on	Wood-fired cast-iron cook stoves come on the market; not in wide use until 1850s
	1825	First cookbook published in Canada
	1827	Matches invented
Rebels in Upper and Lower Canada fight for Representative government	1837	
Upper and Lower Canada joined as Canada West and Canada East	1840	

1764–1850 continued

CANADA EVENTS		HOUSEWIFE EVENTS
Fort Victoria founded on Vancouver Island	1843	
	1845	Oil cloth widely available, giving housewives an easily cleaned table cover
	1849	Nova Scotia geologist Abraham Gesner distills coal oil—which he names kerosene and which burns brighter and cleaner—as a replacement for whale and other oils
	1849	Safety pin invented

1850–1879

CANADA EVENTS		HOUSEWIFE EVENTS
	after 1850	Many urban homes get indoor plumbing
Upper Canada passes Lower Canada in population	1851	Singer treadle sewing machine patented
	1855	Safety matches invented
	1856	Synthetic dyes invented; introduced commercially in 1876
	1856	Pasteurization of milk developed
	1856	Baking powder sold commercially; cakes get lighter and higher
	1858	Mason jar, for home canning, invented
	1858	Can opener invented; better one invented in 1870
	1860 on	Mechanical washing machines with wringers become available

1850–1879 continued

CANADA EVENTS			HOUSEWIFE EVENTS
		1860 on	Montreal opens market buildings in various parts of the city
Population of British North America reaches 3.5 million	1861		
Colonies join to form Canada: Quebec, Ontario, Nova Scotia, New Brunswick	1867	1867	Medical sterilization introduced
		1869	First plastics developed
Hudson's Bay Company turns Northwest over to Canada	1869		
Red River Rebellion over Canadian control of area	1869– 1870	1870s	Sewing patterns sold in various sizes; housewives need no longer rip apart old clothes to make patterns for new
Manitoba joins Confederation	1870		
British Columbia joins Confederation	1871	1871	Timothy Eaton opens his first department store in Toronto
Canadian population 80% rural	1871	1871	School attendance becomes compulsory in Ontario
Plains Indians sign treaties	1871– 1877		
Prince Edward Island joins Confederation	1873		
		1876	Carpet sweeper developed
Intercolonial railway, Nova Scotia to Quebec completed	1876	1876	Feather duster patented
Alexander Graham Bell invents telephone	1876		
Refrigerated ships carry cargo	1877		
Thomas Edison invents incandescent light bulb	1879		

1880–1895

CANADA EVENTS			HOUSEWIFE EVENTS
Settlers move west; buffalo slaughtered	1880 on	1880s	Ice boxes developed for home use
		1880s	First blue jeans sold in Canada
		1880s	Jell-O invented
		1882	Electric iron invented
		1883	First artificial silk developed
		1884	First Eaton's mail-order catalogue produced
		1884	First washing machines with agitator in rotating tub developed; the hardest housewife job gets a little easier
Northwest Rebellion: Métis and Indians against Canadian government	1885		
Railway completed to West Coast	1885		
		1886	Coca-Cola invented
		1889	First mechanical dishwasher developed
Electrical generating facilities in all provinces	1890	1890s	Gas cooking ranges available
		1890s	First electric irons sold
		1892	Publicizing or promoting methods of birth control becomes illegal
		1895	Triscuits crackers on market

1896–1918

CANADA EVENTS			HOUSEWIFE EVENTS
Klondike Gold Rush	1898–1900		
Yukon becomes separate territory	1898		
Automobiles more common on Canada's roads	ca. 1900	1900	Stores stock exotic fruits, vegetables shipped on refrigerated ships, trains
Canada population 62% rural	1901		
		1904	Tea bags invented
		1904	First canned pork and beans

1896–1918 continued

CANADA EVENTS		HOUSEWIFE EVENTS
	1904	Canada Dry ginger ale on sale
	1904	Peanut butter on sale
Alberta, Saskatchewan enter Confederation — 1905	1905	Electric toaster invented
	1907	First Maytag washing machine
	1908	First Hoover vacuum cleaner
	1908	First electrically powered sewing machine
	1909	Instant coffee invented
	ca. 1910	First electric washing machines appear
World War I: Canadian soldiers in Europe — 1914–1918	1915	First mechanical refrigerators for the home appear
	1915	Pyrex dishes on market
Saskatchewan women first to get the vote — 1916	1916	First Campbell's "Cooking with Soup" recipe book

1919–1939

CANADA EVENTS		HOUSEWIFE EVENTS
Worldwide flu epidemic — 1919	1919	Pop-up toaster introduced
	after 1918	Vacuum cleaners readily available—though expensive
	1920s	Sliced bread, packaged cereals, processed cheese, biscuit mix, baby food in jars, appear on grocery shelves
More urban than rural Canadians — 1921	1921	First electric range produced
Vaccines for tuberculosis, diphtheria, whooping cough, tetanus, introduced — 1923–1927	1923	Zipper commercially introduced
	1924	Caesar salad appears
	1927	Homogenized milk and Kool-Aid available

1919–1939 continued

CANADA EVENTS		HOUSEWIFE EVENTS
	1927	Thermostats added to electric irons
	1928	*Chatelaine* magazine begins publication
Worldwide economic depression begins — 1929	1930s	Frozen food sold
	1930s	Most homes have water heaters
	1931	Three doctors at the Hospital for Sick Children in Toronto develop Pablum, an instant cereal for children
	1931	*Joy of Cooking* published
Wheat price drops from $1.02 a bushel in 1929 to 35¢ — 1932		
CCF formed as Canada's socialist party — 1932		
First, limited, unemployment insurance plan — 1934	1934	Cream of mushroom soup available
Unemployed stage On-to-Ottawa protest trek — 1935		
	1937	Kraft macaroni and cheese available

1939–1945

CANADA EVENTS		HOUSEWIFE EVENTS
World War II — 1939– 1945		
Penicillin, first antibiotic, developed — 1940		
Unemployment insurance introduced — 1941		
	1942	Canada Food Rules introduced
	1945	Active dry yeast marketed
	1945	Family allowances established

1946–1959

CANADA EVENTS			HOUSEWIFE EVENTS
		1946	Instant mashed potatoes, TV dinners available
Baby boom generation begins	1947	1947	Refrigerators with freezer units available
		1947	Tupperware seal patented
Cold War days: "Free" World vs. Communist World	1948–1970s		
Newfoundland joins Canada	1949	1949	Cake mixes widely available
		1949	Electric dishwashers available
		1950s	Electric automatic washing machines available
		1950s	Terylene, polyester, dacron fabrics available
		1950s	Laundry detergents become popular
		1950s	Washing machines acquire spin-dryers to replace wringers
		1950s	Plastic parts for vacuum cleaners make them much lighter and easier to use
First Canadian television programs broadcast	1952	1952	Saran wrap marketed
		1953	Cheez Whiz available
Polio vaccine developed	1955		
		by 1959	Almost all rural areas connected to electricity

❧ NOTES AND BIBLIOGRAPHY ❧

NOTES

SALT PORK AND HOMESPUN:
HOUSEWIVES IN ACADIA AND NEW FRANCE
Pages 13–33

Introductory quote: Andrew Clark. *Acadia: The Geography of Nova Scotia to 1760*, p. 89.

1   Ibid., p. 177.

2   Pehr Kalm. *The America of 1750: Peter Kalm's Travels in North America*, pp. 402–3.

3   Dollier de Casson. *A History of Montreal, 1640–1672*, p. 272.

4   Kalm, p. 558.

5   Jesuit Relation, 1636, as quoted in Raymond Douville and Jacques-Donat Casanova, *Daily Life in Early Canada from Champlain to Montcalm*, p. 55.

6   As quoted in Douville, p. 55.

7   Kalm, p. 403.

8   As quoted in Peter Moogk, *La Nouvelle France: The Making of French Canada, A Cultural History*, pp. 6, 63.

9   http://www.maisonsaint-gabriel.qc.ca/en/b/page_b_5a_c8_03.html, consulted 03/03/05.

10 Moogk, pp. 231–33.

11 Dollier de Casson, p. 347.

12 *Journal des Campagnes du Chevalier de Lévis*, as quoted in Moogk, p. 64.

CANDLES, COMPLAINTS, AND A STIFF UPPER LIP:
HOUSEWIVES IN THE BACKWOODS
Pages 35–59

Introductory quote: Catherine Parr Traill. *The Backwoods of Canada*, pp. 183–84.

1   Mary O'Brien. *The Journals of Mary O'Brien, 1828–1838*, p. 141.

2   As quoted in Edwin Guillet, *Early Life in Upper Canada*, p. 268.

3   Parr Traill. *Backwoods of Canada*, p. 308.

4   Susanna Moodie. *Roughing It in the Bush, or, Life in Canada*, pp. 156–160.

5   Anne Langton. *A Gentlewoman in Upper Canada: The Journals of Anne Langton*, p. 150.

6   Ibid., p. 107.

7   *Cook Not Mad, or Rational Cookery*, No. 212.

8   Ibid., No. 247.

9   Ibid., No. 249.

10 Parr Traill. *Backwoods of Canada*, p. 47.

11 Parr Traill. *The Canadian Settlers' Guide*, p. 184.

12 Langton, p. 77.

13 Parr Traill. *The Canadian Settlers' Guide*, p. 181.

14 Ibid., p. 192.

15 *The Cook Not Mad*, No. 238.

16 Kalm, p. 639.

17 O'Brien, pp. 231 ff.

18 Ibid., p. 197

19 Ibid., p. 198.

20 Anna Jameson. *Winter Studies and Summer Rambles*, Vol. II, p. 150.

21 Kathryn Carter, ed. *The Small Details of Life: 20 Diaries by Women in Canada, 1830–1996*, pp. 66 ff.

22 Rev. Thomas Radcliff, ed. *Authentic Letters from Upper Canada*, p. 117.

THE TRUE DESTINY OF WOMEN: THE VICTORIAN HOUSEWIFE

Pages 61–87

1   Intoductory quote, *The Home Cook Book*, p. 9. *Book of Household Management*, n.p. http://etext.library.adelaide.edu.au/b/beeton/isabella/.

2   Margaret Gray Lord. *One Woman's Charlottetown*, Evelyn J. MacLeod, ed., various pages.

3   Toronto *Globe*, June 29, 1897.

4   Toronto *Globe*, January 12, 1889.

5   B.G. Jefferis and J.L. Nichols. *The Household Guide or Domestic Cyclopedia*, p. 376.

6   Lord, pp. 135–36.

7   Toronto *Globe*, Sept. 9, 1898.

8   Toronto *Globe*, January 23, 1854.

9   *The Girl's Own Paper*, May 1892, pp. 476 ff.

10 Paine's advertorial, June 16, 1894.

11 *Mainland Guardian*, New Westminster, B.C., August 20, 1871.

12 Toronto *Globe*, April 16, 1892.

13 Jefferis, p. 25.

14 Mrs. W.H. Beecher. *All Around the House—or, How to Make Homes Happy*, p. 73.

15 Toronto *Globe*, August 5, 1893.

DUST AND ITS DANGERS: INTO THE NEW CENTURY
Pages 89–117

Introductory quote: Women's Institute of Saltfleet fonds, Library and Archives Canada.

1   http://timelinks.merlin.mb.ca/referenc/db0015.htm.

2   Children's Aid Society of Toronto annual report 1907, pp. 32–35 in http://ohq.tpl.toronto.on.ca/gr8-intro-2c-src1.jsp.

3   Nellie McCLung. *In Times Like These*, p. 51.

4   TM, 22 August 1917, *Grain Growers' Guide*, as quoted in Barbara E. Kelcey and Angela E. Davis, eds., *A Great Movement Underway*, p. 161.

5   Annie B. Juniper. *Girls' Home Manual of Cookery, Home Management, Home Nursing and Laundry*, pp. 116–17.

6   Toronto *Globe*, June 18, 1905.

7   *Maclean's*, July, 1917.

8   *Metropolitan Cook Book*, p. 3.

9   Toronto *Globe*, June 23, 1902.

10 Jell-O pamphlet, 1905, Library and Archives Canada.

11 Margaret Taylor and Frances McNaught. *Early Canadian Galt Cook Book*, p. 23.

12 Annie B. Juniper. *Girls' Home Manual of Cookery, Home Management, Home Nursing and Laundry*.

13 *Maclean's*, July 1917.

14 Toronto *Globe*, Oct. 10, 1908.

15 Ibid.

16 *Halifax Herald*, May 8, 1908.

17 Toronto *Globe*, Jan. 3, 1900.

18 Ibid., Feb. 18, 1905.

19 Juniper, pp. 160 ff.

20 http://www.von.ca/english/aboutframe.htm.

21 "Motherhood," British Chemists Company (Toronto, 1900) as quoted in Beth Light and Joy Parr eds., *Canadian Women on the Move, 1867–1920*, p. 146.

22 "Report on Infant Mortality," Ontario Sessional papers No. 66, 1910, 30, 35-6, as quoted in Beth Light and Joy Parr eds., *Canadian Women on the Move, 1867–1920*, pp. 148–49.

23 Anne Anderson papers, Acc. 77.236, Provincial Archives of Alberta, as quoted in *Canadian Women on the Move, 1867–1920*, p. 34.

24 Alice B. Stockham. *Tokology: A Book for Every Woman*, p. 323.

25 Ibid., p. 325.

26 Sept. 5, 1891.

27 Toronto *Globe*, June 13, 1905.

28 *Halifax Herald*, May 8, 1903.

29 Toronto *Globe*, January 25, 1916.

30 Ibid., Dec. 13, 1917.

31 Mrs. A. W. McDougald, in "The Call To Arms, Montreal's Roll of Honour, European War, 1914," http://www.rootsweb.com/~qcmtl-w/IODE.html.

SOD HUTS AND CATALOGUE CLOTHES: SETTLING THE PRAIRIES

Pages 119–43

Introductory quote: "Mrs. St. John's Diary," January 2, 1903 to March 30, 1904, pp. 25–30.

1 Saskatchewan Homesteading Experiences Collection, Library and Archives Canada R2206-0-2-E.

2 *Janey Canuck in the West*, p. 74.

3 *A Lady's Life on a Farm in Manitoba*, p. 55.

4 Mrs. John Irwin Jameson, as quoted in Beth Light and Joy Parr eds., *Canadian Women on the Move, 1867–1920*, p. 174.

5 Walter and Rachel Weber fonds, Nov. 6, 1911.

6 Ibid.

7 *Family Herald and Weekly Star*, November 18, 1914, as quoted in Norah L. Lewis, ed., *Dear Editor and Friends*, p. 118

8 Elvira Backstrom, "Pioneer Parents," p. 21

9 "A Prairie Wife's Tale," p. 22.

10 Ibid.

11 Gertrude Quelch fonds.

12 Mrs. H.C.C., Saskatchewan Homesteading Experiences Collection.

13   *Free Press Prairie Farmer*, July 2, 1912 as quoted in Norah L. Lewis, ed., *Dear Editor and Friends*, p. 99

14   Sheila Kerr. *Early Prairie Remedies*.

15   Harry Piniuta, ed. *Land of Pain, Land of Promise: First Person Accounts by Ukrainian Pioneers 1891–1914*, p. 59.

16   Judy Schultz. *Mamie's Children: Three Generations of Prairie Women*, p. 97.

17   Olive K. Murdoch. "Homesteading in Alberta, Reminiscences of the Heathcote Family," *1894–1901*.

18   May 13, 1903, as quoted in Beth Light and Joy Parr eds., *Dear Editor and Friends*, p. 29.

19   As quoted in Norah L. Lewis, ed., *Dear Editor and Friends*, p. 30.

20   Weber, November 28, 1911.

21   Nellie McClung. *In Times Like These*, p. 109.

22   April 12, 1905, *Farmer's Advocate*, as quoted in Beth Light and Joy Parr eds., *Dear Editor and Friends*, p. 37.

23   Eaton's Catalogue, 1905.

24   Saskatchewan Homesteading Experiences Collection.

SCIENCE, THE NEW WOMAN, AND MAKING DO: HOUSEWIVES IN THE '20s AND '30s

Pages 145–75

Introductory quote 2: From City of Saskatoon Archives, City Clerk Record, box 5887b, Relief-S, 1932, File 308, # 20, as quoted in "Engendering Resistance: Women Respond to Relief in Saskatoon, 1930–1932," by Theresa Healy, in David DeBrou and Aileen Moffat eds., *Other Voices: Historical Essays on Saskatchewan Women*, p. 94.

1   Dr. Benge Atlee. "The Menace of Maternity," *Canadian Home Journal*, May 1932, p. 84.

2   Toronto *Globe*, March 26, 1935.

3   Phillip H. Adams. "Instalment Buying—Its Advantages and Disadvantages in Relation to Banking, Commerce and the Community," *Journal of the Canadian Bankers Association*, Oct. 1930, p. 63, as quoted in Veronica Strong Boag, *The New Day Recalled: Lives of Girls and Women in English Canada, 1919–1939*, p. 115.

4   "Address on Community Kitchens. Given by Mrs. Oag at a Meeting of the United Women Voters," *Women's Century*, April 1919, p. 37, as quoted in Veronica Strong Boag, *The New Day Recalled*, p. 120.

5   *Chatelaine*, March 1928, p. 71.

6   Helen Campbell. "When the North Wind Doth Blow," *Chatelaine*, February, 1933, p. 49.

7   *Just Look at These Wonderful Jams and Jellies*, Certo booklet.

8   *Chatelaine*, February, 1933, p. 48.

9   Toronto *Globe*, April 6, 1935.

10 Hoover vacuum advertisement, *Maclean's*, Oct. 15, 1922, p. 39.

11 Ibid.

12 *McClary's Household Manual*, p. 21.

13 Aberson, Jane. *From the Prairies with Hope*, p. 31.

14 *Gaslights to Gigawatts*, p. 33.

15 *McClary's Household Manual*, p. 37.

16 *Chatelaine*, March, 1928, p. 32.

17 Frances M. McNally, "When Someone Is Sick," *Canadian Home Journal*, February 1927, p. 54.

18 Ibid., p. 17.

19 Dr. Alan Brown. "Keeping the Well Child Well," *Maclean's*, October 15, 1922, p. 20.

20 Letter to the *Birth Control Review*, May 1927, as quoted in Beth Light and Ruth Roach Pierson, *No Easy Road*, p. 123.

21 *Chatelaine*, March 1928, p. 34.

22 Toronto *Globe*, April 3, 1935.

23 *Canadian Home Journal*, December 1926, p. 23.

RATION BOOKS AND KNITTING SOCKS:
HOUSEWIVES ON THE HOME FRONT
Pages 177–93

Introductory quote: *Chatelaine*, June 1941, p. 72.

1   *Chatelaine*, June 1943, p. 4.

2   *Chatelaine*, July 1943, p. 15.

3   *Chatelaine*, January 1943, p. 32.

4   Helen Campbell. "The New Cooking," *Maclean's*, September 15, 1942, p. 53.

5   Carol Joy Dennison. *The Women's Institutes in British Columbia 1909–1946: Housewives for Home and Country*, p. 128.

6   Toronto *Globe and Mail*, Feb. 17, 1943.

7   Dr. Elizabeth Chant Robertson. "They Shall Inherit the Earth," *Chatelaine*, March 1943, p. 13.

8   Jean Bruce. *Back the Attack*, interview with Vancouver woman, p. 70.

9   Lotta Dempsey. "You'll Be So Nice To Come Home To," *Chatelaine*, June 1943, p. 13.

MIRACLE FABRICS AND MARSHMALLOW SALADS:
HOUSEWIVES IN THE '50s
Pages 201–29

Introductory quote: *Globe and Mail,* May 20, 1946.

1   Beverly Gray. "Housewives Are a Sorry Lot," pp. 27, 37.

2   *Chatelaine,* June 1950, pp. 64 ff.

3   *Canadian Home Journal,* January 1946, pp. 33 ff.

4   *Globe and Mail,* April 15, 1948.

5   Kate Aitken fonds.

6   Kate Aitken fonds.

7   *Claresholm Local Press,* July 15, 1948.

8   M. Lois Clipsham. "With Best Wishes to a Housekeeper," *Chatelaine,*
    December 1946, p. 94.

9   *Globe and Mail,* January 17, 1959.

10 Ibid., May 4, 1946.

11 Ibid., February 14, 1947.

12 Author interview, Victoria woman.

13 As quoted in Beth Light and Ruth Roach Pierson, *No Easy Road,*
    p. 174.

14 *Chatelaine,* October 1958, pp. 23 ff.

15 Ibid., January 1959, p. 14.

16 Ibid., January 1946, p. 2.

17 Ibid., "Should Canada Change Its Abortion Law?" August 1959, p. 105.

18 Ibid., December, 1959, p. 116.

BIBLIOGRAPHY

BOOKS

Aberson, Jane L. *From the Prairies with Hope*. Regina: Canadian Plains Research Centre, 1991.

Abrahamson, Una. *God Bless Our Home: Domestic Life in Nineteenth Century Canada*. Toronto: Burns & MacEachern, 1966.

Aitken, Kate. *Feeding Your Family in Wartime*. Montreal: The Standard, n.d. ca. 1943.

Audet, Bernard. *Se Nourrir au Quotidien en Nouvelle-France*. Sainte-Foy, Québec: Éditions GID, 2001.

Baillargeon, Denyse. *Making Do: Women, Family and Home in Montreal during the Great Depression*. Yvonne Klein, tr. Waterloo: Wilfrid Laurier University Press, 1999.

Barss, B. *Pioneer Cook: A Historical View of Canadian Prairie Food*. Calgary: Detselig, 1980.

Baxter, Judith, and Beth Quigley, eds. *Life and Times: Recollections of Eliza Cox Carter*, Hull: Canadian Museum of Civilization, Mercury Series Paper 48, 1997.

Beecher, Mrs. W.H. *All Around the House—or, How to Make Homes Happy*. Toronto: J. Ross Robertson,1881.

Bridge, Katherine. *Henry & Self*. Victoria: Sono Nis, 1996.

Brodie, Jean, ed. *A Guide to Good Cooking*. Montreal: Lake of the Woods Milling Company, 1938.

Bruce, Jean. *Back the Attack: Canadian Women During the Second World War—at Home and Abroad*. Toronto: Macmillan of Canada, 1985.

Carter, Kathryn, ed. *The Small Details of Life, Twenty Diaries by Women in Canada, 1830–1996*. Toronto: University of Toronto Press, 2002.

Choy, Wayson. *All That Matters*. Toronto: Doubleday, 2004.

Clark, Andrew. *Acadia: The Geography of Nova Scotia to 1760*. Saint John, N.B.: The New Brunswick Museum, 1934.

Conrad, Margaret, Toni Laidlaw, and Donna Smyth, eds. *No Place Like Home: Diaries and Letters of Nova Scotia Women, 1771–1938*. Halifax: Formac, 1988.

The Cook Not Mad, or Rational Cookery. Kingston, U.C.: James MacFarlane, 1831.

La Cuisinière Bourgeoise. Québec: A. Germain, 1825.

Daubeny, Charles. *Journal of a Tour through the United States and Canada during the Years 1837–38*. Oxford?: 1843.

DeBrou, David, and Aileen Moffat, eds. *Other Voices: Historical Essays on Saskatchewan Women*. Regina: Canadian Plains Research Center, University of Regina, 1995.

de Casson, Dollier. *A History of Montreal, 1640–1672*. Ralph Flenley, tr. London: J.M. Dent & Sons, 1928.

Dennison, Carol Joy. *The Women's Institutes in British Columbia 1909–1946: Housewives for Home and Country*. Victoria: University of Victoria, 1983.

Dièreville, Sieur de. *Relation of the Voyage to Port Royal in Acadia or New France*. Mrs. Clarence Webster, tr. New York: Greenwood Press, 1968.

Douville, Raymond, and Jacques-Donat Casanova. *Daily Life in Early Canada from Champlain to Montcalm*. New York: The Macmillan Company, 1967.

Edwards, Devonna. *Wartime Recipes from the Maritimes 1939–1945*. Halifax: Nimbus, 2001.

Errington, Elizabeth Jane. *Wives and Mothers, Schoolmistresses and Scullery Maids: Working Women in Upper Canada, 1790–1840*. Montreal: McGill-Queen's University Press, 1995.

Farrant, M.A.C. *My Turquoise Years*. Vancouver: Greystone, 2004.

Finnigan, Joan, ed. *Some of the Stories I Told You Were True*. Ottawa: Deneau, 1981.

Five Roses Cook Book, Bread Pastry Etc. Montreal: Lake of the Woods Milling Company, 1915; reissued, Whitecap Books, 1999.

Gaslights to Gigawatts: BC Hydro Power Pioneers. Vancouver: Hurricane Press, 1998.

Gillett's Pure Flake Lye. Toronto: E.W. Gillett Co., 1913

Goudie, Elizabeth. *Woman of Labrador*. Toronto: Peter Martin Associates, 1973.

Grieve, Maud. *A Modern Herbal*. New York: Dover Publications, 1971.

Guillet, Edwin. *Early Life in Upper Canada*. Toronto: University of Toronto Press, 1933.

———. *The Pioneer Farmer and Backwoodsman*. Toronto: Ontario Publishing Co., 1963.

Hall, Mrs. Cecil. *A Lady's Life on a Farm in Manitoba*. London: W.H. Allen, 1884.

Hiemstra, Mary. *Gully Farm: A Story of Homesteading on the Canadian Prairies*. Toronto: McClelland and Stewart, 1955.

Hoffman, Frances, and RyanTaylor. *Much to Be Done: Private Life in Ontario from Victorian Diaries*. Toronto: Natural History/Natural Heritage, 1996.

The Home Cook Book. Toronto, 1878; reissued Whitecap Books, 2002.

Home and Health and Compendium of Useful Knowledge: A Cyclopedia of Facts and Hints for all Departments of Home Life, Health, and Domestic Economy and Hand Book of General Information. London: 1883.

Hopkins, Monica. *Letters from a Lady Rancher*. Calgary: Glenbow Museum, 1981.

Jameson, Anna. *Winter Studies and Summer Rambles*. London : Saunders and Otley, 1838.

Jefferis, B.G., and J.L. Nichols. *The Household Guide*. Toronto: Nichols Company Limited, 1894.

Jefferys, C.W. *The Picture Gallery of Canadian History*, Vol. I–III. Toronto: The Ryerson Press, 1950.

Jell-O. Toronto: 1905.

Jones, Jo Fraser, ed. *Hobnobbing with a Countess: The Diaries of Alice Barrett Parke, 1891–1900*. Vancouver: UBC Press, 2001.

Juniper, Annie B. *Girls' Home Manual of Cookery, Home Management, Home Nursing and Laundry*. Victoria: Minister of Education, 1913.

Just Look at These Wonderful Jams and Jellies. Cobourg?: Douglas Packing Co., 1926.

Kalm, Pehr. *The America of 1750: Peter Kalm's Travels in North America*. Adolph B. Benson, ed. New York: Dover Publications, 1966, 1937.

Kelcey, Barbara E., and Angela E. Davis, eds. *A Great Movement Underway: Women and The Grain Growers' Guide, 1908–1928*. Winnipeg: Manitoba Record Society, 1997.

Kelowna Hospital Women's Auxiliary Cook Book. Kelowna: 1936.

Kerr, Sheila. *Early Prairie Remedies*. Calgary: Barker Gifts, 1981.

Korinek, Valerie J. *Roughing It in the Suburbs: Reading Chatelaine Magazine in the Fifties and Sixties*. Toronto: University of Toronto Press, 2000.

Labtec Cook Book. Saskatoon Academy of the Canadian Society of Laboratory Technologists, 1938.

Langdon, Eustella. *Pioneer Gardens at Black Creek Pioneer Village*. Toronto: Holt Rinehart and Winston, 1972.

Langton, Anne. *A Gentlewoman in Upper Canada: The Journals of Anne Langton*. H.H. Langton ed., Toronto: Clarke, Irwin & Company, 1950.

Lewis, Norah L., ed. *Dear Editor and Friends: Letters from Rural Women of the North-West, 1900–1920*. Waterloo: Wilfrid Laurier University Press, 1998.

Light, Beth, and Joy Parr, eds. *Canadian Women on the Move, 1867–1920*. Toronto: New Hogtown Press and The Ontario Institute for Studies in Education, 1983.

Light, Beth, and Alison Prentice, eds. *Pioneer and Gentlewomen of British North America, 1713–1867*. Toronto : New Hogtown Press, 1980.

Light, Beth, and Ruth Roach Pierson. *No Easy Road: Women in Canada 1920s to 1960s*. Saskatoon : Western Producer Prairie Books, 1978.

McClary's Household Manual. London: McClary's, 1922.

McClung, Nellie. *In Times Like These*. Toronto: University of Toronto Press, 1972.

McIntosh, Dave. *When the Work's All Done This Fall: Voices of Early Canada, the Settling of the Land*. Toronto: Stoddart, 1989.

MacLeod, Evelyn J., ed. *One Woman's Charlottetown: Diaries of Margaret Gray Lord 1863, 1876, 1890*. Hull: Canadian Museum of Civilization, 1988.

MacTaggart, John. *Three Years in Canada: An Account of the Actual State of the Country in 1826-7-8*. London: H. Colburn, 1829.

Marie de l'Incarnation. *Word from New France: The Selected Letters of Marie de l'Incarnation*. Toronto: Oxford University Press, 1967.

Metropolitan Life Cook Book. Canada: Metropolitan Life Insurance Company, 1918.

Moodie, Susanna. *Roughing It in the Bush*. Toronto: Hunter, Rose, 1871.

Moogk, Peter. *La Nouvelle France: The Making of French Canada, a Cultural History*. East Lansing: Michigan State University Press, 2000.

Mother Hubbard's Cupboard, or, Canadian Cookbook. Hamilton: G.C. Briggs & Sons, 1881.

Murphy, Emily (Ferguson, Emily). *Janey Canuck in the West*. Toronto: Cassell and Company, 1910.

National Council of Women of Canada. *Our First Annual Meeting*. Toronto?: 1894.

La Nouvelle Cuisinière Canadienne. Montreal: L. Perrault, 1840.

O'Brien, Mary. *The Journals of Mary O'Brien, 1828–1838*. Audrey Saunders Miller, ed. Toronto: Macmillan of Canada, 1968.

Ottawa Ladies Hebrew Benevolent Society. *The Economical Cook Book*. Ottawa: 1915.

Parr Traill, Catherine. *The Backwoods of Canada, Being Letters from the Wife of an Emigrant Officer*. London: Charles Knight, 1836.

———. *The Canadian Settler's Guide*. Toronto: McClelland and Stewart, 1969.

Peel, Lucy. *Love Strong as Death: Lucy Peel's Canadian Journal, 1833–1836*. J.I. Little, ed. Waterloo: Wilfrid Laurier University, 2001.

Piniuta, Harry, ed. *Land of Pain, Land of Promise: First Person Accounts by Ukrainian Pioneers 1891–1914*. Saskatoon: Western Producer Prairie Books, 1978.

Potter-Mackinnon, Janice. *While the Women Only Wept: Loyalist Refugee Women*. Montreal: McGill Queen's University Press, 1993.

Prentice, Alison, et al. *Canadian Women: A History*. Toronto: Harcourt Brace Canada, 1996.

Preservation of Food. Victoria: Department of Agriculture, Bulletin No. 83, 1942.

Radcliff, Rev. Thomas, ed. *Authentic Letters from Upper Canada*. Toronto: Macmillan, 1953.

Richards, Amy G. *Cookery*. Montreal: E.M. Renouf, 1895.

Roberts, Kenneth, compiler. *March to Quebec: Journals of the Members of Arnold's Expedition*. New York: Doubleday, Doran, 1938.

Robertson, Una. *The Illustrated History of the Housewife, 1650–1950*. Phoenix Mill, UK: Sutton, 1997.

Schultz, Judy. *Mamie's Children: Three Generations of Prairie Women*. Red Deer: Red Deer College Press, 1997.

Silverman, Eliane Leslau. *Last Best West: Women on the Alberta Frontier, 1880–1930*. Montreal: Eden Press, 1984

Stockham, Alice B. *Tokology: A Book for Every Woman*. Toronto: McClelland & Goodchild, 1893?.

Strange, Kathleen. *With the West in Her Eyes: The Story of a Modern Pioneer.* New York: Dodge, 1937.

Strong Boag, Veronica. *The New Day Recalled: Lives of Girls and Women in English Canada, 1919–1939*. Toronto: Copp Clark Pitman, 1988.

Talbot, Edward Allen. *Five Years' Residence in Canada*. London: Longman, Hurst, Rees, Orme, Brown and Green, 1824.

Taylor, Margaret, and Frances McNaught. *The Early Canadian Galt Cook Book*. Toronto: William Briggs, 1898; Coles facsimile edition, 1980.

Trofimenkoff, Susan Mann, and Alison Prentice. *The Neglected Majority: Essays in Canadian Women's History*. Toronto: McClelland and Stewart, 1977.

Tyrer, Alfred Henry. *Sex, Satisfaction and Happy Marriage*. Toronto: Marriage Welfare Bureau, 1936.

Watkins Cook Book. Winona, Minn: J.R. Watkins Co., 1936.

Webster, John Clarence. *Acadia at the End of the Seventeenth Century: Letters, Journals and Memoirs of Joseph Robineau de Villebon*. Saint John: New Brunswick Museum, 1934.

What Women Say of the Canadian North-West. Montreal: Canadian Pacific Railway Company, 1886.

Women of Canada: Their Life and Work. Compiled by the National Council of Women of Canada, 1900.

MAGAZINES, NEWSPAPERS, AND OTHER PUBLISHED WORKS

A variety of Canadian newspapers and general interest and women's magazines were consulted during the writing of this book. Issues of *Chatelaine* (1928–1960), the *Canadian Home Journal* (1926–1958), *Maclean's* (1916–1960), *Canadian Homes and Gardens* (1924–1960); the Toronto *Globe* (1844–1936; then, the *Globe and Mail*), the *Halifax Herald*, the *Montreal Gazette*, the *Vancouver Sun*, the *Winnipeg Free Press*, and the *Calgary Herald* were among the most valuable. Individual citations are endnoted within the chapters.

Also consulted:
Eaton's catalogue [microform], 1884–1959
Girl's Own Paper, May 1892
Ladies' Home Journal, June 1905
Toronto Mail
Halifax Evening Mail

PERIODICAL ARTICLES

Backstrom, Elvira. "Pioneer Parents." *Alberta Historical Review*, Autumn 1973.
McCorkindale, Mrs. H., and Mrs. Jean Thomas. "Homesteading at Indian Head." *Saskatchewan History*, Vol. 4, #2.
St. John, Mrs. S.T. "Diary." *Saskatchewan History*, Vol. 2, #2 and #3.
Storer, Effie Laurie. "Home Remedies in Pioneering." *Saskatchewan History*, Vol. 42, #9.
Thompson, Shirley Keyes. "A Prairie Wife's Tale." *Saskatchewan History*, Vol. 44, No. 1.

UNPUBLISHED SOURCES

LAC=Library and Archives Canada
Alice Rendell fonds, LAC R1668-0-2-E.
Eliza Jane Wilson fonds, Glenbow Archives M 1320.
Georgina Sackville fonds, Genbow Archives M 6549, Birth Control or Prevention of Conception, Calgary, 1929.
Gertrude Quelch fonds, LAC MG29-C120.
James and Catherine Neil fonds, Glenbow Archives, M 888, M 4116.
Jopling recipe book, in Jopling family material, LAC R10119-7-7-E.
Kate Aitken fonds, Box 33, LAC R4490-0-0-E.
Kathleen Blake Coleman fonds, LAC R7767-0-4-E.
Martha Field cookbook: ca 1842–1858, LAC R4369-0-2-E; MG24-K48.
Mary A.B. Campbell fonds, 1887–1913; LAC MG55/30-No.53.

Olive K. Murdoch, Homesteading in Alberta, Reminiscences of the Heathcote family, 1894–1901, LAC MG55/31-No. 6.

Saskatchewan Homesteading Experiences Collection, LAC R2206-0-2-E.

Sempronius Stretton, sketchbooks, LAC.

Seel papers, University of Victoria Special Collections, The Last Pioneer: My Canadian Diary.

Walter and Rachel Weber fonds, Glenbow Archives M9035.

Women's Institute of Saltfleet fonds, LAC R5209-0-4-E.

WEB PAGES

http://www.maisonsaint-gabriel.qc.ca/en/.

http://collections.ic.gc.ca/heirloom_series/volume1/chapter5/164–169.htm.

http://www.civilization.ca/vmnf/popul/habitant/famile.htm.

http://www.lacefairy.com/Giroux/Toussaint.html.

http://etext.library.adelaide.edu.au/b/beeton/isabella/.

http://www.rootsweb.com/~qcmtl-w/IODE.html.

http://archive.salon.com/mwt/feature/1999/11/17/then/.

✦ Index ✦

Page numbers in bold indicate photographs or sidebars.

Photo Credit: Tony Owen

⇜ ABOUT THE AUTHOR ⇝

Rosemary Neering never thought she would write a book about housewives. A devotee of the cleaning woman, the restaurant, and the craft show, she has tremendous respect for the homely arts, especially as practised by someone else. Nonetheless, while researching and writing this book, she changed the bag on her vacuum cleaner, made raspberry jam, replaced her heritage sewing machine. She is knitting—and has been knitting for a year—a sweater. She still doesn't know how to make soap from scratch.

The author of several books (including *Wild West Women: Travellers, Adventurers and Rebels*, *Down the Road: Journeys through Small-Town British Columbia*) she lives in Victoria, BC, with her husband, Joe Thompson, where she trolls the roadside stands for fresh fruit and vegetables and the plant nurseries for plants that might thrive in her Garry-oak-shadowed garden.